GW00372170

# Insider's Guide to Dublin, Wicklow and the Boyne Valley

Paul Cullen and Ken Boyle

GILL & MACMILLAN

Published in Ireland by
Gill & Macmillan Ltd
Goldenbridge
Dublin 8
with associated companies throughout the world
© text Paul Cullen and Ken Boyle 1994
© maps Gill & Macmillan 1994
0 7171 2123 2
Designed by Design Image, Dublin
Print origination by
Seton Music Graphics Ltd, Bantry, Co. Cork
Printed by
ColourBooks Ltd, Dublin

A catalogue record is available for this book from the British Library.

Maps in this book are based on
the Ordnance Survey by permission
of the Government (Permit No. 5905).

1   3   5   4   2

# CONTENTS

# INTRODUCTION TO THE GUIDE

Dublin is above all a *modest* city. Without an imperial past, Ireland's capital lacks the pomp and grand architecture that define so many other great cities of Europe. Even today, there are few signs of the trappings of financial power and ostentatious wealth to be seen elsewhere. Economically, too, Ireland remains the poor relation of Western Europe. And although the population of Dublin has grown in recent decades to over a million people — still small in comparison with other major capitals — the place retains all the intimacy of an overgrown village.

This modesty extends to the geography of the city. Nestling between the gently sloping Wicklow hills and the curving sea of Dublin Bay, Ireland's capital reveals its charms slowly, even shyly. It may not have the imposing castles, boulevards and monuments that fill the guidebooks of other cities, but what it can boast is a more indefinite attraction — call it atmosphere, vibrancy, buzz — that is found in few other places. Like gems buried in the earth, its beauties are hidden, revealed only to the persistent and observant seeker. Everything is less than it seems, yet the total is undoubtedly greater than the sum of the individual parts.

There are many reasons for Dublin's special place in literature, history and people's hearts. For one, it is a capital city, home to migrants from all over Ireland. In fact, a third of 'Dubliners' were actually born elsewhere in Ireland, and another third are the sons and daughters of country-people. As such, it's a meeting-place of town and country, of urban and rural, and of their different traditions. Dublin is also a sort of spiritual capital to countless people of Irish descent throughout the world — forty million of them in North America alone. And as the main city of the only independent Celtic nation, it serves as the conduit through which thousands of years of Gaelic culture reach the outside world.

The history of Dublin is lightly peppered with periods of prosperity and glory: at the beginning of the eighteenth century, for example, it was the second largest city in the British Empire, after London. However, the essence of Dublin — and the font of inspiration for its many writers and poets — is more the wit, debate and animated conversation of its inhabitants. The achievement of Dublin is, therefore, essentially the achievement of Dubliners. It is a wry, inestimable world whose door is always open — if the visitor can only find it. The purpose of this guide is to set the visitor 'on the inside track' which will reveal the true beauty of Dublin.

*Insider's Guide to Dublin, Wicklow and the Boyne Valley* has been designed as the ultimate visitor's companion book to the region, but in fact it will be of use to anyone who wishes to know Dublin better, whether he or she intends to stay just a few days, several months or a complete lifetime. Its authors are Dubliners who love their home city deeply and hope that this affection shines through.

The guide aims to be encyclopedic, comprehensive and — as far as possible — objective. The listings are extensive and cover restaurants, accommodation, entertainment, daytime activities and shopping. There are few specific recommendations of places to eat or stay; instead, the intention is to give you, the reader, a gentle nudge in the direction of quality and value, and thereby to enable you to choose your own path through the city.

There is also a complete set of tour itineraries, covering all the most interesting attractions in the city and beyond. A series of ecotours serves as an introduction to urban and rural nature and geology in the area and can be followed by foot, bicycle, public transport, car or any combination of these. In addition, it is hoped that the writing on every page of this guide will in itself convey a flavour of what is a uniquely special city.

# Acknowledgments — Guide

I would like to acknowledge the research assistance of Judith Devlin and Paul Gannon in the preparation and checking of the copy. Thanks are also due to the staff of the Central Library in Dublin's ILAC Centre for helping me locate research materials, and to Roisín O'Kane of Dublin & East Tourism and Catherine Gorman of Midlands & East Regional Tourism, for keeping me informed on the latest developments in tourism in their areas, as well as to Edward Sharkey of Bord Fáilte. Last but not least, I would like to thank my mother, for her patience and support.

Paul Cullen
March 1994

# INTRODUCTION TO THE ECOTOURS

The ecotours are written as non-technical guides to the ecology of three separate regions, the Boyne Valley, Dublin city and the Wicklow mountains. Each ecotour is complete and sets out to describe what it is that is special about these three areas. In the Boyne Valley the ecotour is focused on the river and a disused canal which flows in tandem with the river. Dublin city has a wealth of habitats along its coastline and in its rivers and parks. Among Dubliners, this wealth of nature is taken for granted and often ignored. For the visitor curious about nature, Dublin is a city that has plenty of offer. Wicklow has, at its heart, a vast, unspoilt area of upland peats, rivers and lakes. This wilderness is only a half-hour drive from Dublin city and many days, weeks or years can be spent getting to know it. I have tried to convey some of the workings of the ecology of these three areas and hope that the reader is at least prompted to look a little more closely at what can be seen around them.

The ecotours can be dipped into in search of information and used in conjunction with other tours described in the book. If you are walking in Wicklow, be sure to tell others where you intend to go and when you expect to arrive. Take no chances on the mountains: the weather can change suddenly and walkers have been lost in all months of the year.

## ACKNOWLEDGMENTS — ECOTOURS

In writing this series of ecotours I have had recourse to experience gained through years of walking over and talking about hills, coastlines, woodlands, and canal and river banks. Many people accompanied me on those walks, but the most constant companion and sound adviser on all things has been Orla Bourke. Lecturers, post-grads and students in both the Faculty of Agriculture, University College Dublin and at the Dublin Institute of Technology, Cathal Brugha Street have taught me both to see things and what it is that is interesting about nature.

Ken Boyle
March 1994

# THE WEATHER

The Irish climate is mild and frequently damp. Prevailing south-westerly winds and the influence of the warm Gulf Stream in the Atlantic ensure that Ireland escapes the extremes of temperature experienced in other regions at similar latitudes, such as Newfoundland or Poland. January and February are the coldest months, when air temperatures average 4–7°C. The warmest months, July and August, boast average temperatures of 14–16°C. Extremely high or low temperatures are virtually unknown; it is rare indeed when the thermometer shows over 25°C.

There are compensations, however; the weather changes continually, so bad weather doesn't stay for longer than a few days. Dublin lies on the more sheltered eastern coast, and enjoys a drier, less windy climate than much of the rest of the country (average annual rainfall is 31 inches/ 785 mm). Even in winter, the pattern of rainy, windy weather is regularly punctuated by cold, dry spells that are ideal for outdoor activities such as hill-walking.

May tends to be the sunniest month with an average of six to seven hours of sunshine per day. Most summers bring with them at least one spell of warm, sunny weather, the problem being that no one has as yet managed to predict just when in June, July and August the sun will appear for any decent length of time.

The weather in Wicklow, particularly in the hills, is often damp. Since the going underfoot is almost always boggy, stout walking shoes and water-proof clothes are recommended here. Anyone venturing into the heart of the Wicklow hills on foot should take the usual mountaineering precautions of bringing a map and compass, as well as emergency provisions and a first-aid kit.

# LIST OF PHOTOGRAPHS

# LIST OF MAPS

# DUBLIN

Dublin gets its name from the 'dark pool' ('linn dubh' in Gaelic) where the waters of the River Poddle meet those of the Liffey, near the spot where the first settlers in Dublin Bay made their home some time over 5,000 years ago. The city's official name in Gaelic is Baile Átha Cliath, 'the town of the ford of the hurdles', a reference to the first crossing-point of the Liffey in the area, which formed part of one of the great roads of Ireland and led to the seat of the High Kings at Tara.

Little is known of the early hunters and fisherfolk who inhabited the region, although neolithic farmers built their tombs at the foot of the Dublin Mountains, and the Greek geographer Ptolemy wrote about the town of Eblana — presumed to be Dublin — in the second century AD.

Legend has it that Saint Patrick, the patron saint of Ireland, visited Dublin in AD 448 and converted many of the people to Christianity. In the following centuries, monasteries and hermit cells were built north and south of the Liffey and the first churches were erected, but none of these survives today.

Scandinavian pirates were first sighted off Ireland at the end of the eighth century. In the succeeding decades, Vikings from modern-day Norway and Denmark pillaged much of the east coast and in AD 841 a Viking fortress was built near where Christ Church Cathedral now stands. The invaders set up a port and used the site for further raids inland. Though forced to flee for a time, the original Vikings were followed by others who firmly established Dublin (or 'Dyflin', as they called it) as a town. The Viking attacks were met by fierce resistance from the native Irish, but the Scandinavian presence in Ireland was consolidated by their victory in the Battle of Dublin in December 919.

Subsequently, Dublin became an important trading outpost in the Viking empire, and crafts such as weaving, tanning, shipbuilding and bronzework

1

# DUBLIN SUBURBS

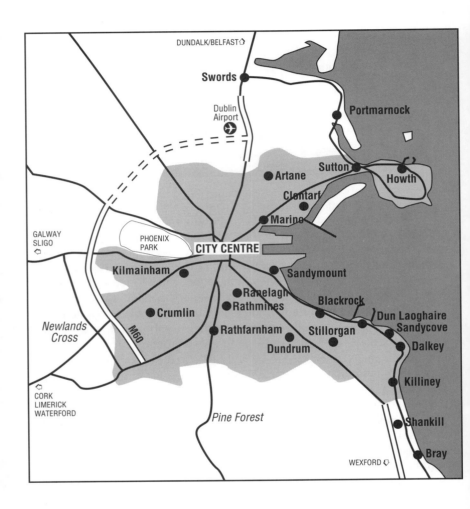

prospered. Although Scandinavian power was finally broken in the decisive Battle of Clontarf in 1014, Viking culture became a permanent feature of Irish life as the Norse and Danish settlers intermarried with the Gaelic Irish. Place-names like Howth ('Hovud' for headland) and Leixlip ('Laxlep' for salmon leap) commemorate the Scandinavians today.

After the Battle of Clontarf there was a period of relative peace in which Dublin became the largest town in Ireland. The first churches were established on the sites of Christ Church and St Michan's and a merchant class developed. However, the temporary unity of the Gaelic clans against the Scandinavians quickly fractured. The next wave of invaders came at the invitation of the Irish, when Normans from south Wales landed in modern-day County Wexford in 1169. These well-armed and aggressive warriors were responding to a Gaelic chieftain, Dermot McMurrough, who had appealed to the Norman King Henry II for support to recover his kingdom. Within two years, Dublin had been overwhelmed by the Norman force, and Henry II granted the city its first charter.

The Normans quickly set about erecting fortifications, churches and other urban edifices in Dublin. The oldest surviving buildings in the city date from this period, including the two cathedrals of Christ Church and St Patrick's and the administrative centre, garrison and prison in Dublin Castle, as well as other churches and the medieval wall surrounding the town.

Street-names such as Bull Alley, Cornmarket, Winetavern Street and Fishamble Street recall the thriving commercial life of this period. Dublin traded with England and continental Europe, exporting agricultural produce and importing wine and luxuries such as fruit and spices. One estimate of the population at this time put it at about 8,000.

Within the city an early form of apartheid was in operation, and the Gaelic Irish were excluded from a civic life controlled by the Norman ruling class, although outsiders continued to trickle in and intermarriage, especially among the working classes, took place just as when the Vikings were in control. Beyond the walled town and a surrounding area that became known as 'the Pale', however, the Irish chieftains ruled supreme, and regularly attacked the city from their secure mountain bases to the south in County Wicklow.

These attacks grew in frequency and ferocity in the thirteenth and fourteenth centuries as Norman power in Ireland declined. Outside Dublin the Normans intermarried and became 'more Irish than the Irish themselves', but within the city English customs and the English language prevailed, albeit tenuously. To make matters worse, the city suffered fires, intensely cold winters and a series of plagues culminating in the Black Death; an epidemic in 1348 is estimated to have killed about half the population.

Ireland remained in ferment in the fifteenth and sixteenth centuries. This unrest culminated in the quixotic revolt of the Anglo-Irish Lord

Thomas Fitzgerald, better known as Silken Thomas, who, believing that his father had been hanged in London, rode to Dublin in 1534 at the head of a company of cavalry. Thomas burst into the Council meeting in the Chapter House of St Mary's Abbey and flung his sword of state upon the table, divesting himself of his allegiance to the English King Henry VIII. However, this defiance and the subsequent revolt were brutally suppressed and, together with his five uncles, Thomas was executed in London in 1537.

An act of more lasting consequence for Irish history occurred in 1536, when Henry VIII, who had proclaimed himself King of England and Ireland, brought the Reformation to Ireland. Monasteries were dissolved, religious lands acquired and a new wave of immigrants arrived to run the English operations. Although the rest of Ireland staunchly resisted the Reformation, Dublin gradually became Protestant. As a result, the city gained new importance as the nerve-centre of English military, legal and administrative procedures in Ireland, and the size of the Pale expanded as royal authority was carried into parts of the country never before subdued.

Crowning the achievements of the newly ascendant Protestant ruling class, 'the College of the Holy and Undivided Trinity of Queen Elizabeth', better known as Trinity College, was founded in 1592 on land confiscated from the Priory of All Hallows. Established as an exclusively Protestant institution designed to promote the Reformation, Trinity has played an illustrious if at times controversial role in Dublin's history over the past four centuries.

The defeat of the Irish chieftains by the army of Elizabeth I at the Battle of Kinsale in 1601 ushered in a bleak century for the native Irish. In contrast, Dublin's importance as the base for England's military operations grew yet further. Ireland was used as a pawn in the Civil War in England between King Charles and parliament, with Dublin supporting the royalist cause. Oliver Cromwell landed in the city in 1649 with a large army and proceeded to sack Drogheda and Wexford with a savagery that has lived long in the collective Irish memory.

The rest of Ireland lay in ruins after decades of war, but Dublin made a swift recovery, especially after the restoration in 1660. New streets and bridges were constructed, extensive building was undertaken north of the Liffey for the first time, and St Stephen's Green was developed. The Phoenix Park was laid out and the earliest public buildings of note were erected, including the Royal Hospital (now the Irish Museum of Modern Art) and the old Bluecoat School in Blackhall Place. In the same period, Dublin's linen and wool trade prospered, and literary and cultural life flourished. The Philosophical Society was founded in Trinity College and Smock Alley theatre opened its doors.

In 1685 the Catholic King James II succeeded to the throne. In rapid consequence, Ireland became the battleground for a war of religion involving most of the major powers of Europe, and several factions within the country. James paid two noteworthy visits to Dublin: in 1688, when he was welcomed with great enthusiasm; and in 1690, when he fled through the city with indecent haste after losing the historic Battle of the Boyne to the forces of the Protestant Prince William of Orange.

The price paid by Ireland for backing the losing side in the Williamite Wars was high. Catholics were robbed of their remaining rights by the Penal Laws, Gaelic culture was driven underground, and even the Protestant merchants of Dublin found their commerce crippled by a series of tariffs imposed by London. Victimisation by the English bred a sense of common cause and eventually a separatist identity among all communities, and this was later to provide the foundation for a full-blown struggle for Irish autonomy.

Notwithstanding the difficulties of the period, the eighteenth century was Dublin's finest hour. The Mansion House, the Custom House, Parliament House (now the Bank of Ireland on College Green) and Marsh's Library were built, and Jonathan Swift returned to the city of his birth in 1713 to become Dean of St Patrick's Cathedral. The author of *Gulliver's Travels* and *Drapier's Letters*, Swift was a cantankerous but charitable genius who concentrated much of his literary talent on denouncing the wrongs done to Ireland.

As the wealthy built themselves lavish townhouses and sought amusement for their considerable leisure-time, the city became a magnet for actors, debaters and *bon viveurs*. In 1742 Handel came to Dublin and gave the first performance of *Messiah*. Plasterers and other craftspeople came from abroad to put the finishing touches to the extravagant new residences constructed on Merrion Square and Fitzwilliam Square. The city teemed with rakes, scholars, fops and brawlers.

In the Irish parliament, Henry Grattan pressed for free trade between Ireland and England and for additional autonomy for Ireland. He obtained these concessions, and Dublin's growth continued apace. The Royal and Grand Canals were built, the Custom House was completed, and the Four Courts was erected in 1786.

However, this golden age was short-lived. The benefits of the era were enjoyed by only a small section of the Anglo-Irish aristocracy, and certainly not by the majority Catholic community. Demands for further reform and for Catholic franchise grew louder towards the end of the eighteenth century. Wolfe Tone, a Protestant lawyer from County Kildare, succeeded in uniting diverse strands of opposition under a republican banner, but his revolt in 1798 proved abortive and Tone committed suicide in prison.

The British response to insurrection in Ireland was swift and severe. The Irish parliament was bribed out of existence and Ireland was brought under direct rule from London by the Act of Union passed in 1800.

The effect of this legislation was immediate. Almost overnight, Dublin lost its cultural and social sparkle, as the aristocracy and their hangers-on decamped to London. The Act of Union dealt a real blow to the trades and crafts, as the city's fine residences were abandoned by their occupants, to become boarding-houses or schools.

Catholic emancipation was achieved in 1829, largely through the efforts of Daniel O'Connell, a leading nationalist politician and one-time Lord Mayor of Dublin. The economic fortunes of Catholics, who made up 70 per cent of the city's population, improved modestly, and a Catholic middle class developed. For the first time in its history, Dublin was becoming a distinctly Irish city.

The Great Famine of the late 1840s was caused by the failure of three successive potato crops due to blight. It is estimated that one million people died between 1845 and 1848, and that another million emigrated. While Dublin escaped the worst effects of this catastrophe, the city became even more crowded as migrants flooded in from the surrounding countryside. Already squalid slums became even more dismal and diseases such as typhus and cholera were rampant.

The present layout of central Dublin dates from this period. In 1834 the opening of the railway between Dublin and Kingstown (Dún Laoghaire) paved the way for the expansion of the suburbs. The General Post Office was erected on Sackville (O'Connell) Street and, opposite it, Nelson's Pillar, Dublin's best-known and most controversial landmark until it was blown up in 1966.

Under the Protestant leader Charles Stewart Parnell, from Avondale in County Wicklow, the case for Irish autonomy was argued with con-summate skill in the English parliament at Westminster. Parnell died prematurely in 1891 — his funeral procession through the streets of Dublin was attended by over 200,000 people — and there followed a period of political apathy, though this vacuum was filled by the great cultural movement known as the Irish Literary Renaissance.

George Moore, George Russell, James Stephens, Lady Gregory, John Millington Synge and, most notably, William Butler Yeats were all prolific writers in the early years of the twentieth century and helped to spearhead this revival of national pride. The Abbey Theatre, founded in 1904, became the focus for the movement and dedicated itself to the reworking of ancient Irish legends in order to revitalise the national consciousness. In the same year, James Joyce left Ireland, the better to be able to write about Dublin with a skill and attention to detail that would eventually be recorded in *Ulysses*, published in 1922.

Also at the end of the nineteenth century, movements to revive the Irish language (the Gaelic League) and Gaelic sports of hurling and football (the Gaelic Athletic Association) were blossoming. Politically, these forms of cultural nationalism were eventually to find their fullest expression in

Sinn Féin — 'Ourselves Alone', a political movement advocating a boycott of the English parliament. The pace of events quickened in the second decade of the new century, with the Great Lockout in 1913 — Ireland's first major labour dispute, pitting striking workers against (largely Catholic) employers in Dublin — and a gun-running episode carried out in Howth by republican militants in the following year.

The high point of the Gaelic revival was also the nadir of Dublin poverty. Conditions for the poor at the beginning of the twentieth century were among the worst in Europe, with high infant mortality and frequent epidemics of cholera. Surveys recorded four families living to a room in the decaying eighteenth-century mansions that once were the glory of Dublin. These were now reduced to 'the bare bones of a fanlight/Over a hungry door', in the words of the poet Louis MacNeice. Indoor toilets were unknown, and up to sixty people might have to share a single earth closet in the back-yard. Only at the end of the nineteenth century were the first purpose-built houses constructed for the poor of the city.

With the outbreak of the First World War, some Sinn Féin members saw 'England's difficulty as Ireland's opportunity'. On Easter Monday 1916, fewer than 2,000 militants occupied strategic sites around Dublin, made the General Post Office their headquarters and declared Ireland a republic. Six days' bitter fighting ensued, leaving the city centre in ruins and 300 dead, before the rebels surrendered to British forces. In May, fifteen of the rebel leaders were executed.

Public opinion, initially hostile to the Rising, switched to vehement support after the executions. Sinn Féin won the 1917 elections overwhelmingly and two years later the War of Independence broke out. After two years of sporadic but intense guerrilla fighting between Irish republican and British armies, a treaty was agreed which resulted in the creation of the Irish Free State, comprising twenty-six of the thirty-two counties of Ireland. Six of the nine counties of Ulster, thereafter known as Northern Ireland, remained part of the United Kingdom.

While Dublin had survived the War of Independence relatively intact, it was to suffer extensive damage during the Civil War which broke out between pro- and anti-Treaty factions in the old Sinn Féin the following year. Historic landmarks such as the Custom House and Four Courts came under attack and were badly damaged as those for and against the Treaty fought out their dispute with uncontrolled ferocity. The Civil War lasted only a year, but the bitterness it engendered was to dominate Irish political life for decades after.

The newly independent Free State set about repairing the devastation in Dublin's city centre. Costly renovation began on the General Post Office, the Four Courts and the Custom House, and many of the buildings on O'Connell Street were rebuilt in the 1920s. However, the overcrowded tenements in the city centre were left untouched, as were the bullet-holes in the GPO and in the monument to Daniel O'Connell nearby, which still serve as a reminder of the conflicts of previous years.

After so many centuries of subjugation, Ireland became a sovereign country once again, and Dublin was restored to the status of capital. Yet, the aims of the new Free State Government were modest and its policies were conservative. There would be no return to the golden age of the eighteenth century, or to an earlier period when Gaelic laws and customs held sway. The new rulers were content to take over the administration of the country without making any great adjustments; even the republican administration which came to power in 1932 showed little inclination for radical reform.

As a result, Ireland — and Dublin with it — became a sort of provincial backwater, insulated from, and largely indifferent to, the major developments occurring in the rest of the world. For decades, this meant that the country remained underindustrialised and heavily dependent on agriculture, as well as being strongly influenced by an all-pervading Catholic ethos. On the positive side, the Free State's policy of political neutrality allowed Ireland to escape the carnage of the Second World War (although Dublin was bombed accidentally on several occasions during the war, most notably in May 1941 when German aeroplanes dropped bombs on the North Strand, killing thirty-four people).

The Constitution was introduced in 1937, Ireland became a republic in 1949, but neither event made much difference to the slow pace of life in Dublin, and its steady decline. The great Georgian townhouses of the seventeenth century had long since become filthy slums, home to destitution, disease and hordes of underfed children. At the start of the century, Dublin could even claim to have one of Europe's largest red-light districts. The Free State administration assumed it could get rid of these problems by demolishing the tenements, and so they were pulled down, along with many other fine buildings. Yet the problems of deprivation, unemployment and emigration remained.

The 1950s, when an economic depression caused unemployment and emigration to rise to new heights, was perhaps the most miserable period of recent Irish history. Writers such as Brian O'Nolan (Flann O'Brien), Brendan Behan and Patrick Kavanagh comforted themselves with songs, stories and plenty of drink in Dublin's pubs, perhaps as an antidote to the gloom outside.

Events took a turn for the better in the 1960s. A new Taoiseach (Prime Minister), Seán Lemass, promoted a policy of modernisation and industrialisation as the solution to Ireland's economic ills, and the importance of Dublin, as the main urban centre, grew in consequence. Television arrived and acted as a liberalising influence. Censorship laws were eased, and a ban on Catholics attending Trinity College was lifted in 1970. Ireland was admitted to the European Economic Community in 1973.

Sadly, the architectural fabric of the city suffered more in these decades of progress and economic growth than it had in the dark days of the 1950s and before. Greedy developers pulled down many of the finest buildings in Georgian Dublin while the authorities stood idly by. Modern architecture in the city was almost always bleak and cheap. In the 1970s, efforts to save Wood Quay, under which lay a treasure trove of Viking history, came to nothing as the city corporation pressed on with its plans to build ugly new offices for itself behind Christ Church Cathedral.

The violent conflict in Northern Ireland which began in 1969 has had a deep impact on Irish life, but it has touched Dublin directly on very few occasions. The worst incident took place in 1974, when twenty-five people were killed in bomb explosions in the city centre.

In recent years, Dublin has grown rapidly and boasts the youngest population of any city in Europe. Today, its population is about 500,000, and that of the county of Dublin is about one million. The constant scourge of unemployment is greater than ever, and has been joined by those of drug abuse and crime. In spite of all this, Dublin could be said

Arms of the City of Dublin

· OBEDIENTIA · CIVIUM · URBIS · FELICITAS ·

to be muddling along better than ever. The Millennium in 1988, which celebrated the city's thousandth birthday (the arithmetic was a bit askew), helped to crystallise and copperfasten Dubliners' sense of their own identity and their own specialness; the achievements of U2, Bob Geldof and other celebrated natives have helped too. Today, a highly educated population feels it has more control over its destiny than any generation before.

Dublin's motto is *Obedientia Civium Urbis Felicitas* — 'Happy the city where citizens obey'. The arms of the city have evolved through several versions since the thirteenth century. A seal from this period shows a miniature city under siege with three towers being staunchly defended by archers, while trumpeters sound the alarm. In a gruesome reminder of early barbarities, the heads of the city's enemies are depicted over the main entrance.

The heads were dropped, so to speak, in the forerunner of the modern version, dating from 1607. Urging vigilance among the population, these arms show three gates, each of which has turrets on fire. Look out for this design on street lamps, official buildings and elsewhere, sometimes displayed in a crest flanked by two figures representing Justice and the Law.

---

**Miscellaneous facts about Dublin**
— The roaring lion used in the introduction to MGM films came from Dublin Zoo, which is the second oldest in the world.
— The Phoenix Park, at 1,760 acres/713 hectares, is the largest enclosed urban park in Europe.
— Handel conducted the first performance of *Messiah* at the Musick Hall, Fishamble Street, on 13 April 1742.
— The Guinness Brewery in Dublin is the world's largest producer of stout.
— The Rotunda Hospital, founded in 1745 and opened on Parnell Street 12 years later, is the world's oldest maternity hospital.
— Soda water was the invention of a Dublin man, Augustine Thwaites. The discovery was made in 1776 while Thwaites was a medical student.
— Dublin's Municipal Art Gallery was the first public collection in the British Isles exclusively devoted to modern art.
— Dubliners eat more kebabs and go to the cinema more often than the inhabitants of any other city in Europe.
— The Bank of Ireland has a windowless façade.

# ESSENTIAL INFORMATION

Listed below in alphabetical order is information vital during a stay in the Dublin area, with accompanying telephone numbers. Remember the prefix (usually 01) is used only if you are ringing from outside the prefix area.

## BANKS

All banks (except the one in Dublin Airport) close on Saturdays, Sundays and bank holidays. The traditional opening hours of the four main banks — Bank of Ireland (BoI), Allied Irish Banks (AIB), National Irish Bank (NIB) and Ulster Bank — are in the process of being extended. All banks in the city are open from 10 a.m. to 3 p.m. weekdays; busier branches remain open until 4 or 5 p.m.

The bank at Dublin Airport is open every day (except Christmas Day) from 6.45 a.m.–10 p.m. (6.45 a.m.–9 p.m. October–March), telephone 01–8420433.

The main banks have numerous branches in Dublin city centre and suburbs, many of them with 'hole-in-the-wall' cash points for after-hours banking. These cash points accept cards issued by all the main banks, as well as Visa, Access and other internationally recognised cards. Eurocheque cards can also be used to withdraw money at some cash points, provided the user has been issued with a PIN number by his or her own bank.

American Express operates a cash dispenser at the Bord Fáilte (Irish Tourist Board) office at 14 Upper O'Connell Street.

## BICYCLE HIRE AND REPAIR

Cycling in Ireland has undergone a boom since Stephen Roche won the Tour de France in 1987. It has always been the quickest way to get around Dublin's city centre, though a steady nerve is called for in negotiating a seemingly endless series of potholes, illegally parked cars and other obstacles. The existing small network of bicycle lanes is being extended slowly, but with little regard for the safety or convenience of cyclists. Remember to keep your bicycle locked (always to an immovable object) at all times when unattended — Dublin's bike thieves are persistent, skilled and work fast.

You can hire a bicycle, or have one repaired, from:
Bike Store, 56 Lower Gardiner Street (behind the Custom House), telephone 01–8744246
C. Harding, 30 Bachelor's Walk (off O'Connell Bridge), telephone 01–8732455
Mike's Bikes, George's Square, Dún Laoghaire Shopping Centre, telephone 01–2800417.
Bicycle manufacturers Raleigh operate a rental scheme through a number of bike shops, further information from Raleigh Rent-a-Bike, telephone 01–6261333.
The following Raleigh agents also rent and repair bikes:
Joe Daly, Main Street Lower, Dundrum, telephone 01–2981485;
Little Sport, Fairview, telephone 01–8332405;
McDonald's Cycles, 38 Wexford Street, telephone 01–4752586.
The Square Wheel Cycleworks, Temple Lane South (off Dame Street), telephone 01–6790838, will repair all types of bicycle and offers a supervised bike park in a central location. Open 8.30 a.m.–5.30 p.m. Monday to Friday.
Bikes can be transported on mainline trains but not on the DART suburban line.

## BUREAUX DE CHANGE

Changing money in Dublin is in general much less of a problem than in other big cities such as Paris or London. Virtually all commercial banks will cash traveller's cheques and exchange currency. Traveller's cheques and major credit cards are accepted by most hotels, large shops, travel and transport companies. Just remember to bring along your passport or other means of identification.

Bureaux de Change are also operated by:

American Express, 116 Grafton Street, telephone 01–6772874 and 14 Upper O'Connell Street, telephone 01–8747303

Dublin & East Tourism, 14 Upper O'Connell Street, telephone 01–8747733

First Rate, 1 Westmoreland Street, telephone 01–6713233

JWT Forex, 69 Upper O'Connell Street, telephone 01–8725536

Thomas Cook, 118 Grafton Street, telephone 01–6771307.

# CAR HIRE

Car hire in Ireland is expensive and should be booked in advance in the peak season. All the major car rental companies are represented, as are a number of Irish firms. All you need is a valid national driver's licence; note, however, that some companies operate age restrictions, and will rent cars only to drivers over twenty-three and under seventy years of age.

Avis Johnson & Perrott, 1 Hanover Street East, telephone 01–6774010 and Dublin Airport, telephone 01–8444466

Budget, Dublin Airport, telephone 01–8445919 and Dublin City, telephone 01–8379611

Hertz, Dublin Airport, telephone 01–8429333, Dún Laoghaire pier, telephone 01–2801518, 149 Upper Leeson Street, telephone 01–6602255/6604504

Murray's Europcar, Baggot Street Bridge, telephone 01–6681777 and Dublin Airport, telephone 01–8444179

Practical, 19 Nassau Street, telephone 01–6715540

# CAR REPAIRS/24-HOUR PETROL SUPPLIES

The downtown office of the Automobile Association (AA) is at 23 Suffolk Street, telephone 01–6779481 (shop and breakdown services). Opening hours are 9 a.m.–5 p.m. Monday–Friday, and 9 a.m.–12.30 p.m. Saturday.

The headquarters of the AA are located at 23 Rock Hill, in the southern suburb of Blackrock, telephone 01–2833555.

## 24-hour petrol stations

Artane Service Station, Malahide Road, telephone 01–8312138

Belmont Service Station, 126 Sandford Road, Ranelagh, telephone 01–4978209

East Wall Self-Serve Service Station, East Wall Road, telephone 01–8363455

Huntsman Service Station, Fox & Geese, Long Mile Road, telephone 01–4503596

Riverside Service Station, Shankill, telephone 01–2824672

Service Station, Dublin Airport

## 24-hour on-the-spot mobile puncture service

Glasnevin Tyres, 9 St Ita's Road, Glasnevin, telephone 01–8375622/8376847

Mobile Tyres, Old Blessington Road, Tallaght, telephone 01–4511824/4511156. After hours, telephone 088–592364.

Wheel Fix It Tyre Centre, Monkstown Farm, Dún Laoghaire, telephone 01–2809330/2802729

## 24-hour on-the-spot breakdown service

A1 24-Hour Towing, 92 Baggot Lane, telephone 01–6600596

Alley Cats Garage, telephone 01–4544552, evenings 01–6265286

Tom Kane Motors, telephone 01–8338143, evenings 01–8315983/088–555504

Most garages carry out small repairs; a full list is obtainable under 'Garages' in the Golden Pages telephone directory. The same book also lists further emergency repair services under 'Towing & Breakdown Service'.

# CHURCHES

Catholic mass times are usually posted outside churches. In the city centre, there are daily services in the University Church on St Stephen's Green South and in the Pro-Cathedral, Marlborough Street. Mass is sung in Latin in the Pro-Cathedral on Sundays at 11 a.m. and on Fridays at 5.05 p.m. Vespers are sung by the boys of the Palestrina Choir.

Dublin's two cathedrals are both Church of Ireland (Anglican). In Christ Church Cathedral, Lord Edward Street (telephone 01–6778099) on Sundays, there is sung Eucharist at 11 a.m. and Choral Evensong at 3.30 p.m on Sundays (6 p.m. on Thursdays except July and August).

The Cathedral Choir School associated with St Patrick's Cathedral, Patrick Street, was founded in 1432. Sung Eucharist or Matins is at 11.15 a.m. on Sundays and Choral Evensong is at 3.15 p.m. on Sundays and 5.45 p.m. on Tuesdays.

A list of the times and locations of the main Christian services (other than Catholic, which would be too numerous to mention) is published each Saturday in *The Irish Times*. There is a mosque at the Dublin Islamic Centre, 163 South Circular Road, telephone 01–4533242.

There are synagogues at 37 Adelaide Road, telephone 01–6761734, and Rathfarnham Road, Terenure, telephone 01–4905969.

# CRÈCHE AND BABYSITTING SERVICES

Euro-placements, 59 Waterloo Road, telephone 01–6603926 will mind children for hours, days, weekends or even longer.

Information on kindergartens is available in the Golden Pages telephone directory under 'Schools — Nursery & Kindergarten'. Centrally located crèches (long-stay) include:
Grosvenor Crèche, 9 Grosvenor Road, Rathmines, telephone 01–4979657
Step by Step, 30 Mountjoy Square East, telephone 01–8744612.

The voluntary childcare agency, Barnardo's, operates an advisory service for parents on crèches, childminders and nurseries, telephone 01–4530355.

The following suburban (except St Stephen's Green) shopping centres provide crèche facilities for small children while their parents use the centre: Nutgrove, Stillorgan, Swan Centre Rathmines, Crumlin, Santry, The Square Tallaght, Dún Laoghaire, Blackrock and the St Stephen's Green Centre. All branches of Superquinn supermarkets (see Golden Pages) also provide 'playhouses' for children. Shop and supermarket noticeboards are useful places to find babysitters locally.

# EMBASSIES

Embassies are listed under 'Diplomatic and Consular Missions' in the telephone directory. They include:
American, telephone 01–6688777
Australian, telephone 01–6761517
British, telephone 01–2695211
Canadian, telephone 01–4781988
Dutch, telephone 01–2693444
French, telephone 01–2694777
German, telephone 01–2693011
Italian, telephone 01–6601744
Spanish, telephone 01–2691640
Swiss, telephone 01–2692515.

# EMERGENCIES AND MEDICAL MATTERS

In cases of emergency, ring 999 from any telephone, and say which service you require — fire brigade, police or ambulance. The call is free.

The following Dublin hospitals are 'on call' to deal with emergencies:

**North City:**

Beaumont Hospital, Beaumont Road, telephone 01–8377755

Mater Misericordiae, Eccles Street, telephone 01–8301122

**South City:**

St James's, James's Street, telephone 01–4537941

Meath, Heytesbury Street, telephone 01–4536555

St Vincent's, Elm Park, telephone 01–2694533.

If you need a doctor, ask at your accommodation or consult the Golden Pages telephone directory.

The Dublin Dental Hospital, 20 Lincoln Place, telephone 01–6620766, has emergency facilities and information on dentists offering emergency care.

Other useful numbers:

AIDS Helpline, telephone 01–8724277

Rape Crisis Centre, telephone 01–6614911/6614564

Samaritans, who help the lonely, depressed and suicidal, telephone 01–8727700

Women's Aid, telephone 01–4961002.

# GARDAÍ (POLICE)

If an emergency arises ring 999 and ask for the Gardaí/Police. This call is free.

The main city-centre police station on the south side is at Pearse Street, near Trinity College, telephone 01–6778141. Territory covered by this station includes the shopping area around Grafton Street, up to St Stephen's Green. The building itself has been cleaned recently, and looks pristine. Watch out for the carvings of policemen over the door.

North of the Liffey, the main station covering the shopping area of O'Connell Street and Henry Street is at Store Street (near Busáras, the central bus station), telephone 01–8742761.

Other city-centre stations:

Fitzgibbon Street, telephone 01–8363113

Harcourt Terrace, telephone 01–6763481

Kevin Street, telephone 01–4543841.

## Note

Crime is as much a problem in Dublin as it is in any other big city. Acts of violence are rare, but the frequency with which tourists are robbed has prompted the Gardaí to issue special warnings to visitors.

Handbags, wallets, cars and their contents are favourite targets. Visitors are advised to take good care of their valuables, not to leave luggage unattended, and to keep wallets and cash out of sight. Always lock a car and remove or hide the luggage before leaving it. City-centre areas with a reputation for being dangerous, especially at night, include the side-streets east of O'Connell Street, and the area around the Guinness Brewery.

# GAY DUBLIN

Homosexual activity for consenting males aged 18 and over was finally legalised in 1993. As a result, the gay scene is moving out of the closet, though discretion is still the watchword. Gay pubs include the George and Loft, South Great George's Street, and the Parliament Inn in the street of the same name. Shaft, 22 Ely Place (off St Stephen's Green) is the most prominent gay nightclub, while Fifi's in Dame Court attracts a mixed gay and lesbian crowd.

The Horse and Carriage, at 15 Aungier Street, telephone 01–4783537 is a newly opened gay hotel, with an associated health club behind.

Full gay listings are published fortnightly in *In Dublin* magazine. A useful contact number is the Gay Switchboard, telephone 01–8721055, which operates 8–10 p.m. Sunday–Friday, and 3.30–6 p.m. Saturday.

## LATE-OPENING SHOPS

Slowly but surely, Dublin is becoming a 24-hour city. Many neighbourhood shops stay open until 9 p.m. and beyond, and stock a good range of food and other essentials. The following shops stay open until at least 3 a.m.:

AM-PM Stores, 153 Rathmines Road Upper, telephone 01–4961545
Park Stores (24 hours), 24 Marino Mart, telephone 01–8330526
Spar, 64 Ranelagh, telephone 01–4971549
Spar 24 Hours, Malahide Road, Artane, telephone 01–8316717
Spar, Lower 101 Rathmines Road, telephone 01–4971497
Spar, 23/25 Upper Baggot Street, telephone 01–6603326.

## LAUNDERETTES

Launderettes are concentrated in the areas with the highest density of flat-dwellers, such as Rathmines and Phibsborough. This means there are none in the city centre. Gold Star Launderette & Dry Cleaners, 52 Rathgar Avenue, Rathgar, telephone 01–4965157, is open seven days a week until 9 p.m. (6 p.m. on Sundays).

The Laundry & Dry Cleaning Shop has late-opening branches (8 a.m.–10 p.m. daily, including Sunday) in:

118 Rathmines Road Lower, telephone 01–4962467
365 North Circular Road, telephone 01–8308558
23 Sandymount Green, telephone 01–6683962.

Dry-cleaning services are more widely available. The following are just a few:
Baggot Dry Cleaners, 33 Baggot Street Upper, telephone 01–6681286
Crown Cleaners, 81 Camden Street Lower, telephone 01–4753584
Georgian Dry Cleaners, 72 Pearse Street, telephone 01–6710747
Grafton Cleaners, 32 South William Street, telephone 01–6794309
Marlowe Cleaners, 58 Upper O'Connell Street, telephone 01–8731050
New York Dry Cleaners, 68 Middle Abbey Street, telephone 01–8730929.

## LIBRARIES

The Dublin Central Library, telephone 01–8734333, is located in the ILAC Shopping Centre on Henry Street. Opening hours are 10 a.m.–8 p.m. Monday–Thursday and 10 a.m.–5 p.m. on Fridays and Saturdays. Much more than a mere collection of books, the ILAC library boasts special music and business sections, language and computer learning facilities, a lively programme of cultural activities and weekly conversation groups in French, Spanish, German, Italian and Irish.

Visitors are entitled to use the reference facilities in the library on production of an ID. An Irish resident has to act as guarantor before a visitor is allowed to borrow books. Other city-centre libraries:

Charleville Mall, North Strand, telephone 01–8749619
Gilbert Library, 138 Pearse Street, telephone 01–6777662
Rathmines, 157 Rathmines Road, telephone 01–4973539.

The Community & Youth Information Centre, Sackville House, Sackville Place (off O'Connell Street, behind Clery's), telephone 01–8786844, carries a wide range of information of interest to young people, including tourist, employment and accommodation listings.

# PHARMACIES

Pharmacies generally follow normal shop-opening hours (9 a.m.–5.30 p.m.), though many open for a few hours on Sunday mornings. The following pharmacies open late (in most cases, until 10 p.m.) and on Sundays:
Crowley's Pharmacy, 6 Upper Drumcondra, telephone 01–8373462
Drumcondra Pharmacy, 149 Lower Drumcondra Road, telephone 01–8373436
O'Connell's, 55 O'Connell Street, telephone 01–8730427
O'Connell's, 6 Henry Street, telephone 01–8731077 (not Sunday)
Ranelagh Pharmacy, 21 Ranelagh, telephone 01–4972190 (not Sunday)
Unicare, 282 Rathmines Road, telephone 01–4970750
Walsh's Late Night Pharmacy, 290 Harold's Cross Road, telephone 01–4923769.

# POST OFFICES

The General Post Office (GPO) on O'Connell Street (telephone 01–8728888) is open 8 a.m. to 8 p.m. on weekdays, and on Sundays and bank holidays from 10.30 a.m. to 6 p.m. Other centrally located post offices such as those at St Andrew Street (off Wicklow Street) and South Anne Street (off Grafton Street) are open from 9 a.m. to 6.00 p.m. Monday–Friday only (South Anne Street also opens on Saturdays).

# PUBLIC HOLIDAYS

New Year's Day, 1 January
Saint Patrick's Day, 17 March
Easter Monday
May holiday (first Monday in May)
June holiday (first Monday in June)
August holiday (first Monday in August)
October holiday (last Monday in October)
Christmas Day, 25 December
St Stephen's Day, 26 December
Good Friday is not a statutory public holiday, although it is generally observed as such.

# TAXIS

Taxi-drivers in Dublin are generally a friendly and talkative lot, though sometimes hard to find. Hailing a taxi in the street is difficult, especially at peak hours or when it is raining (that is, when you most need one), so it is best to ring one (under 'Taxi Cab Ranks and Shelters' in the telephone directory) or to proceed to a taxi rank. Beware, especially, of looking for a taxi after the pubs close — around midnight — on Fridays and Saturdays. The main ranks in the city centre are at Eden Quay (off O'Connell Bridge), College Green and St Stephen's Green; elsewhere, ask the locals.
Standards of taxis vary enormously, though they are improving. Make sure the meter displaying the fare is running; there are extra charges for each passenger, baggage and night journeys. The 6 mile/10 km journey from the airport to the city centre costs about £12; don't pay any more.
Some taxi companies:
Blue Cabs, telephone 01–6761111
Co-Op, telephone 01–6766666

Metro, telephone 01–6683333
National Radio Cabs Co-Op, telephone 01–6772222/6776528
VIP Taxis, telephone 01–4783333.

# TELEPHONE SERVICES

Public pay phones are located in street booths and in pubs and shops. Currently, a local call costs 20p for three minutes. More and more phones are now card-operated; callcards in denominations of 10, 20, 50 and 100 units can be purchased in any post office and many newsagents. Phoning from your hotel room may be up to three times as expensive. Direct dialling is in operation throughout the country, but you can also dial 10 for operator assistance. All Dublin's phone numbers are being converted to seven digits. The numbers in this guide are as up-to-date as possible. However, if you have difficulties with a six-digit number, call the operator.

International calls can be made from virtually all the public phones in the Dublin area. The international prefix from Ireland is 00. It costs between 54p and 72p per minute to ring other EC countries from a pay phone, and £1 to ring North America. Reduced rates for international calls are available at weekends and from 6 p.m. Monday to Friday for Europe (further reductions are available from 10 p.m. for North America). Directory enquiries:

Ireland 1190
UK 1197
International 114 (also for reverse-charge calls).

# TOURIST INFORMATION OFFICES

The Tourist Information Office at 14 Upper O'Connell Street, Dublin, is open all year from 9 a.m. to 5 p.m. on weekdays, 9 a.m. to 3.30 p.m. on Saturdays. The opening hours are longer in summer: the office is open until at least 6 p.m. on Saturdays from June to mid-September.

In July and August the opening hours are 8.30 a.m.–8 p.m. Monday–Saturday and 10.30 a.m.–2 p.m. on Sundays. In the peak season it gets very busy, so go in early. Telephone 01–8747733.

The office of Bord Fáilte (Irish Tourist Board), Baggot Street Bridge, telephone 01–6765871, also supplies local tourist information. Opening hours here are 9.15 a.m.–5.15 p.m. Monday–Friday.

The Tourist Information Office in the arrivals hall of Dublin Airport is open daily from 8 a.m. to 6 p.m. (until 8 p.m. from May to mid-June, and 10.30 p.m. from mid-June to mid-September), telephone 01–8445387/8445533.

There is also a Tourist Information Office (near the ferry terminal) in the southern suburb of Dún Laoghaire, at St Michael's Wharf. The opening hours here are 7.30 a.m.–9 p.m. on weekdays in June–September (open Sunday, 4–9 p.m. in September). For the rest of the year, the opening hours are 9 a.m.–8 p.m. (except January, when it is open Monday–Friday, 9 a.m.–5 p.m.). Telephone 01–2806984/5.

All these tourist offices sell the 'Dublin Cultural Connection', which is a single booklet of tickets providing entry to many of the heritage centres and other historical sites worth visiting in the city, at a reduced rate compared to the sum of individual admission charges.

# TRAVEL

Most of the sights of Dublin lie within a one-mile radius of the city centre, so walking is a good way to see everything. With its one-way system, complex street structure and poor signposting, Dublin's centre is not recommended territory for visiting car-drivers,

A Georgian doorway on St Stephen's Green

who are best advised to find a secure car park, leave all valuables out of sight, and resort to walking, buses or taxis.

## Arriving in Dublin

Most visitors arrive in Dublin through the airport or through one of two ferry-ports. Dublin Airport, 6 miles/10 km to the north of the city is well served by international and domestic airlines. There is a bureau de change and post office in the arrivals hall and a branch of the Bank of Ireland in the departures hall. There is also a Tourist Information Office, and all the main car hire companies are represented.

A taxi provides the quickest way of getting to the centre; the journey should take about thirty minutes and cost no more than £12. Dublin Bus (telephone 01–8366111) operates an airport coach to Busáras, the central bus station in town, which leaves from outside the arrivals hall every thirty minutes. The service runs all day, from 7.30 a.m. to 11 p.m. Simply pay the driver on the bus. The cheapest way of getting into the city centre is to wait for one of the regular double-decker buses which stop at the airport. Buses 41/41A/41B/41C begin and end at Eden Quay.

Ferries travel to and from Britain via the ports at Dublin's North Wall and Dún Laoghaire. B&I Line boats go from Alexandra Road on the North Wall (bus 53A from Beresford Place; direct connections also from Busáras and Heuston Station) to Holyhead, from where there are bus and train connections to London and elsewhere. The voyage time on the Irish Sea is approximately 3.5 hours, but it takes about 11 hours to reach London. For more information contact any travel agent or B&I Line, 16 Westmoreland Street, telephone 01–6797977. Stena Sealink services the route from Dún Laoghaire to Holyhead (bus 46A or take the DART). Contact Stena Sealink, 15 Westmoreland Street, telephone 01–2808844.

Dublin has two main train stations, both situated in the city centre. Connolly Station, on Amiens Street, serves towns on a north–south axis — between Rosslare Harbour/Wexford and Belfast — and also those north-west of Dublin, such as Sligo. Heuston Station, upriver by the Liffey and the Guinness Brewery, is the main-line station for the south and the west, including Galway, Limerick, Killarney and Cork (buses 24 and 26 from Essex Quay). There is no direct bus connection to Dublin Airport. Bus 90 shuttles between the two stations and also stops at Busáras.

## Buses

Buses start running from about 6.30 a.m. on weekdays (9.30 a.m. on Sundays). Most routes run on a north–south axis, with the last bus leaving the city centre at about 11.30 p.m. Night buses operate at the weekends until 3 a.m. on selected routes to the suburbs. Tickets for these services are sold from a mobile bus parked on Westmoreland Street on Friday and Saturday nights.

Daytime fares average about £1, depending on the length of the journey. Monthly passes may be purchased from Dublin Bus, 59 Upper O'Connell Street, telephone 01–8734222. Daily, weekly and family bus (and combined bus and suburban train) passes can be obtained from Dublin Bus and selected newsagents. The Dublin Explorer Ticket is a four-day pass allowing travel on all Dublin bus and DART services. It can only be used after 9.45 a.m. but there are no evening restrictions. This ticket is available from the Dublin Bus Booking Office, 59 Upper O'Connell Street. Dublin Bus publishes a timetable annually, but asking the locals may well be the best way of finding out how to reach a particular destination. Otherwise, information on all public transport services can be obtained by telephoning 01–8734222 (Monday–Saturday, 9 a.m.–7 p.m.). Beware, though: bus services in Dublin have improved somewhat in recent years, but arrival times are still approximate.

Information on bus tours around Dublin and beyond can also be obtained from Dublin Bus.

Last but not least, the use of Irish on buses can prove confusing to visitors. If in doubt just ask someone in the bus queue, but the one destination worth remembering is An Lár, which means city centre.

## Hitch-hiking

Hitch-hiking in Ireland is easy enough though often slow. Drivers are not loath to give lifts to strangers, but in summer the numbers at the main hitching-points can pose a problem. Traffic off main roads can be very light and very slow-moving, so patience is called for. Don't even try to hitch in Dublin; use public transport to get to the outer boundaries of the city before heading off west, south or north. Those heading north towards Dundalk or Belfast are best advised to take bus 41/41C from Eden Quay towards Santry and Swords. Newlands Cross (bus 51/51B/51C from Fleet Street) is the acknowledged starting-point for access to the main road to Cork and Kerry. The road west to Galway passes through the Kildare towns of Leixlip and Maynooth (bus 66/67/67A from Middle Abbey Street). Finally, the Stillorgan dual carriageway (bus 46A from Fleet Street) leads south to Wexford and Rosslare Harbour.

## Suburban trains

The DART electric rail service occupies pride of place in Dublin's public transport system. Trains on the route snake along the shores of Dublin Bay every five minutes at peak times, from Bray in the south to Howth in the north, offering passengers comfort and splendid views. The DART starts each day at 6.30 a.m. (9.30 a.m. on Sundays), finishing at about 11.45 p.m., and costs slightly more than the equivalent bus journey. Tickets can be bought at the stations; the Irish Rail Travel Centre, 35 Lower Abbey Street, telephone 01–8366222, sells weekly and monthly passes. Bikes cannot be transported on the DART.

See also the DART tour on page 105.

Less frequent suburban train services also connect Connolly Station with Dundalk to the north, Arklow to the south, and Mullingar inland.

## Tours

Bus Éireann, telephone 01–8366111, Dublin Bus, telephone 01–8734222, Vision Tours, telephone 01–6797588 and Grayline Tours, telephone 01–6619666, all run three- to four-hour city sightseeing tours that visit the main attractions in the city centre.

Bus Éireann also offers day tours to country destinations that leave from the main bus station, Busáras, near the Custom House in Dublin. Dublin Bus conducts north- and south-city coastal tours in the summer months.

City Cycle Tours offers bicycle tours of central Dublin, departing from Temple Bar. The price includes hire of a bicycle and helmet. Telephone 01–6715606/6715610.

There is a wide variety of guided walking, pub, literary and other special interest tours

# DART & SUBURBAN RAIL NETWORK

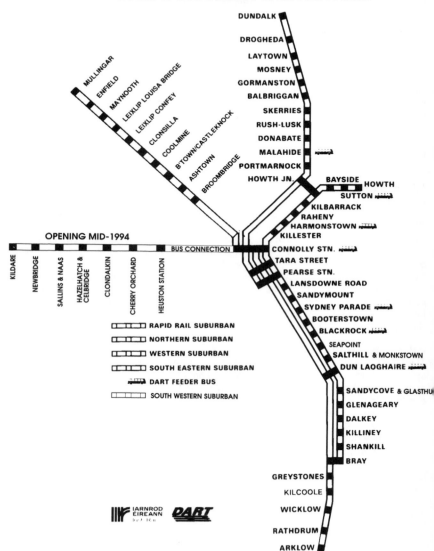

on offer, particularly in the summer months. These include Old Dublin tours from Christ Church Cathedral, tours of Trinity College given by students at the university, and a four-hour City Cycle tour from Temple Bar.

Historical walking tours begin from the front gate of Trinity College at 11 a.m., 12 noon and 3 p.m. daily (also 2 p.m. on Sundays) in the summer months. These are given by history graduates at the university and combine a sightseeing tour of Dublin's historic buildings with lectures on Irish history since 1798. The tour lasts about two hours. For more information telephone 01–8450241 or 01–4535730.

Last but not least, there is a Literary Pub Crawl that visits many of Dublin's more famous (or infamous) bars on Monday to Thursday evenings between May and September. The usual starting-point is the Bailey pub on Duke Street, off Grafton Street, at 7.30 p.m., but it's advisable to check with the tourist office in advance or telephone 01–4540228.

Since arrangements for these tours change from season to season, it is best to contact any Tourist Information Office for precise details.

## Travel information

Aer Lingus, flight information, telephone 01–7056705, passenger booking, telephone 01–8444777

British Midland, flight information, telephone 01–8422011, reservations, telephone 01–2838833

Ryanair, flight information, telephone 01–8444411, reservations, telephone 01–6774422

B&I Line, telephone 01–6797977, after office hours, telephone 01–6606666

Irish Ferries, telephone 01–6610511

Stena Sealink Line, telephone 01–2808844

Bus Éireann, telephone 01–8366111

Dublin Bus, telephone 01–8734222

Irish Rail, telephone 01–8366222

USIT Travel, 19 Aston Quay (by O'Connell Bridge), telephone 01–6798833, is the main travel agency for students and young people, and specialises in reduced-rate tickets to the UK, Europe and North America. There is also a noticeboard that may be of use to visitors looking for a ride or accommodation. (Two other useful noticeboards for would-be hitch-hikers or flat-dwellers can be found just inside the front gate of Trinity College, and also in the Students' Union offices in the university, at No. 6.) In summer it gets chaotic, so arrive early.

## TV/RADIO

Most homes and hotels in Dublin can receive State-run Irish TV (RTE 1 and Network 2) as well as a selection of British and other stations. One channel shows the national news from Germany, France, Italy and Spain, consecutively each evening.

Radio 1 (88.5 Mhz) is the main radio station for news. A number of State-run and commercial stations offer a non-stop diet of pop music.

# FESTIVALS AND SPECIAL EVENTS

## March

17 March is St Patrick's Day, Ireland's national holiday, marked by parades and celebrations throughout the country (and the world). Dublin's parade of marching bands and commercial exhibits is the biggest in Ireland, and takes several hours to wind its way through the centre of the city. Get there by mid-morning for a good view; the main review stand is in front of the GPO on O'Connell Street.

The Dublin Feis Ceoil, a classical and traditional Irish music competition, takes place at about the same time.

The Dublin Film Festival at the start of the month mixes the best of modern international cinema with revivals of screen classics and lectures and seminars on all aspects of the world of cinema.

The Irish Motor Show and the Irish Dog Show both take place in this month in the Royal Dublin Society (RDS), Ballsbridge.

## April

Irish Grand National. The highlight of the National Hunt season (horse-racing with jumps), a sport much loved by the Irish. Held on Easter Monday at Fairyhouse racecourse, north of Dublin.

The Dublin Grand Opera Society has its spring season in the Gaiety Theatre.

An Early Music Festival is held in the Royal Hospital, Kilmainham.

## June

The Spring Show, at the grounds of the RDS in Ballsbridge, was for decades the centrepiece of Ireland's agricultural year and a jovial meeting-ground of city and country. However, in recent years, its popularity declined sharply and it has now been replaced by a more broadly based fair called the RDS Summer Festival and held over the June bank holiday weekend.

The events of James Joyce's *Ulysses* took place on 16 June 1904, and the anniversary — Bloomsday — is commemorated each year with readings, dramatisations, fancy-dress parties and pilgrimages throughout the city centre.

The Irish Derby, the highlight of the flat-racing calendar, is held at the Curragh in Co. Kildare, 31 miles/50 km west of Dublin.

## July

Rose judging at St Anne's Park

## August

The Dublin Horse Show, held in the second week of August, is at once Ireland's premier show-jumping event and a highlight of the Dublin social calendar.

Irish Antique Dealers' Fair in the Mansion House

Dublin Regatta, Liffey powerboat-racing

Air Show in Baldonnel, in south-west County Dublin

## September

The first and third Sundays in September are traditionally the dates for the All-Ireland finals in Gaelic hurling and football.

Dún Laoghaire Festival

Liffey Descent (canoeing)

## October

Thousands of runners participate in the Dublin City Marathon, which takes place on the bank holiday Monday at the end of this month.

Dublin Theatre Festival. A two-week celebration of the best in Irish and international drama.

## November

Irish National Stamp Exhibition

## December

The Dublin Grand Opera Society has its winter season in the Gaiety Theatre.

Arts and Crafts Fairs in the Mansion House and the Tower Design Centre on Pearse Street

# WHERE TO STAY

A number of modern luxury hotels have been built in Dublin over the past few years, joining in competition with the city's more traditional establishments such as the Shelbourne. Less expensive and more intimate, family hotels and guesthouses offer good value to the economy-conscious visitor. At the cheaper end of the market, there is a wide choice of bed & breakfast accommodation (B&Bs) in private houses, mostly in the suburbs, and a handful of modern and comfortable hostels.

Bord Fáilte (Irish Tourist Board) operates a central reservation service for all types of accommodation at 14 Upper O'Connell Street, telephone 01–8747733. The fee for this service is £1 for local bookings and £2 for bookings outside Dublin. Especially in peak season (mid-March, Easter, July and August), it is advisable to book accommodation in advance.

There follows a list of some of the best hotels, guesthouses and hostels; information on the many B&Bs in the Dublin area can be obtained from Bord Fáilte. All the accommodation listed below is approved by Bord Fáilte; look out for the sign displaying a shamrock or saying 'ITB approved'. There are many more unapproved B&Bs, guesthouses and hotels and, although standards vary considerably, some at least offer good value and good quality. They can be found by consulting the telephone directory or calling to the premises.

Guesthouses and hotels usually provide a traditional (and very filling) Irish breakfast of cereal, fried bacon/eggs/sausages, brown bread and toast. Give some advance warning if you would prefer a 'continental' or vegetarian breakfast. In many hotels, the price of breakfast is extra.

Bord Fáilte grades hotels and guesthouses separately, depending on facilities. Hotels range from five-star international-style, to modest, usually family-run, one-star establishments. Guesthouses are classified separately, from four stars to one star. As prices vary according to season and inflation, only a rough indication is given here, based on the cost of overnight single accommodation (double accommodation can cost up to 50 per cent less for two people sharing). The categories are as follows:

| | |
|---|---|
| Economy: | £15 to £25 |
| Budget: | £25 to £35 |
| Moderate: | £35 to £45 |
| High: | £45 to £60 |
| Very high: | £60 and more |

When asking the price, check whether a service charge is added.

# DUBLIN CITY CENTRE

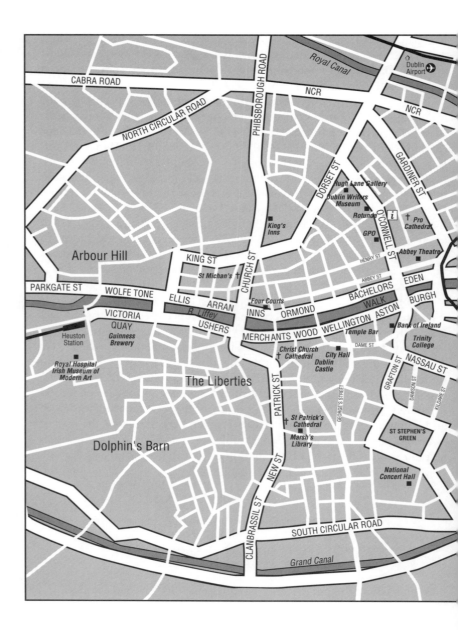

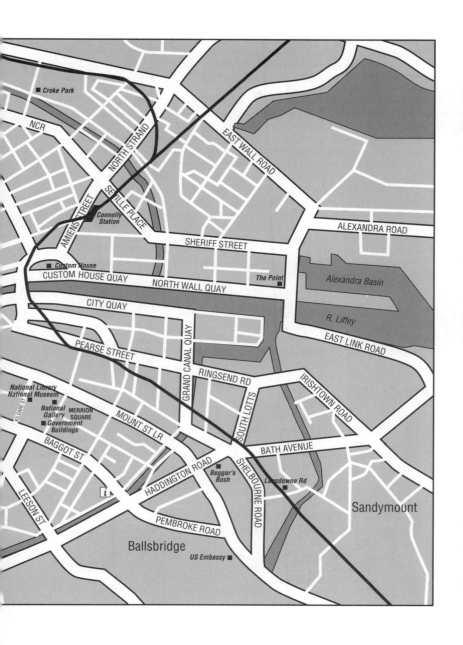

# HOTELS

## City centre

*Belvedere Hotel*, Great Denmark Street, telephone 01–8741413. Grade *. Rating: budget.

*Blooms Hotel*, Anglesea Street, telephone 01–6715622. Grade ***. Central location in Temple Bar. Modern and comfortable hotel with 86 bedrooms. A little plain, though. Restaurant and nightclub in the building. Rating: very high.

*Buswell's Hotel*, Molesworth Street, telephone 01–6764013. Grade ***. A largely political clientele gives this old-world hotel near the Dáil (Irish parliament) a whiff of intrigue. Rating: high.

*Clarence Hotel*, 6/8 Wellington Quay, telephone 01–6776178. Grade **. Traditional hotel which has found new popularity as a result of its central location in Temple Bar. Now owned by rock group U2. Rating: moderate.

*Conrad Hotel*, Earlsfort Terrace, telephone 01–6765555. Grade *****. Modern international-style hotel near St Stephen's Green. Rating: very high

*Georgian House*, 20 Lower Baggot Street, telephone 01–6618832. Grade **. Small hotel located in the heart of Georgian Dublin. Rating: moderate.

*Gresham Hotel*, Upper O'Connell Street, telephone 01–8746881. Grade ****. Long-established hotel on Dublin's main thoroughfare. Less fashionable than it once was, but the hotel has been completely refurbished in the past decade. Rating: very high.

*Kelly's Hotel*, 36 South Great George's Street, telephone 01–6779277. One of the last family-run hotels in the city centre. Good location close to the main sights. Grade *. Rating: budget.

*O'Brien's Hotel*, 38/39 Gardiner Street, telephone 01–8745203. Grade *. Rating: economy/budget.

*Shelbourne Hotel*, St Stephen's Green, telephone 01–6766471. Grade *****. Dublin's most celebrated hotel for over a century, the Shelbourne is invariably the favoured resting-place of star visitors to the city. An old-world hotel where no two rooms are the same size, the Shelbourne also boasts a fine restaurant and a pair of lively bars patronised by lawyers, politicians and journalists. Rating: very high.

*Westbury Hotel*, off Grafton Street, telephone 01–6791122. Grade *****. Modern international hotel located near the main shopping area. Rating: very high.

## South city

*Berkeley Court Hotel*, Lansdowne Road, telephone 01–6601711. Grade *****. International-style hotel with shopping centre, hair salons, swimming pool. Popular with business travellers. Rating: very high.

*Burlington Hotel*, Upper Leeson Street, telephone 01–6605222. Grade ****. The first and largest of Dublin's modern hotels, the Burlington still possesses a 1960s feel. Restaurant and nightclub in the building. Rating: very high.

*Jury's Hotel*, Pembroke Road, telephone 01–6605000. Grade *****. Popular with business people and package tourists. Accommodation for disabled guests. Rating: very high.

*Lansdowne Hotel*, Pembroke Road, telephone 01–6762549/6682522. Grade **. A small hotel popular with business people and rugby fans. Restaurant and bar. Rating: high.

*Orwell Lodge Hotel*, Orwell Road, Rathgar, telephone 01–4977258/9. Grade *. Small hotel in a settled suburb 3 miles/5 km from the city centre. Rating: budget.

*Rathgar Hotel*, 33/34 Kenilworth Square, telephone 01–4976392. Grade *. Rating: economy.

## City environs

*Court Hotel*, Killiney, telephone 01–2851622. Grade ***. Accommodation for disabled persons. Rating: budget/moderate in low season, high in summer.

*Dalkey Island Hotel*, Dalkey, telephone 01–2850377. Grade *. A converted two-storey nineteenth-century mansion 8 miles/13 km south of the city, with views of the small Dalkey Island. Rating: moderate.

*Howth Lodge Hotel*, Howth, telephone 01–8321010. Grade ***. Family-run hotel in its own grounds overlooking Ireland's Eye. Rating: moderate/high.

*Royal Marine Hotel*, Marine Road, Dún Laoghaire, telephone 01–2801911. Grade ***. A refurbished nineteenth-century hotel with fine views of the harbour. Rating: very high.

# GUESTHOUSES

## South city

*Ariel House,* 52 Lansdowne Road, telephone 01–6685512. Grade ****. Restored Victorian house located near DART rail service, 1 mile/1.5 km from the city centre. Rating: high.

*Beddington*, 181 Rathgar Road, telephone 01–4978047. Grade ***. 2 miles/3 km from city centre. Rating: budget.

*Kilronan House*, 70 Adelaide Road, telephone 01–4755266/4751562. Grade ***. Family-run guesthouse with a thirty-year reputation for friendliness, five minutes' walk from St Stephen's Green. Rating: moderate.

*Mount Herbert*, 7 Herbert Road, telephone 01–6684321. Grade ***. Family-run establishment located in the quiet inner suburb of Ballsbridge. Rating: moderate.

*St Aiden's*, 32 Brighton Road, Rathgar, telephone 01–4902011/4906178. Grade ***. Friendly guesthouse 3 miles/5 km from city centre. Rating: budget.

*Carrick Hall*, 69 Orwell Road, Rathgar, telephone 01–4922444. Grade **. Rating: economy.

Dublin contrasts: St Stephen's Green (*above*) and the bustle of Moore Street (*over*)

## North city

*Egan's House*, 7 Iona Park, Glasnevin, telephone 01–8303611. Grade ***.
Accommodation for disabled guests. Rating: economy.
*Iona House*, Iona Park, Glasnevin, telephone 01–8306217/8306855. Grade ***.
Good-value family guesthouse in a converted Victorian house. Rating: budget.
*Othello House*, 74 Gardiner Street, telephone 01–8743460/8740442. Grade **.
Originally associated with a group of actors, Othello House was refurbished in 1990.
Rating: budget.
*Parkview House*, 492 North Circular Road, telephone 01–8742208/8743697. Grade **.
Rating: economy/budget.

## City environs

*Abrae Court*, 9 Zion Road, Rathgar, telephone 01–4922242/4967133. Grade ***.
Rating: budget.
*Bayside*, Seafront, 5 Haddington Terrace, Dún Laoghaire, telephone 01–2804660.
Rating: budget.
*Kingswood Country House*, Kingswood, Naas Road, telephone 01–4592428. Grade ***.
Rating: moderate.
*Sea View*, Strand Road, Portmarnock, telephone 01–8462242. Grade *.
Rating: economy.

# HOSTELS

The number and standard of hostels is improving. Most offer a choice between
dormitories, multi-bed and single rooms, as well as cooking facilities and restaurants,
and are open all year round, twenty-four hours a day.

## An Óige (Irish Youth Hostel Association)

Dublin International Youth Hostel, 61 Mountjoy Street (near Dorset Street), telephone
01–8301766/8301396. Newly converted hostel (it was a convent) a few minutes' walk
from O'Connell Street. Open all day. Bicycle hire. Non-members of An Óige or other
national youth hostelling organisations can stay for a small extra charge.

## Other hostels (Tourist Board approved)

Avalon House, 55 Aungier Street, telephone 01–4750001. A converted medical school offering rooms with en suites, self-catering facilities, restaurant, launderette.
ISAAC's, 2 Frenchman's Lane (off Gardiner Street), telephone 01–8749321/8363877. The longest-established and currently the cheapest independent hostel, with self-catering kitchens, restaurant and bicycle hire.
Kinlay House, 2 Lord Edward Street, telephone 01–6796644. A nineteenth-century house refurbished for use as low-budget accommodation. Bureau de change. Accommodation for disabled persons.
Marlborough Hostel, 81/82 Marlborough Street, telephone 01–8747629. Directly beside the Pro-Cathedral. Self-catering kitchen, laundry facilities, security lockers.
The Young Traveller, St Mary's Place, off Dorset St, telephone 01–8305000/8305319. Four-bedded rooms, each with shower, towels, soap, sheets and duvet supplied. Coin-operated launderette, TV lounge.
YWCA Radcliffe Hall, St John's Road, Sandymount, telephone 01–2694521. No. 3 bus goes to the door. Open all year except Christmas.

## CAMPING AND CARAVAN SITES

Visitors to Dublin are advised against pitching tents in parks or other unapproved sites. There are two approved caravan and camping parks in the area, but both of them are more than 10 miles/16 km from the city centre.
North Beach Caravan and Camping Park, Rush, telephone 01–8437131/8437602, is located by the sea in North County Dublin and can be reached by taking the 33 bus from Eden Quay. Open all year round.
Shankill Caravan and Camping Park, Shankill, telephone 01–2820011, lies on the main Dublin–Wexford road, 10 miles/16 km south of the city. Open all year round.

## SELF-CATERING AND UNIVERSITY ACCOMMODATION

Several thousand on-campus rooms at Dublin's universities become available in summer, when Ireland's student population takes flight for North America and the rest of Europe. Rooms can be booked for single nights, but this option represents better value for visitors seeking accommodation for several weeks or months.
Demand for accommodation is heaviest at Trinity College, where many of the rooms are over 200 years old. More information can be obtained from the Accommodation Office, telephone 01–7021177.
The same university also has rooms available at Trinity Hall, Dartry Road, 3 miles/5 km south of the city centre. Telephone 01–4971772.
The other universities in Dublin offer accommodation in summer in modern and comfortable purpose-built blocks. University College Dublin rents out rooms in three locations, two of them on the main campus at Belfield, 3 miles/5 km south of the city centre:
Roebuck Hall, Belfield, telephone 01–2693244
UCD Village, Belfield, telephone 01–2697111
Blackrock Campus, Carysfort Avenue, Blackrock, telephone 01–7068797.
Dublin City University, Glasnevin, telephone 01–7045736/7045000, also rents rooms for the summer in its newly constructed accommodation block.
Bord Fáilte (Irish Tourist Board), telephone 01–2841782, keeps lists of houses, apartments and other self-catering accommodation available for weekly and monthly rent. Advance booking is essential in peak season.

# WHERE TO EAT

Eating out regularly is a newly acquired habit for most Irish people. Until very recently, going out for a meal was regarded as a treat reserved for special occasions and, even then, the venue was usually a hotel restaurant.

All this has changed in the past twenty years. Dublin now boasts numerous international-class restaurants — with prices to match. At the other end of the market, there are the ubiquitous fast-food outlets, selling burgers, kebabs, sandwiches, pizzas and oriental food, as well as an increasing number of coffee shops, pubs and vegetarian cafés serving good-quality food at affordable prices.

In between, standards vary hugely. Some restaurants offer great atmosphere and poor food. With others, the opposite is the case. As many French, German and Italian readers will discover, many establishments can't even be bothered to get the spellings on their menus right.

There are two reasons for the variation in quality. First, Ireland has no tradition of *haute cuisine* on which to fall back (there are only two 'Irish' restaurants in Dublin, both listed below). Most of the city's good restaurants are relative newcomers, founded in the past twenty years. Although standards are rising fast, there is still plenty of room for improvement. Second, Irish people are notoriously shy when it comes to complaining about poor quality, so even restaurants with low standards manage to survive far longer than they should.

There may not be a specifically Irish cuisine; there is, however, a wealth of fine food ingredients produced throughout the country. As the capital of a largely agricultural land, Dublin has ready access to wonderfully fresh natural foods. Be sure to try at least some of the following during your stay: fresh and smoked salmon and trout, sole, turbot, monkfish, prawns, mussels, lobsters, oysters, beef, lamb and pork, wholemeal and soda bread, and farmhouse cheeses.

It would be impossible to list every eating-place in Dublin; however, the list below is fairly comprehensive and includes the best of each type of restaurant, from low-budget to very expensive. A quick-reference guide is provided at the end.

It does not include fast-food outlets, which are the same in Dublin as anywhere else, except more numerous. A special mention must be made here for Dublin's fish and chip shops ('chippers'), many of them run by expatriate Italians who came to Ireland after World War II. Real fish and chip shops sell chips made from freshly chopped potatoes, not the reconstituted, synthetic or frozen varieties sold in many fast-food joints. The most famous chipper in Dublin is Burdock's in Werburgh Street, close to Christ Church Cathedral, which serves positively monstrous portions of cod, ray, haddock and whiting together with traditional chips. Another good one is Beshoff's in Westmoreland Street.

Hotel restaurants are not included. All the major Dublin hotels have their own restaurants but, although the quality in these places is sometimes excellent, atmosphere is usually lacking and the prices are high.

The list below covers only the best coffee houses and cafés throughout central Dublin. There are many more which serve excellent salads, sandwiches and light meals, especially at lunchtime. Of these, the most famous is undoubtedly Bewley's, with branches in Grafton Street, Westmoreland Street and South Great George's Street (see pages 82–3). These shops now open up to midnight and beyond on most nights, giving modern Dublin its first proper taste of café society.

In addition, an increasing number of pubs now offer good-quality food. The Stag's Head in Dame Court merits a special mention here for the tastiness of its grilled food and the friendliness of the staff; see 'Publife', page 51, for more information on this and other bars. For those who wish to, it should be easily possible to eat lunch for about £5.

Most good restaurants are located on the south side of the Liffey, near the main business and upmarket shopping streets. Anyone wanting to choose a restaurant on sight is advised to head for Temple Bar or St Andrew Street (near the bottom of Grafton Street), two areas with a particularly high concentration of restaurants.

Most restaurants sell wine, but beer is harder to come by. However, licensing laws have been liberalised recently, so more and more restaurants are allowed to sell beer and spirits; this is shown in the list.

All restaurants are required by law to display their menu and prices outside the premises. The list below is not in any sense a 'good food' guide, though some indication is usually given as to what can be expected from a restaurant. The ratings used refer to the approximate price of a meal for one person, wine not included. They are as follows:

| | |
|---|---|
| Economy: | under £5 |
| Budget: | under £10 |
| Moderate: | under £15 |
| High: | over £15 |
| Very high: | over £25 |

## SOUTH CITY CENTRE

*Bad Ass Café*, 9 Crown Alley, telephone 01–6712596. American pizzas and pasta in an upbeat warehouse atmosphere. Children's menu. Open 9 a.m.–11 p.m. every day. Rating: budget.

*Blazes Restaurant*, 11/12 Lower Exchange Street, telephone 01–6711261. Restaurant with full bar located in Temple Bar. Live music. Open seven days, 6 p.m.–12 midnight and sometimes later. Rating: moderate.

*Blazing Salads*, Powerscourt Townhouse Centre, Clarendon Street, telephone 01–6719522. Salads and vegetarian-inclined menu. Open 9 a.m.–6 p.m. Monday–Saturday. Rating: budget.

*Bucci*, 7 Camden Street, telephone 01–4751020. Italian restaurant serving both pizzas and pasta. Location a little out of the way, but the food is very good for the price. Open 12 noon onwards Monday to Saturday for lunch, 6 p.m. until late every day for dinner. Rating: budget to moderate.

*Le Caprice*, 12 St Andrew Street, telephone 01–6794050. Italian restaurant with appropriate interiors. Well established on the St Andrew Street strip. Open 6 p.m.– 12.45 a.m. every day. Rating: moderate to high.

*Captain America's*, Grafton Court, Grafton Street, telephone 01–6715266. Dublin's original burger restaurant, with a full bar which also serves cocktails. Children welcome. Open seven days, 12 noon to 12.30 a.m. Rating: budget to moderate.

*Castle Vaults Bistro*, Dublin Castle, telephone 01–6770678. Lunch specials and a salad bar, home-baked patisseries in pleasant surroundings. Open Monday–Friday 8.15 a.m.– 5.30 p.m., Saturday/Sunday 12 noon to 5.30 p.m. Rating: economy to budget.

*La Cave*, 28 South Anne Street, telephone 01–6794409. French/North African cuisine. Turns into a wine bar after midnight. Open 4.30–11.30 p.m. every day. Rating: budget to moderate.

*Cedar Tree*, 11a St Andrew Street, telephone 01–6772121. Lebanese and Middle Eastern cuisine. Rating: moderate.

*Cellary*, 1 Fownes Street (Temple Bar), telephone 01–6710362. Vegetarian lunches, à la carte restaurant upstairs in the evenings. Open 8 a.m.–12 midnight, 12 noon to 10.30 p.m. Sunday. Rating: economy to budget.

*City Arts Centre Café*, 23/25 Moss Street, telephone 01–6770643. Simple, affordable lunches and sandwiches. Open Monday–Friday 8 a.m.–5.30 p.m. Rating: economy.

*Coffee Bean*, 4 Nassau Street, telephone 01–6797140. Mostly vegetarian lunches. Nice view of Trinity College opposite. Open Monday–Friday 10.30 a.m.–3.30 p.m. Rating: economy.

*Coffee Inn*, 6 South Anne Street (off Grafton Street), telephone 01–6770107. Bohemian place with good coffee. The food — mainly pasta and burgers — is cheap but unremarkable. Seats outside in the summer when the sun shines. Open Monday–Saturday 11 a.m.–2 a.m., Sunday 6 p.m.–1 a.m. Rating: economy.

*Cooke's Café*, 14 South William Street (behind Powerscourt Centre), telephone 01–6790536. Fashionable restaurant serving Mediterranean/Californian food. Delicious desserts. Advance booking recommended. Open 9 a.m.–11 p.m. Monday–Saturday. Also open for breakfast 8–11 a.m. Sunday brunch 11 a.m.–3 p.m. Rating: high.

*Le Coq Hardi*, 35 Pembroke Road, telephone 01–6684130/6689070. Very expensive French cuisine, good wine cellar. Open 12.30–2.30 p.m., 7–11 p.m. Monday to Saturday. Rating: very high.

*Cornucopia*, 19 Wicklow Street, telephone 01–6777583. Affordable and tasty vegetarian food. Open Monday–Friday 8 a.m.–9 p.m., Saturday 9 a.m.–6 p.m. Rating: economy.

*Cottonwood Café*, 7 Johnson's Court (off Grafton Street), telephone 01–6712276. Late-opening restaurant with reasonable prices and live music on some nights. Open 9 a.m.–1 or 2 a.m. Monday–Saturday. Rating: budget to moderate.

*Dobbins Wine Bistro*, 15 Stephen's Lane, telephone 01–6764670. Pricey but fashionable. Open 12.30–3 p.m. and 8 p.m.–midnight, Monday to Saturday. Rating: high.

*Eastern Tandoori*, 34/35 South William Street, telephone 01–6710506. One of the best Indian restaurants in town. Full licence. Open 12.30–2.30 p.m. Monday–Saturday, 6 p.m.–12 midnight every day. Rating: moderate to high.

*Elephant & Castle*, 18 Temple Bar, telephone 01–6793121. Busy and frequently noisy restaurant serving good salads and hamburgers. Good for weekend brunches too. Open 8 a.m.–11.30 p.m. Monday–Thursday, 8 a.m.–midnight Friday, 10 a.m.–midnight Saturday, 12 noon to 11.30 p.m. Sunday. Rating: moderate to high.

*Fitzers*, National Gallery restaurant, Merrion Square West, telephone 01–6686481. Interesting menu, reasonable prices. Popular on Sundays. Open 11 a.m.–5.30 p.m. Monday–Saturday (until 8.30 p.m. Thursday), 2–5 p.m. Sunday. Rating: budget.

*Les Frères Jacques*, 74 Dame Street, telephone 01–6794555. Expensive French restaurant with excellent reputation. Open 12.30–2 p.m. Monday–Friday, 7–11 p.m. Monday–Saturday. Rating: high.

*Gallagher's Boxty House*, 20/21 Temple Bar, telephone 01–6772762. Unspectacular Irish cuisine (boxty is a kind of traditional potato pancake). Pleasing traditional Irish décor and taped folk music. Open 12.30–11.30 p.m. every day. Rating: moderate to high.

*George's Bistro*, 29 South Frederick Street, telephone 01–6797000. Late-night restaurant popular with lawyers and politicians working nearby. Late-night music and singing sometimes. Open 12 noon to 3 p.m. Monday–Saturday, 7 p.m. to about 2 a.m. Tuesday–Saturday. Rating: high.

*Imperial*, 12a Wicklow Street, telephone 01–6772580. Good-quality Chinese restaurant. Open noon–midnight daily. Rating: moderate to high.

*Kingsland*, 15 Dame Street, telephone 01–6798286. Long-established and popular Chinese restaurant. Sedate atmosphere. Open 5.30 p.m.–12.30 a.m. Monday–Thursday, 12.30 p.m.–12.30 a.m. Friday–Saturday, 1–11 p.m. Sunday. Rating: moderate.

*Little Lisbon*, 2 Fownes Street Upper (beside Central Bank), telephone 01–6711274. Unpretentious Portuguese food, big helpings. Bring your own wine if you like. Open 12–11 p.m. every day. Rating: moderate.

*Locks*, 1 Windsor Terrace, telephone 01–4543391. Meat and fish specialities in a converted pub with canal view. Long-established restaurant with consistently excellent reputation. Open 12.30–2 p.m. Monday–Friday, 7.15–11 p.m. Monday–Saturday. Rating: high.

*Lord Edward*, 23 Christ Church Place, telephone 01–4542420. Renowned seafood restaurant, above pub of same name by Christ Church Cathedral. Open 12.30–2.30 p.m. Tuesday–Friday, 6–10.45 p.m. Tuesday–Saturday. Rating: high.

*Marks Brothers*, 7 South Great George's Street, telephone 01–6771085. Cheap soups, salads and excellent sandwiches. Popular with students and all sorts. Open 10 a.m.–5 p.m. Monday–Saturday. Rating: economy.

*La Mezza Luna*, 1 Temple Lane, telephone 01–6712840. Inexpensive Italian cuisine in a busy restaurant. Open 12–11 p.m. Monday–Thursday, 12–11.30 p.m. Friday/Saturday, 4–10.30 p.m. Sunday. Rating: budget to moderate.

*Mitchell's Cellars*, 21 Kildare Street, telephone 01–6680367. Varied menu, good wines. Lunch only. Open 12.15 to 2.30 p.m. Monday–Saturday. Rating: moderate.

*Nico's*, 53 Dame Street, telephone 01–6773062. One of the oldest Italian restaurants in Dublin, and one of the most comfortable. Traditional cuisine. Open 12.30–2.30 p.m. Monday–Friday, 6 p.m.–12.30 a.m. Monday–Saturday. Rating: moderate.

*Oisin's*, 31 Upper Camden Street, telephone 01–4753433. Expensive Irish cuisine. Open 6.30–10.30 p.m. Tuesday–Saturday. Rating: high.

*Old Dublin*, 91 Francis Street, telephone 01–4542028. Russian/Scandinavian cuisine. Open 12.30–2.30 p.m., 7.30–10.30 p.m. Monday–Saturday. Rating: high.

*Pasta Fresca*, Chatham Street, telephone 01–6792402. Small restaurant, busy atmosphere. Fresh pasta a speciality. Also serves a good breakfast. Advance bookings not accepted. Open 7.30 a.m.–7.30 p.m. Monday, 7.30 a.m.–11 p.m. Tuesday–Saturday. Rating: budget to moderate.

*Patrick Guilbaud*, 46 James Place, Lower Baggot Street, telephone 01–6764192. Nouvelle cuisine French restaurant with a good reputation. Open 12.30–2 p.m., 7.30–10.15 p.m. Monday–Saturday. Rating: very high.

*Pigalle*, 14 Temple Bar, Merchant's Arch, telephone 01–6761060. Excellent upmarket French restaurant. Rating: high.

*Pizzeria Italia*, 23 Temple Bar, telephone 01–6778528. Great pasta and pizzas, little room. Friendly staff. No advance booking or credit cards. Open 12 noon to 11 p.m. Tuesday–Saturday. Rating: moderate.

*QV 2*, St Andrew Street, telephone 01–6773363. The successor to Quo Vadis, a firm favourite with Dubliners for many years. Italian-influenced cuisine, lively atmosphere, good lunch specials. Interesting wine list. Open 12 noon to 2.45 p.m., 6 p.m.–12.30 a.m. every day. Rating: moderate to high.

*Rajdoot Tandoori*, 26/28 Clarendon Street, telephone 01–6794274. Excellent Indian restaurant. Open 12.30–2.30 p.m., 6.30–11.30 p.m. Monday–Saturday. Rating: moderate to high.

*Restaurant Tosca*, 20 Suffolk Street, telephone 01–6796744/6797536. Italian cuisine, cool interior. Owned by Bono's brother, so there's often a rock star or two in the place. Open 9 a.m.–12 midnight Sunday–Wednesday, 9 a.m.–1 a.m. Thursday–Saturday. Rating: moderate.

*Rock Garden Restaurant*, 3a Crown Alley, telephone 01–6799114. Upbeat, noisy joint serving burgers and Mexican food. Open noon–midnight every day. Rating: budget.

*South Street Pizzeria*, South Great George's Street, telephone 01–4752273. Home-made pizzas and pasta. Good late-night alternative to fast food. Open 12 noon–2 a.m. every day. Rating: budget.

*La Stampa*, 35 Dawson Street, telephone 01–6778611. Posh Italian establishment worth a visit for the sumptuous décor alone. Booking advisable at the weekend. Open noon to 11.30 p.m. Monday–Saturday. Rating: high.

*Tante Zoe's*, 1 Crow Street (Temple Bar), telephone 01–6794407. Dublin's first cajun restaurant. Open 12 noon to 3 p.m. Monday–Saturday, 6 p.m.–12 midnight every day. Rating: moderate.

*Trocadero*, 3 South Andrew Street, telephone 01–6775545. Popular with theatre and media people, who go for the atmosphere more than the food. Open 6 p.m.–12.30 a.m. daily (Sunday 11.30 p.m.). Rating: moderate to high.

*Vertigo*, South Richmond Street, Portobello. A real neighbourly diner situated just before you reach the canal, going in the direction of Rathmines. Monster breakfasts served at any time and scrumptious desserts. Friendly staff too. Open 12 noon to 1 a.m. (to 4 a.m. Thursday–Saturday). Rating: budget.

*Well Fed Café*, Dublin Resource Centre, 6 Crow Street, telephone 01–6771947. Cheap cooperative restaurant serving vegetarian dishes. Big helpings. Open 10 a.m.–4.30 p.m. Monday, 10 a.m.–8.30 p.m. Tuesday–Saturday. Rating: economy.

# NORTH CITY CENTRE

*Chapter One*, Dublin Writers' Museum, 18/19 Parnell Square, telephone 01–8732266/8732281. Full bar. Irish food, including venison, salmon, lamb and duckling. Offers lunch and pre-theatre menus, and à la carte in the evening only. Open 12 noon to 2.30 p.m., 6–11 p.m. Monday–Saturday. Rating: high.

*Flanagan's*, 61 Upper O'Connell Street, telephone 01–8731388. Steak, fish, chicken and pasta dishes. Open 8 a.m.–12 midnight daily. Rating: moderate.

*Gallagher's*, 83 Middle Abbey Street, telephone 01–8729861. Steak restaurant. Open noon–midnight Monday–Thursday and Sunday, 12 noon to 1 a.m. Friday/Saturday. Rating: moderate.

*Mahoganí Gaspipes*, 17 Manor Street, Stoneybatter, telephone 01–6798138. Chinese/Irish/American food. Late-night jazz at the weekends. Rating: moderate.

*101 Talbot*, 100/101 Talbot Street, telephone 01–8745011. Good-value food served up in a lively ambience. Popular for lunches and pre-theatre. Open 9.30 a.m.–4 p.m. Monday, 9.30 a.m.–10.30 p.m. Tuesday–Saturday. Rating: budget to moderate.

*Sheries*, 3 Lower Abbey Street, telephone 01–8747237. Diner in curious chrome. Open 8 a.m.–6 p.m. Monday–Saturday. Rating: budget.

*Winding Stair Bookshop and Café*, 40 Lower Ormond Quay (by the Ha'penny Bridge), telephone 01–8733292. Lovely place to have soup and a sandwich overlooking the Liffey. Open 10.30 a.m.–6 p.m. Monday–Saturday. Rating: economy.

## SOUTH DUBLIN AND ENVIRONS

*Ayumi-Ya*, Newpark Centre, Blackrock, telephone 01–6620233. Brilliant Japanese cuisine. Beer licence. Open 7–11 p.m. Monday–Saturday, 6–10 p.m. Sunday. Rating: high.
*De Selby's*, 17/18 Patrick Street, Dún Laoghaire, telephone 01–2841761/2. Family-run fish restaurant. Beer licence. Open 5.30–11 p.m. Monday–Friday, 12 noon to 10 p.m. weekends. Rating: moderate to high.
*Killakee House*, Killakee Road, Rathfarnham (below Hellfire Club, 8 miles/13 km from city centre), telephone 01–4932645. Pricey table d'hôte/à la carte in a mountain setting. Open for lunch Monday–Friday, dinner Monday–Saturday. Rating: high.
*Restaurant na Mara*, 1 Harbour Road, Dún Laoghaire, telephone 01–2806767/2800509. Seafood restaurant overlooking harbour. Beer licence. Open 12.30–2.30 p.m., 7–10.30 p.m. Monday–Saturday. Rating: high to very high.

## NORTH DUBLIN AND ENVIRONS

*Abbey Tavern*, Howth, telephone 01–8390307. Seafood restaurant popular with tourists. Beer licence. Cabaret entertainment. Open 7–11 p.m. Monday–Saturday. Rating: high.
*Adrian's Restaurant*, Abbey Street, Howth, telephone 01–8391696. Fish restaurant in port of Howth. Four-course dinner menu; table d'hôte only. Open for lunch seven days, dinner Monday–Saturday. Last orders 9.30 p.m. Rating: moderate to high.
*Bon Appetit*, 9 St James's Terrace, Malahide, telephone 01–8450314. Fish and meat dishes in an elegant Georgian building in Malahide, 8 miles/13 km north of Dublin. Beer licence. Open 12.30–2.30 p.m. Monday–Friday, 7–11 p.m. Monday–Saturday. Rating: high.
*King Sitric*, East Pier, Howth, telephone 01–8325235. Popular tourist destination serving fish caught locally. Beer licence. Seafood and oyster bar open noon–3 p.m. in the summer months. Open 6.30–11 p.m. Monday–Saturday. Rating: high to very high.
*Old Schoolhouse*, Swords, telephone 01–8402846. Open 12.30–2.30 p.m., 7–10.30 p.m. Rating: high.

### BREAKFAST IN DUBLIN

The Irish rise late, but still manage to consume vast breakfasts washed down with lashings of tea. This traditional model is perhaps not as universally true as it once was, but there's no doubt that a hearty, if cholesterol-rich, breakfast of eggs, bacon, sausages with brown bread or toast is still very popular. Black or white pudding, made from the less mentionable parts of the pig, is another local favourite.

Some restaurants and cafés have come up with healthier variations on this bill of fare, and also serve cereals, fruit and muesli. The following establishments offer the best breakfasts in Dublin and are open from 8 a.m. and sometimes earlier (see full list for addresses):

Any Bewley's (Grafton, Westmoreland or South Great George's Street)
Cooke's Café (upmarket brunch)
Cornucopia (for the vegetarian version of a traditional Irish fried breakfast)
Elephant & Castle (another brunch specialist)
Kitty O'Shea's (see page 53; weekend brunch a speciality)
Montague, 4b Montague Street (coffee shop on side-street off Harcourt Street)
Pasta Fresca (the Italian influence)
Vertigo (big portions for the late riser — open from noon)

## QUICK-REFERENCE GUIDE TO EATING IN DUBLIN

### American Food/Burger Restaurants
Captain America's
Elephant & Castle
Rock Garden Restaurant
Vertigo

### Chinese
Kingsland
Imperial

### French
La Cave
Le Coq Hardi
Les Frères Jacques
Patrick Guilbaud
Pigalle
La Stampa

### Indian
Eastern Tandoori
Rajdoot Tandoori

### Irish
Gallagher's Boxty House
Oisin's

### Italian/Pizzerias
Bad Ass Café
Bucci
Le Caprice
La Mezza Luna
Nico's
Pasta Fresca
Pizzeria Italia
Tosca

### Late-opening (midnight and later)
Bewley's
Blazes
La Cave
Cottonwood Café
Dobbins Wine Bistro
George's Bistro
South Street Pizzeria
Trocadero
Vertigo
QV 2

### Other
Ayumi-Ya (Japanese)
Cedar Tree (Middle Eastern)
Cooke's Café (Mediterranean/Californian)
Little Lisbon (Portuguese)
Old Dublin (Russian/Scandinavian)

### Seafood
Abbey Tavern
Adrian's
King Sitric
Lord Edward
Restaurant na Mara

### Vegetarian
Blazing Salads
Cellary
Coffee Bean
Cornucopia
Marks Brothers
Well Fed Café
Winding Stair Bookshop and Café

# SHOPPING

Normal shopping hours are 9.30 a.m.–5.30 p.m., Monday to Saturday, though there are significant variations. City-centre shops stay open until 8 p.m. on Thursdays and suburban shopping centres stay open until 9 p.m. on Thursdays and Fridays. In addition, many neighbourhood grocery stores stay open until late; see page 15 for a list of such shops.

Consumer laws in Ireland are similar to those elsewhere in the EC, so if an article is defective, bring it back and demand a refund. In case of difficulties, ring the Office of the Director of Consumer Affairs, telephone 01–6606011.

Value-added tax (VAT) is levied at 21 per cent on most non-essential items, but visitors from outside the EC who are buying goods for export should remember they can claim this back. The 'Cashback' scheme is easy to use; ask about it at the time of purchase, keep your receipt and present this at the special 'Cashback' desk at the airport. The refund is given on the spot in the currency of your choice. (For more information telephone 01–8427573.) Other-

Grafton Street

wise, refunds can be claimed from individual shops on returning home; make sure the customs stamp the relevant form before you leave Ireland. Many shops will also ship goods overseas; there is a shipping charge, but VAT is deducted at point of sale.

Dubliners love to go shopping, and 'town' on a busy Saturday afternoon is a spectacle in itself. On offer is an interesting mix of department stores, shopping centres, designer boutiques, specialist shops and lively street markets, and all within a fairly compact area in the city centre. Products for which Ireland is famous worldwide include linen, knitwear, tweed and glass or crystal, but there are many more quality articles to be had if you hunt around. Pottery from the Kilkenny Design Centre, leather from the Westbury Mall, or clothes from Irish designers such as John Rocha's China-town or Louise Kennedy in the Powerscourt Townhouse Centre all make for original and distinctive purchases for the visitor.

Every Dubliner knows the four main department stores in the city: Brown Thomas and Switzers on Grafton Street, Clery's on O'Connell Street, and Arnotts, whose main branch is on Henry Street. Brown Thomas is the most sophisticated, Clery's is the cheapest and most characteristically Irish, while the other two lie somewhere in between in terms of price and range. There are other department stores too — such as Marks & Spencer, Roches Stores and Dunnes Stores — which offer good value but less atmosphere or choice.

**Grafton Street** and the surrounding area south of the river is Dublin's most fashionable and expensive shopping district. This part of the city is also home to Dublin's ever-increasing community of buskers, who'll keep you entertained (for a fee) as you go about your business. Expect also to have at least one collection-box rattled in your direction during the day. If you feel so inclined, contribute early on, make sure you get a badge, display it prominently and shop in peace. Other regulars you'll encounter on the streets include pavement-artists, face-painters, hair-braiders, poetry-readers, flower-sellers, newspaper-sellers, sign-holders and beggars.

**Dawson Street**, parallel to Grafton Street, is notable for its two large bookshops and its designer clothes shops, including Jasper Conran, Kamouflage and the Irish designer Mariad Whisker. There are more fashion shops in the **Royal Hibernian Way**, an exclusive but intimate shopping arcade leading from Dawson Street to Grafton Street.

The **Powerscourt Townhouse Centre**, on the other side of Grafton Street, down Johnson's Court, is worth visiting for the building alone. A once-fashionable townhouse built in 1774, Powerscourt was used for many years by a wholesale textile company (this business still thrives elsewhere along South William Street) until it was converted to commercial use in the late 1970s. The interior courtyard is completely roofed in, and two floors of galleries above are filled with craft shops interspersed with cafés and restaurants. Of special note is the gallery of the Craft Council of Ireland, which exhibits the best work by Irish designers.

The **St Stephen's Green Centre**, at the top of Grafton Street, is Dublin's largest shopping mall. Although its mock-Victorian ironwork and showboat shape demonstrate little regard for architectural sensibilities, it has nonetheless proved extremely popular with Dubliners who flock here for household goods, clothes and crafts. The centre was built on the site of the old Dandelion Green, scene in the 1970s of U2's first concerts.

On **Henry Street**, north of the river, the streetlife is the same but the shopping is different. This area is more downmarket, less chic. The lower-priced department stores such as Roches and Dunnes Stores compete fiercely with bargain-basement shops and street hawkers for your custom. The stalls on nearby **Moore Street** are as famous for the women who own them as for the colourful displays of vegetables and fruit on sale. In 1986 the women fought the city authorities for the right to keep their stalls in the middle of Dublin's busiest shopping district without having to pay a licence for the privilege. Needless to say, they won. The mazy interior of the ILAC Shopping Centre is home to Dunnes Stores, countless boutiques and cafés, as well as the Central Library.

Clery's has been on **O'Connell Street** for over fifty years, opposite the GPO. It is an institution that has long been a favourite with value-conscious shoppers, especially those up from the country. These days, however, it is struggling hard to keep up with changing tastes, though it retains a slightly old-fashioned and familiar air. With the exception of Eason's, a large newsagents and booksellers, the rest of O'Connell Street is a disappointment for shoppers, with burger joints and tinselly gift shops predominating.

Grafton Street and Henry Street were formerly two distinct worlds, but now they are joined by a thread of shopping activity stretching through **Temple Bar**, over the celebrated Ha'penny Bridge and down Liffey Street to the ILAC Shopping Centre. Indeed, Temple Bar with its assortment of second-hand shops, craft workshops and record stores is one of the most interesting shopping areas in the city these days, especially for the young. The best advice here is to browse, particularly in the streets behind the towering Central Bank.

There are many other shopping areas away from this main axis. Back on the south side, on **Francis Street**, in the heart of old Dublin known as the Liberties, you can find a collection of antique shops selling a mixture of old and unusual furniture, paintings, bric-à-brac, and often just plain junk. Nearby, on **Thomas Street**, there are open-air stalls and a number of bargain-basement stores. One of these, Frawleys, is legendary for the wide range and rock-bottom prices of its unfancy goods.

The **South City Markets**, off South Great George's Street, west of Grafton Street, is an original Victorian market housing a variety of stalls selling second-hand clothing, plants and bric-à-brac. There's also Jenny Vander, an interesting vintage clothing shop full of twenties dresses, period jewellery and platform shoes.

Somewhat removed from the main shopping areas, the **Tower Design Centre** (Pearse Street, off Grand Canal Quay, telephone 01–6775655) houses almost thirty craft firms, located in a converted 1862 sugar-refining tower. Among the attractions here are workshops devoted to heraldry, stained glass and Irish pewter, as well as displays of hand-painted silks, hand-knits and silver jewellery. There's a restaurant on the first floor. Take bus 3 from Clery's on O'Connell Street.

## WHAT TO LOOK FOR

### Antiques

For years, Ireland's antiques, the products of her magnificent eighteenth- and nineteenth-century craftspeople, were plundered for sale overseas. As the great houses and mansions became idle, they were stripped of their possessions, legally or illegally. Furniture, fittings and even fireplaces were removed in the rush to profit from misery. Today, there is an increased and more widespread appreciation of the country's remaining treasure of antiques, and the flow of goods abroad has slowed. The antiques trade continues to thrive and there are dozens of such shops around the city, ranging from bric-à-brac stalls to large furniture showrooms.

The main area in which to browse is the Liberties, especially Francis Street, as mentioned above. There are also some shops in nearby Patrick Street, in the Iveagh Buildings. Clanbrassil Street, straight out by St Patrick's Cathedral on the new dual carriageway, is not as busy as it used to be, but still has some shops selling furniture, mirrors and other objects.

Along the river, Bachelor's Walk and the quays above it have some wonderfully dusty old furniture and antique shops and warehouses crammed from floor to ceiling with bric-à-brac.

For smaller things, check out the Powerscourt Townhouse Centre, as well as the more expensive shops on Dawson and Molesworth Street. The principal salesroom for antiques, fine art and paintings is James Adam, on the corner of Kildare Street and St Stephen's Green. Check the 'Fine Arts' section in Saturday's *Irish Times* for up-to-date information on sales and auctions.

## Art galleries

There are over fifty art galleries, both public and private, in Dublin. The visual arts never ranked as high as literature throughout the history of the city, possibly because of a lack of patrons. Today, the art scene is modest but thriving, and encompasses a wide variety of tastes and styles.

Most of the commercial art galleries are small and concentrated on the south side of the city. These include the popular Kerlin Gallery, Dawson Street, telephone 01–6779179, a purpose-built gallery space which focuses on the work of new, emerging Irish artists. Worth a visit too are the Caldwell Gallery, 31 Upper Fitzwilliam Street, telephone 01–6688629, Temple Bar Gallery & Studios, 48 Temple Bar, telephone 01–6710033, and the City Arts Centre, Moss Street, telephone 01–6770643, which also has a café.

Taylor Galleries, 34 Kildare Street, telephone 01–6766055, is the longest-established private gallery dealing with twentieth-century art. Solomon Gallery, Powerscourt Townhouse Centre, telephone 01–6794237, exhibits paintings, sculpture and ceramics of contemporary Irish artists in an extravagant Georgian setting. In the same centre, the Crafts Council Gallery, telephone 01–6797368, displays visiting crafts and the best of Irish design, traditional and modern.

The Boulevard Gallery is not a gallery at all, but an open-air exhibition held on the railings of Merrion Square opposite the National Gallery every Sunday. The painters are amateurs, and their work ranges in quality from the ordinary to the excellent, so the challenge for the buyer is to spot real talent.

## Arts and crafts

The Kilkenny Design Centre groups together over 400 artists and craftworkers whose produce is sold through the Kilkenny Shop (Nassau Street, opposite Trinity College, telephone 01–6777066). One side of the shop is devoted to clothes, especially woollens, linen and tweed. The other half contains a wide variety of Irish glass, pottery, ceramics and metalwork. Look out for pottery from Stephen Pearce, knitwear from Lainey Keogh, Jerpoint Glass and jewellery by Sonia Landweer.

The Tower Design Centre, Pearse Street, was mentioned above (see page 39). A similar craft centre is located at Marlay Park, Rathfarnham, 6 miles/10 km south of the city centre, where the stables and workshops have been converted into the Marlay Crafts Courtyard (telephone 01–4942083, bus 47B) and leased to professional designers. The main specialities here are bookbinding and glassware.

The Crafts Council Gallery, Powerscourt Townhouse Centre, telephone 01–6797368, displays crafts by Irish and international designers, including ceramics, fabrics, wood and metalwork. As the headquarters of the Crafts Council of Ireland, the gallery holds frequent exhibitions and also runs a retail shop.

## Books

As you might expect in such a literary city, Dublin boasts an impressive collection of bookstores, which stay open longer than most other shops (including Sundays, in many cases). The rise of the native publishing industry has been one of the country's modern-day success stories, and this combination of good writing and attractive design makes an Irish-published book an excellent present.

Two of the biggest bookstores are Waterstone's and Hodges Figgis, which face each other near the bottom of Dawson Street. Both are open until 8.30 p.m. most evenings as well as on Sundays. Around the corner in Dawson Street is Fred Hanna's, which carries a huge number of titles and has a wonderfully knowledgable staff. The shop is much favoured by students from Trinity College across the street, who buy their textbooks there. Eason's, on O'Connell Street, is another large store selling books, stationery, art materials and a variety of other goods. It is also the place with the widest range of magazines and foreign newspapers, so come here if you can't find a publication anywhere else.

Other bookshops are more intimate and pleasant to browse through. Top of the list is Books Upstairs, facing Trinity College on College Green, a left-of-centre place with good media, poetry and specialist coverage (such as gay fiction and feminist writing). George Webb on Crampton Quay is more old-fashioned and stands as a last reminder of the era when the quays of Dublin were packed with booksellers displaying their wares on barrows out front. The Dublin Bookshop is centrally located on Grafton Street, while Connolly Books, on East Essex Street, is a small shop run by Ireland's minuscule Communist Party, and which specialises — not surprisingly — in Marxist economics, history, politics and third world issues.

There are countless second-hand bookshops in Dublin. Perhaps the most famous is Greene & Co., on Clare Street, whose upstairs floor is a dusty wonderland for bibliophiles. Greene's still keep books on barrows outside the shop for browsers to sift through, and they also sell new books of Irish interest. There's even a post office in the shop.

The Winding Stair Bookshop and Café on Ormond Quay, facing the Ha'penny Bridge, is another highlight of the Dublin book world. Here, there are second-hand books on three floors, and the view from the café over the Liffey is incomparable. Among the best-known antiquarian shops specialising in books, maps and prints of Irish interest are Cathach Books on Duke Street and Cathair Books at Essex Gate, in Temple Bar.

Books Upstairs, College Green, telephone 01–6796687
Cathach Books, 10 Duke Street, telephone 01–6718676
Cathair Books, 1 Essex Gate, telephone 01–6792406
Dublin Bookshop, 24 Grafton Street, telephone 01–6775568
Eason's, 40 Lower O'Connell Street, telephone 01–8733811
Fred Hanna, 27/29 Nassau Street, telephone 01–6771255
Greene & Co., 16 Clare Street, telephone 01–6762554
Hodges Figgis, 41 Dawson Street, telephone 01–6774754
Library Shop, Trinity College, telephone 01–6772941
Waterstone's, 7 Dawson Street, telephone 01–6791415
George Webb, 5 Crampton Quay, telephone 01–6777489

## Crystal, china, ceramics, cutlery

Waterford Crystal is a famous product closely associated with Ireland. It is expensive, though small pieces can be purchased relatively cheaply. The price doesn't vary, so there's no point in shopping around. Other Irish glass firms, from Galway, Cavan, Tyrone and Tipperary, are now challenging Waterford, and are usually cheaper. The best places to buy glass are the Kilkenny Shop and the Blarney Woollen Mills, both on Nassau Street, and Best of Irish, Westbury Hotel. Switzers also sells the entire range of Waterford cut glass, and Tierneys, in the St Stephen's Green Centre, is another specialist shop. At Dublin Crystal (Carysfort Avenue, Blackrock, Co. Dublin, telephone 01–2887932), visitors can watch the crystal being cut.

All the above outlets also sell Irish ceramics, from Belleek, Donegal and Galway. One shop worth a special mention is Read's, a knife and cutlery shop on Parliament Street which is the oldest shop in Dublin. This establishment has been in continuous occupation on this site since 1670, when the Reads were the official swordmakers for Dublin Castle.

## Department stores

Arnotts, 12 Henry Street, telephone 01–8721111
Brown Thomas, 15 Grafton Street, telephone 01–6795666
Clery's, O'Connell Street, telephone 01–6786000
Dunnes Stores, ILAC Centre, Henry Street, telephone 01–8730211 and St Stephen's
Green Centre, telephone 01–4751111
Eason's, O'Connell Street, telephone 01–8733811
Marks & Spencer, 24 Mary Street, telephone 01–8728833 and 28 Grafton Street,
telephone 01–6797855
Roches Stores, 54 Henry Street, telephone 01–8730044
Switzers, 92 Grafton Street, telephone 01–6776821

## Fashion

When it comes to fashion, Dublin is certainly no match for Paris or Milan. The Irish in general don't seem to have the instinctive feel for colour and tone of, say, the Italians. Moreover, the climate is constantly conspiring against fashion and sophistication — solid, practical shoes are needed to keep the rain out, while dark colours are required wearing for hiding the city's grime. Indeed, on dull, rainy days it sometimes appears as though the entire population of Dublin is dressed in monotonous shades of grey or black.

However, a closer look reveals a slightly different story. Young Dubliners may not follow the rules of high fashion (most of them couldn't afford to do so, anyway), but they increasingly possess an elegance that is both very individualistic and effortlessly casual. Put this bohemian chic together with the natural free-spiritedness of the Irish, and it's easy to understand why Dublin has become one of the 'hippest' cities in Europe.

And it's not just the young who are growing more fashion-conscious and demanding of quality. People of all ages are more aware than before of the fashion options open to them. In response, a new generation of Irish designers and shops has developed, offering native reworkings of classical designs. At the same time, the traditional tweed and knitwear sectors have adapted to changing tastes, and have largely abandoned the kitschy patterns that previously passed for traditional Irish clothing.

At the upper end of the market, one of the best places to go is *Brown Thomas*, on Grafton Street. This department store stocks many international brands, especially Italian ones, but it also features a number of Irish designers in its Private Lives section, notably Paul Costelloe (whose customers include the Irish President, Mary Robinson, and Britain's Princess Diana) and Michelina Stacpoole.

Similarly, the *Design Centre* in the Powerscourt Townhouse Centre, Clarendon Street (telephone 01–6795718) is a superb showcase for Irish fashion, particularly from young designers. The names to look out for here include Mariad Whisker, Louise Kennedy, Lainey Keogh, Glynis Robins and Michael Mortell, whose clothes are also on sale in Firenze in the Westbury Mall, Balfe Street.

*Sybil Connolly*, 71 Merrion Square, telephone 01–6767281, is probably the longest-established designer of *haute couture* in the city. Other leading designers include *Ib Jorgensen*, 29 Molesworth Street, telephone 01–6619758, and *Pat Crowley*, 3 Molesworth Place, off Molesworth Street, telephone 01–6615580.

*A Wear*, with branches in Grafton and Henry Street, is a good-value alternative to the upmarket boutiques, and sells both men's and women's clothes. The Chinatown range (again, for men and women) from John Rocha, another leading designer, is sold here. For men, the choices are more limited. *Alias Tom* (telephone 01–6715443) on Duke Lane, off Grafton Street, has a good reputation for stylish, modern clothing. *Louis Copeland*, with branches on Wicklow Street, Pembroke Street and Capel Street, is the classic men's tailor in the city. Businessmen and politicians flock to Copeland for his grey and navy pinstripes, but there's probably something with a bit more colour somewhere in the depths of these large emporiums. The top of Grafton Street is the location for a number of well-known men's shops, including *F.X. Kelly.* *Kennedy and McSharry*, on Nassau Street, is a long-established firm of bespoke tailors which makes suits from Donegal handwoven tweed. *Kevin & Howlin*, further up the same street, also sells tweeds and woollens.

## Food and drink

Supermarkets came to Ireland in the late 1960s and quickly grew to dominate the market. The biggest of them — Dunnes Stores, Quinnsworth and Superquinn — have enormous power and enjoy a greater share of the food retail business than in any other Western country.

Sadly, this situation has led to the demise of most of the small family-run grocery stores and other specialist food shops that prevailed in Dublin as recently as the 1950s. (In this era, pubs often doubled as grocers. In Kehoe's of South Anne Street, or Toner's of Merrion Row, you can still see original shop fittings such as the countless drawers and cupboards used to store provisions.) The best shops, of course, have survived and even prospered into the 1990s, when the pendulum has swung once again in favour of personal service and intimate scale.

In addition, there is a new generation of shop-owners who concentrate on providing quality, farm-fresh produce for consumers who are prepared to pay a little extra for this standard.

For basic provisions (as opposed to gifts), there are very few general food shops in the centre of Dublin. The nearest supermarkets are Quinnsworth in Merrion Row and Upper Baggot Street, and Dunnes Stores in the St Stephen's Green and ILAC shopping centres. All these branches also sell alcohol.

Street markets on Moore Street and Camden Street are the cheapest places to buy fruit and vegetables, but better quality and a wider range of produce can be obtained in shops on Anne Street, Nassau Street and the Powerscourt Townhouse Centre. There are health food shops on Upper Camden Street, South Great George's Street, and in the St Stephen's Green and ILAC shopping centres.

Food and/or drink makes an ideal gift from Ireland. The delicatessen at Dublin Airport is well stocked with fish, cheese, bread, biscuits, chocolate and many other food items, and the duty-free shop is one of the largest in Europe.

Wild Irish salmon (make sure it's wild, not farmed) is delicious and provides a lovely and distinctive gift. The following shops will post salmon overseas:

Dunn's, 6 Upper Baggot Street, telephone 01–6602688

Hanlon's, 20/21 Moore Street, telephone 01–8733011

McConnell & Nelson, 38 Grafton Street, telephone 01–6774344.

Magill's, 14 Clarendon Street, telephone 01–6713830, is a first-class continental delicatessen. John Caviston, 59 Glasthule Road, Sandycove, south of the city, makes fine soda bread, and sells good cheese and salmon. Mogerley's, a long-established butchers at Leonard's Corner, 104 South Circular Road, reputedly sells the best sausages in Dublin. The Gallic Kitchen, Mother Redcap's Market, 40/48 Back Lane, near Christ Church, telephone 01–6761872, makes excellent and cheap pastries, savouries and desserts, and is open to the public Friday–Sunday. Orders are taken over the phone on other days.

In recent years small Irish companies have begun making hand-crafted chocolates, and the most prominent firm, Butlers Irish, has a little shop at the top of Grafton Street. Bewley's also sells its own range of handmade chocolates and its selection of teas and coffees is renowned.

Apart from Guinness, the most distinctively Irish drinks are whiskey, the liqueur Irish Mist, and Bailey's Irish Cream and its imitators. Irish whiskey isn't just spelt differently from scotch; it tastes different too. Look for the Jameson, Bushmills and Middleton brand names; Paddy and Powers are cheaper varieties.

## Footwear

Dublin is one of the cheapest cities in Northern Europe in which to buy a pair of shoes. And the cheapest place in Dublin is at the back of the ILAC Shopping Centre, where the stallholders are the spiritual first cousins of the redoubtable women in the Moore Street market around the corner. Doc Martens, so popular with Irish young people, not least because they last so long, are the speciality here. Don't be rushed into choosing the right pair, and be prepared to haggle a little.

Back on the high streets, Dublin is awash with shoe shops, many of them filled with cheap imports. The better shops on Grafton Street include Thomas Patrick at No. 77, Fitzpatricks next door and Carl Scarpa at No. 25. The Natural Shoe Store, 25 Drury Street (telephone 01–6714978) specialises in comfort shoes. Tutty's, Powerscourt Townhouse Centre (telephone 01–6796566) has been making made-to-measure shoes in classic styles for over fifty years. DV8, 4 Crown Alley in Temple Bar (telephone 01–6798472) lies at the other end of the spectrum, with its wild range of punk styles heavily influenced by the selfsame Doctor Martens.

## Knitwear

Aran sweaters were first knitted by the women of the Aran Islands, west of Galway, to provide work clothes that were comfortable yet warm and weatherproof. The motifs used in the designs were derived from religious and folk traditions and served as a means of identifying different families and the village from which they came. Today, these Celtic motifs live on in Irish fashion, and are used extensively in knitwear, pottery and jewellery. Hand-knitted woollens have always been an excellent gift to buy in Dublin, where prices are often a fraction of those in the top boutiques of New York or Paris.

The best-known shops include:

Blarney Woollen Mills, 21/23 Nassau Street, telephone 01–6710068

Cleo, 18 Kildare Street, telephone 01–6761421

Dublin Woollen Company, 41 Lower Ormond Quay, telephone 01–6775014

Irish Scene, Powerscourt Townhouse Centre, telephone 01–6794061

Monaghan's, Grafton Arcade, off Grafton Street, telephone 01–6770823

Sweater Shop, 9 Wicklow Street, telephone 01–6713270

## Jewellery

Today's Irish craftworkers make use of traditional materials — gold, silver and marble — and native Celtic designs to create modern pieces of art. Gold and silver Claddagh rings are among the most popular souvenir buys, and prices are often very reasonable. The Powerscourt Townhouse Centre is the workplace of a number of gold- and silversmiths, including Patrick Flood and Emma Stewart Liberty. The Tower Design Centre (see page 39) is a good place to see these craftworkers in action. Weir and Sons, 96 Grafton Street, telephone 01–6777275, is a traditional and somewhat imposing store selling watches, clocks and jewellery.

## Markets

Dublin's markets are small but at least there are plenty of them. There is a traditional open-air flea market held every Saturday morning (go as early as possible) on *South Cumberland Street*, near the top of O'Connell Street. However, the future of this market, which sells junk and second-hand clothes, is threatened by new housing developments in the area. As an alternative, several sheltered markets selling bric-à-brac have sprung up in recent years and these are detailed below.

The stallholders at *Mother Redcap's Market* on Back Lane, near Christ Church, sell antiques and other bric-à-brac, books and cheese. The market is open Friday–Sunday, 10.30 a.m.–5.30 p.m. Nearby, at the top of Francis Street, is the traditional *Iveagh Market* selling second-hand clothes, bric-à-brac and some furniture throughout the week. This is a strange but atmospheric place, long past its best days. It remains empty most of the week, when the piles of used clothes are left covered with blankets like so many corpses laid out to rest. The *Liberty Market*, close by on Meath Street, is very noisy and sells new clothes and household goods at the weekend. All these markets are indoor.

The *Blackberry Fair* on Rathmines Road, just over Portobello Bridge, seems to thrive every weekend. From the advertising signs outside, you'd think it sold only bean bags, but in fact there's a huge range of junk, antiques, books, records and other second-hand goods inside. *Blackrock Market*, 5 miles/8 km south of Dublin, has a similar mix of stalls on Saturdays and Sundays.

The best known of Dublin markets, for the banter more than anything else, are the fruit and vegetable stalls on *Moore Street*, open 9 a.m.–6 p.m. Monday–Saturday. Shoes are sold around the corner, at the back of the shopping centre. Women also sell fruit and vegetables, as well as flowers and fish, on *Camden Street* and *Thomas Street*.

Finally, there's the unique horse fair held monthly in the ancient area of *Smithfield* (behind the Four Courts), which was settled by the Vikings after the Normans conquered Dublin in the twelfth century. On the first Sunday morning of each month, donkeys, ponies and all manner of nags are traded here by a motley collection of travellers (Irish gypsies), trainers and other horse-fanciers. The fair, with its blacksmiths, horse dealers and out-of-town visitors, is a throwback to an era when Dublin was a village and the horse was king, but it continues to thrive nonetheless. Watch out for the deal-making, which generally starts after noon.

## Music

In the past decade, Irish rock groups led by U2 have taken the world music scene by storm, and Dublin has come to be known as 'the city of a thousand bands'. This description is only a slight exaggeration.

It is surprising, therefore, that the city has so few good specialist music shops. There are, of course, the giant British chainstores: HMV, with branches in Grafton Street and Henry Street; the Virgin Megastore on Aston Quay, near O'Connell Bridge; and Our Price Music on Henry Street. All of these shops sell a broad range of music on CD, cassette and, less and less, vinyl records. Their main emphasis, however, is on Top 40 pop/rock. A newer arrival, Tower Records on Wicklow Street, sells a good selection of soul, jazz, indie and mainstream CDs, and is open daily until midnight.

The following are smaller shops with a greater range of specialist music:
Borderline, 17 Temple Bar, telephone 01–6799097 (punk, rock, indie, dance)
Claddagh Records, 2 Cecilia Street, telephone 01–6770262 (Irish, folk and ethnic)
Comet, 5 Cope Street, in Temple Bar, telephone 01–6718592 (punk, rock, indie)
Gael Linn, 26 Merrion Square, telephone 01–6767283 (Irish music and Irish language).

The best shops for sheet music and instruments are Opus II (sheet music only), 24 South Great George's Street and Walton's, 69 South Great George's Street and 2 North Frederick Street.

Concert tickets can be purchased in HMV, Grafton Street and the various branches of Golden Discs.

## Sports goods

Arnotts, Henry Street (Liffey Street entrance), telephone 01–8721111
Elvery's, Suffolk Street, telephone 01–6776744
Great Outdoors, Chatham Street, telephone 01–6794293
Marathon Sports, ILAC Centre, telephone 01–8728868, and Grafton Street, telephone 01–6795794

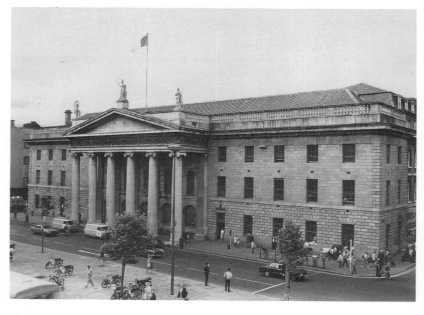

The General Post Office on O'Connell Street (*above*), and an aerial view of O'Connell Bridge, O'Connell Street and environs (*below*).

# WHAT TO DO

Dublin has a well-deserved reputation as one of the liveliest cities in Europe for its size. The fact that the city's social life is centred on the pub may not suit everyone, but this traditional dependence is being weakened as opportunities for good eating and cultural activities increase. There are more and more late-night options as the pub licensing laws are relaxed gently, though Dublin has not yet acquired the status of a 24-hour city.

Some visitors, therefore, may find that an evening out in Dublin starts early and finishes early; the last regular buses leave the city centre at about 11.30 p.m., which is about the time the pubs are closing. Restaurants too generally close at this time, or a little later at the weekend; their busiest time is between 8 p.m. and 9 p.m. Except at the weekend, the last showings in city-centre cinemas start before 9 p.m.

*In Dublin* magazine, which is published every fortnight, contains a full listings service covering music, cinema, theatre and so on. The *Dublin Event Guide*, a weekly magazine which is available free in city-centre shops and cafés, gives the same information, and is especially good on rock music and nightclubs. *Hot Press*, a fortnightly music magazine, also carries concert and cinema listings.

The cinema programme can be checked in the *Irish Times* newspaper, or in one of the city's two evening newspapers, the *Evening Herald* and the *Evening Press*. On Saturdays, *The Irish Times* carries a useful listing of cultural happenings in the week to come, and the same paper also publishes daily a 'what's on' section which includes meetings, readings and other free activities occurring on the day in question.

## MUSIC

Dublin has a lot to offer in terms of musical attractions, from the buskers playing on Grafton Street to the international performers who regularly appear at the giant Point Depot arena. For so long a major centre of folk and traditional music, the city has of late won a reputation as one of the world's rock capitals, largely as a result of the phenomenal success of U2.

### Cabaret

The bigger international hotels, including Jury's and the Burlington, put on cabaret shows in the summer months that are popular with tourists. Jury's cabaret is particularly famous, though not always for the right reasons. It is the type of entertainment you'd expect to find in any big hotel anywhere, imbued with a local flavour — schmaltz Irish-style, you might say. Jury's cabaret starts at 8 p.m. with dinner (optional) at 7.15 p.m. Other popular cabarets are staged at the Abbey Tavern in Howth, telephone 01–8390282, the Braemor Rooms in Churchtown, telephone 01–4988664, and Clontarf Castle, Castle Avenue, Clontarf, telephone 01–8332321. Ask the tourist office for more information or consult one of the evening newspapers.

### Classical

The main venue for classical music is the splendid National Concert Hall, Earlsfort Terrace, telephone 01–6711533 (reservations and credit card booking from 11 a.m. to

7 p.m. Monday–Saturday). The RTE Concert Orchestra and the National Symphony Orchestra are both based at the Hall, which sometimes hosts jazz, opera and traditional music events. The NCH publishes an events listing monthly and this is available from the Hall itself or from tourist offices.

Classical music recitals are also held in a number of churches and halls around the city. Major classical and operatic acts often perform at the Point Theatre, East Link Bridge, telephone 01–8363633. Other important venues include the RDS in Ballsbridge and the Royal Hospital, Kilmainham.

Dublin's diet of classical music is traditional, some would say conservative. However, the Hugh Lane Municipal Gallery of Modern Art (see page 58) often stages concerts of new music on Sundays at noon and the Project Arts Centre in Temple Bar sometimes hosts avant-garde performances of music and dance.

There are two seasons of opera annually — in spring and winter — at the Gaiety Theatre, South King Street, presented by the Dublin Grand Opera Society. The programme consists of the standard repertory of continental opera, supplemented by an occasional performance of a more obscure work. The solo roles are sung by Irish and international singers while the DGOS provides the chorus. A newer group, Opera Theatre Company, stages small-scale, adventurous productions on an intermittent basis.

## Discos/Nightlife

Dublin has some of the worst nightclubs this side of Mecca. The typical 'dive' has a dance-floor the size of your average hotel bathroom, plays records of unredeemable awfulness — and the same ones every week, serves bottles of sugar-sweet plonk at outrageous prices and is full of dubious, drink-filled types whose idea of dancing is to elbow everyone else in the face.

On the other hand — and thankfully there is another side to Dublin nightlife — the situation is improving and there is an increasing number of good clubs now catering for most musical tastes. However, don't expect to be able to drink beer or spirits in most clubs, as the majority still have only a wine licence. A bottle of cheap wine will cost about £20.

Nightclubbing remains a post-pub activity, so things don't start happening until after midnight. The main concentration of clubs lies on Leeson Street, which stays busy until 4 a.m., and later at the weekends.

Expect to pay a cover charge into most places, except perhaps at the start of the week; the exception here is the Leeson Street strip, where entry is free (provided you get past the bouncer) but the wine prices soar in compensation.

*Annabel's*, Burlington Hotel, Upper Leeson Street. Long-established club in the underground car park below the hotel. Broad mix of mainstream music. Popular with young professionals. Full drinks licence.

*Bad Bob's*, East Essex Street. Top 40 disco and live country music. Where the city meets the country in Dublin. Very popular and packed at the weekends. Full licence. Until 2 a.m.

*Club M*, Blooms Hotel, Anglesea Street, in Temple Bar. Top 40 records, Golden Oldies. Reputedly Europe's biggest light show.

*Fibber Magee's*, Parnell Street. New Wave/dance music, depending on the night. Student crowd. Full licence. Closes about 2.30 a.m.

*Lillie's Bordello*, off Grafton Street. Officially members only, but it is possible to talk your way past the bouncers. The place to be seen for models, visiting rock stars, etc. Full licence.

*McGonagle's*, South Anne Street. New Wave/heavy metal, depending on the night. Very young crowd.

*Night Train*, O'Dwyer's, Lower Mount Street. Rock and blues with live music. Full licence.

*Pink Elephant*, South Frederick Street. Trendy, young crowd. Mixture of dance-style music. Full licence.

*P.O.D. (Place of Dance)*, top of Harcourt Street. Trendy new club situated in a splendidly converted wine vault. Dance/seventies music. Full licence. Until about 3 a.m.

*Rock Garden*, Crown Alley. New Wave/Salsa/African/Techno, depending on the night. Students' club on some nights. Live music downstairs. Closes about 2.30 a.m.

*Strings*, 24 Lower Leeson Street. Top 40 until 4 a.m. or so.

*Suesey Street*, 25a Lower Leeson Street. Probably the most bearable of the Leeson Street clubs. Regular media clientele, eighties/Motown music according to a tried and trusted formula. Comes alive after 3 a.m., when people drift in from other clubs.

*The Kitchen*, Clarence Hotel, East Essex Street. U2-owned club opening in 1994.

## Jazz

In spite of having produced some fine artistes, the jazz scene in Dublin is tiny, although it is growing slowly. Among the general public, the most popular form of jazz is probably the New Orleans type played by middle-aged men in waistcoats and straw hats. However, there are regular weekly sessions that will appeal to more specialist tastes in the following pubs: *The Purty Loft*, Dún Laoghaire, telephone 01–2801257; *The Barge Inn*, Charlemont Street, 01–4780005; and *J.J. Smyth's*, Aungier Street, 01–6752565. *Andrew's Lane Theatre, 01–6795720* has late-night jazz sessions, usually on Fridays. Another venue is *Mahoganí Gaspipes* restaurant in Stoneybatter on Dublin's north side. There are cover charges for some of these events; check listings in the evening papers or in *In Dublin* magazine. And watch out for appearances by Irishman Louis Stewart, one of the world's best jazz guitarists. Other worthwhile local names to follow are Brian Dunning, the singer Honor Heffernan, and Richie Buckley.

## Traditional/Folk

Twentieth-century mass media have left Irish traditional music undiminished, though not unaffected. 'Trad' in Ireland now encompasses a wide diversity of music, from the reels and jigs player, as purist as ever, to crossover folk-rock performers such as Davy Spillane or Dolores Keane. Indeed, talented artists such as Paul Brady easily span the genre, depending on whether their chosen instruments for the night are plugged in or not.

The basic set-piece of traditional music is the 'seisiún' or session, a bland word for an exciting event. Regular sessions — more or less spontaneous outbreaks of singing and music performed on instruments such as the bodhrán (a hand-held drum) or uileann pipes — take place in a number of traditional pubs in Dublin (see 'Publife', page 51 for more details). Excellent sessions are also organised at *Comhaltas Ceoltóirí Éireann* (The Irish Musicians' Fellowship), Belgrave Square, Monkstown, telephone 01–2800925. Take bus 7 or 8 from the city centre, or get the DART train to Monkstown or Seapoint.

Larger traditional concerts occur at various venues around the city. Perhaps the best group to watch out for is Dé Danann, a movable feast of virtuoso musicians that has at one time or another featured all of the leading female folk singers. Many of these — Mary Black, Dolores Keane, Eleanor Shanley — sing solo and are well worth hearing. And watch out too for Sharon Shannon from County Clare, a true angel on the accordion. In the past few years, there has been a tremendous and heartening revival of set-dancing in Ireland. As passionate and elegant as the accompanying music, this form of folk dancing can be witnessed regularly and even tried in *Slattery's* on Capel Street (Tuesday), *Hughes's* on Chancery Street (Monday/Wednesday/Friday) and *The Merchant*, Lower Bridge Street (most nights).

Mention must also be made of country & western, a form of music especially popular in Ireland. Mournful ballads about lost loves in Texas and Nashville are not as inappropriate in an Irish setting as they might first seem; American country & western has its roots in the traditional music brought to North America by Irish emigrants in the last century. Now it has been re-exported to Ireland by US and Irish performers. *Bad Bob's* in East Essex Street, *The Harcourt Hotel* at the top of Harcourt Street and *Whelan's* in Wexford Street are good venues for this type of music.

## Rock

Dublin's new-found status as a leading world rock capital has bemused many of its citizens, but the 'city of a thousand bands' is not inaccurately named. Just about every teenager who can lift a guitar and put together three chords — and, the locals would say, a few who can't — has tried to hit the big-time by joining a rock band.

Most groups don't last very long, but quite a few have achieved success abroad and one — U2, of course — is arguably the biggest rock band in the world. Many reasons have been put forward for the success of Irish rock, among them the high proportion of young people in the population, rampant unemployment, the natural disrespect of the Irish for authority and a rich traditional music scene. All of this was hilariously summed up in *The Commitments* where the group sang Motown soul because 'the Irish are the niggers of Europe . . . an' Dubliners are the niggers of Ireland . . . an' the northside Dubliners are the niggers o' Dublin'.

Whatever the cause, Dublin's rock scene continues to thrive. The city is a regular stamping-ground to, for example, Sinéad O'Connor, Elvis Costello, The Hothouse Flowers and The Pogues, though concerts by these internationally famous artists are rare enough. However, every night, the city's main rock venues stage concerts by the myriad up-and-coming groups, some of whom may turn out to be the U2s of tomorrow. In addition, Dublin is a regular stop for the big international acts on European tour.

The *Point Depot* at the East Link Bridge, telephone 01–8363633, a magnificently restored set of warehouses with middling acoustics, is the main venue for these mega-concerts. Other, smaller venues include the *Rock Garden*, 3a Crown Alley, Temple Bar, telephone 01–6799114 and the *Baggot Inn*, Baggot Street, telephone 01–6761430, both of which feature live music seven nights a week; and *Whelan's*, 25 Wexford Street, telephone 01–4780766, a pub with folk/world music leanings. *McGonagle's*, South Anne Street, telephone 01–6774402, and the *SFX*, 23 Upper Sherrard Street, are irregular venues for New Wave/heavy metal concerts; the *National Stadium* on the South Circular Road is a medium-sized boxing stadium which sometimes hosts sit-down concerts.

At the weekends, the *Olympic*, *Tivoli*, *Gaiety*, *Riverbank* and *Andrew's Lane* theatres are all pressed into service as late-night concert venues with full drink licences. The summer sees occasional free concerts in parks and on the streets, as well as a number of giant outdoor rock events in and near Dublin.

Full listings of rock events are available in the evening newspapers, *In Dublin* or the *Dublin Event Guide*. Another good way to find out what's happening musically in Dublin is to buy the *Hot Press*, a lively and informative fortnightly rock magazine that covers much more than just music.

Dublin Tourism has put together a tour of the city that visits a series of locations claiming historic associations with Irish rock stars (historic meaning over the past twenty years, in this case). Some of the links in the Rock 'n' Stroll tour are tenuous; for example, there's a visit to the Bad Ass pizzeria in Temple Bar, where Sinéad O'Connor once worked as a waitress, and to Captain America's burger restaurant in Grafton Street, where Chris de Burgh warbled for the customers in the 1970s. The best place to visit is the Windmill Lane studios, off Sir John Rogerson's Quay, where U2 recorded many of their albums. The studios have since moved elsewhere, but the graffiti left by adoring fans of the group remain. The walls of the Lane are covered with messages from all over the world, in many languages, acclaiming U2 and informing the readers of many things, such as 'War is like a pizza, it leaves red stains everywhere.'

For all its shortcomings, the Rock 'n' Stroll tour is as valid a way of discovering the city as any. The accompanying guide is available from any tourist office.

# CINEMA

After years of decline, cinema is once again thriving in Dublin — it may come as a surprise that the Irish go to the cinema more often than any other European nationality. There are now over twenty screens in the city centre, and several large multiplex cinemas have been built recently in the suburbs. Although Ireland has of late produced a number of notable films — for instance, *My Left Foot*, *The Field* and *The Commitments* — the local film industry is minuscule and the diet of Dublin cinemas consists mostly of Hollywood thrillers and comedies.

However, there is at the same time a growing market for 'art-house' films and a major development here was the opening in 1992 of the Irish Film Centre, 6 Eustace Street, in Temple Bar. Converted from a former Quaker meeting hall, the IFC is a magnificent home for film and houses two comfortable cinemas, a film bookshop and an archive. Worth a visit just to see the building, the Centre also has a bar and an excellent restaurant. During the summer, it puts on special film programmes for tourists.

The Lighthouse Cinema, in Middle Abbey Street, also shows art-house films, as does the Screen Cinema at the top of D'Olier Street.

Full cinema listings are published each day in *The Irish Times*, *Evening Herald* and *Evening Press*. 'The flicks', as they are known in Dublin, are especially good value in the afternoon and early evening, when admission prices are under £3.

Late-night showings (meaning a screening at about 11 p.m.) take place only on Fridays and Saturdays, although the IFC sometimes shows late films on Thursdays.

The Dublin Film Festival at the start of March mixes the best of modern international cinema with revivals of screen classics and lectures and seminars on all aspects of the world of cinema. There is usually a retrospective dedicated to the work of a particular director, who may be present. The festival is very popular, so it's necessary to book early for the many screenings. An attractive one-week French language film festival is also held in the Screen Cinema in the winter months.

# PUBLIFE

Dublin is defined by its pubs — people even give directions according to the bars along a route. The cadences and the nuances of social life in the city are mirrored in its countless drinking spots, which range from 'spit and sawdust' bars that have changed little since the last century to highly fashionable lounges in the top modern hotels. Drinking in the city is a very democratic business — alcohol isn't cheap, but it costs roughly the same everywhere. And while each bar has its own regular customers, people of all ages, appearances and outlooks are likely to pass through most city-centre pubs.

Just why the Irish 'took to the drink' is unclear; the early emergence of a local whiskey-distilling industry and the establishment of the Guinness Brewery in Dublin in 1759 must have played a part. Another school of thought holds that the removal of the Irish parliament after the Act of Union was passed in 1800 meant there was no serious business to occupy the minds of the city's inhabitants, and a good deal to brood about.

Whatever the reason, these dark, convivial, even confessional places have bestowed on Dublin its justified reputation for gossip, debate, storytelling and merrymaking. There's a pub on every street corner in the city, with its doors open to all comers. Dublin pubs pass in and out of fashion (and anti-fashion) with inscrutable regularity.

Many can lay claim to glorious literary, historical or musical associations, though these golden days may be long past. Others have been renovated, often for the worse, though none of today's customers seems to mind.

More and more pubs sell food, although the majority will usually serve nothing fancier than a toasted sandwich outside mealtimes. Unlike other races, the Irish traditionally eat first and then go drinking and most of us show little inclination to merge the two activities.

The city's staple drink is of course Guinness, that mysterious concoction of black porter crowned with a creamy beige head. There's a world of ritual associated with the drink that visitors can learn only by close observation. Ask for 'a pint', which always means Guinness, and bide your time; a good pint is pulled slowly and allowed to settle before being served up to the customer. Then sip deliberately, swallow gently and slip into easy conversation.

Dockland pubs serve from as early as 7 a.m., but most bars don't open their doors until 10.30 a.m. or later. Since the 'holy hour' (an hour's closing time in the afternoon that was designed to get hard-drinking husbands out of the pubs and back to their families) was abolished in 1988, pubs stay open continuously until 'last orders' at 11.30 p.m. (11 p.m. in winter and on Sundays). Thereafter, customers have a half-hour's 'drinking-up time' in which to finish their drinks; this period is more flexibly interpreted in some establishments than in others. Pubs also close from 2 to 4 p.m. on Sundays, and on Christmas Day and Good Friday.

The best Dublin pubs are at their nicest when half-full in the afternoon or in the early evening. Come the weekend, everywhere is jam-packed, which may or may not suit your tastes. Anyone looking for a quiet drink on a Friday or Saturday night is advised to head for a hotel bar, the suburbs, or just to stay at home.

The list below includes most of the best traditional and musical pubs, as well as other bars noted for their atmosphere, interiors or historical associations:

*Bailey*, Duke Street. Modern, cosmopolitan pub popular with the beautiful people. The front door of 7 Eccles Street, the now demolished home of Leopold Bloom, the hero of *Ulysses*, is upstairs.

*An Béal Bocht*, 58 Charlemont Street. Regular traditional music sessions in the bar; concerts and pub theatre in the lounge. The pub gets its name, which means 'The Poor Mouth', from the title of a comic work by Myles na gCopaleen, an adaptation of which is performed frequently in the lounge. Near the Grand Canal.

*Brazen Head*, 20 Lower Bridge Street. Dublin's oldest pub, first mention of which dates from 1613. Lost some of its charm but none of its popularity when it was renovated and expanded a few years ago. Traditional music in the summer.

*Bruxelles*, 7 Harry Street. The ground-floor bar has one of the finest interiors in Dublin. However, the present clientele, mostly bikers and young people, can be very noisy at the weekends. Occasional jazz sessions.

*Davy Byrne's*, 21 Duke Street. Leopold Bloom had lunch here in *Ulysses* but the pub has changed character a lot since then. It is now an upmarket establishment popular with the local business community.

*Doheny & Nesbitt's*, 5 Lower Baggot Street. A real 'insider's' pub, popular with lawyers, journalists and politicians. Traditional interior with snugs (private compartments for private drinking).

*Hogan's Bar Café*, 35 South Great George's Street. Recently renovated in a continental style — dimmed lights, large smoked windows and a coffee-bar atmosphere that wouldn't be out of place in Amsterdam or Munich. Very trendy and a bit self-conscious. At its best in the afternoon or early evening, but far too crowded on weekend nights.

*Hughes's*, Chancery Street (behind the Four Courts). Unpretentious place with reputedly the best traditional music sessions in town.

*John M. Keating*, 14 Mary Street. A beautifully decorated and relaxing pub (big armchairs upstairs) that has traditional Irish music sessions most evenings. Not too crowded, either.

*Kehoe's*, Anne Street. Rural-style pub in the heart of the city. Décor unchanged since the 1950s. Young crowd.

*Joxer Daly's*, 103 Dorset Street. A finely-decorated northside haunt.

*Kitty O'Shea's*, 23/25 Upper Grand Canal Street, Ballsbridge. Traditional old-style pub with live music most evenings. Popular with the local business community. Famous for its weekend brunches.

*Long Hall*, South Great George's Street. Somehow all the kitsch — clocks, plates, mirrors — hanging on the wall of this pub is just right.

*McDaid's*, Harry Street (off Grafton Street). Famous literary drinking spot in the 1950s. Now newly renovated and more popular with the young and less well read. Live blues music upstairs.

*Mother Redcap's Tavern*, Back Lane, Christ Church. Large, rustic pub decorated in rich pine. Live music — usually folk/traditional — upstairs.

*Mulligan's*, 8 Poolbeg Street. Connoisseurs say it has the best pint of Guinness in the city (though this writer begs to differ). Otherwise, a 200-year-old pub bursting with life, intrigue and journalistic debate.

*Neary's*, 1 Chatham Street (off Grafton Street). Plusher than most traditional pubs, with excellent sandwiches.

*O'Donoghue's*, 15 Merrion Row. The city's most celebrated traditional music pub (the Dubliners started here in their early days). Sawdust on the floor, music in the air. Packed in summer.

*Palace Bar*, Fleet Street. The back room here was the haunt of writers, students and journalists in the 1950s and it still draws a good mix of characters.

*Purty Kitchen*, Old Dunleary Road, Dún Laoghaire. First established in 1728, this traditional Irish bar lies 5 miles/8 km south of Dublin. Traditional and rock music venue upstairs.

*Ryan's*, 28 Parkgate Street (just before entrance to Phoenix Park). A little off the beaten track, but a beautifully fitted pub which serves an excellent pint of Guinness and has individual snugs for that private drink.

*Scruffy Murphy's*, 1 Powerscourt, off Lower Mount Street. Trendy place popular with the business community.

*Slattery's*, 129 Capel Street. One of the best-known pubs for traditional Irish music, though it also plays host to set-dancing, rock and blues.

*Stag's Head*, 1 Dame Court. Perfectly preserved bar established in 1885. Popular with students in the winter. Wonderful pub grub until 7 p.m. and unbelievably friendly staff.

*Toner's*, 139 Lower Baggot Street. Friendly staff, Victorian fittings (look for the shelves and cabinets where groceries were once sold along with the alcohol), bohemian clientele.

A Dublin landmark:
O'Donoghue's of Merrion Row

# THEATRE

Bustling but riven by dissension, Ireland's theatre world still manages miraculously to produce world-class playwrights. The best mainstream Irish plays will most likely be staged at the *Abbey Theatre*, telephone 01–8787222, the national theatre on Lower Abbey Street, or at the Peacock (same telephone number), the more adventurous studio theatre on the same site.

The Abbey first opened its doors in 1904 and quickly became an important centre for the Irish cultural renaissance. After the original theatre burned down in 1951, a blunt modern building was completed on the same site in 1966. The staple diet of Synge, O'Casey and Yeats still accounts for a large part of the Abbey's bill of fare, particularly during the summer tourist season. Increasingly, however, contemporary playwrights — and especially Brian Friel and Tom Murphy — are having their work performed here.

The *Gate Theatre*, Cavendish Row, Parnell Square, telephone 01–6774085, was founded in 1928 by Micheál MacLíammóir and Hilton Edwards, a professional and personal partnership which dominated Irish theatre for decades. The Gate was the scene of Orson Welles' first professional appearance (at the age of sixteen), and has enjoyed great success in recent years with popular contemporary plays and revivals of classics. The *Gaiety*, South King Street, telephone 01–6771717, and the *Olympia*, Dame Street, telephone 01–6777741, are both old music-hall-style theatres providing family entertainment, while *Andrew's Lane Theatre*, 9–11 Andrew's Lane, telephone 01–6795720, and the *Tivoli*, Francis Street, telephone 01–4535998, alternate between popular drama and more highbrow entertainments.

The *Riverbank Theatre*, 13/14 Merchant's Quay, telephone 01–6773370, is a fairly new complex overlooking the Liffey which concentrates on the work of Irish playwrights. At the experimental end of the spectrum lie the *Project Arts Centre*, 39 East Essex Street, telephone 01–6712321, the new *Samuel Beckett Centre* in Trinity College, telephone 01–7021239, and the tiny *Focus Theatre*, 6 Pembroke Place, off Pembroke Street, telephone 01–6763071/6712795, which is dedicated to the Stanislavsky method.

The highlight of the year is the Dublin Theatre Festival, which starts in late September/ early October and continues for two weeks. During this time, every performance space in the city is pressed into service for all manner of theatre, revue, comedy, musical and dance. New works by major Irish playwrights are premièred, and renowned overseas troupes come to perform in the city.

# MUSEUMS AND ART GALLERIES

Dublin's modest treasures are stored in a great number of museums, many of them small and little known. The city lacks the resources to do justice to its long and varied history, and many museums are understaffed and lack space. Several promising archaeological sites in the old city lie untouched, while others have been examined only cursorily before being destroyed by modern-day developers.

Nonetheless, there is something to suit virtually every taste, and Ireland's finest treasures, as displayed in the National Museum, rank alongside those of the most illustrious civilisations anywhere in terms of antiquity and intricacy of design.

## Museums

Most museums remain closed on Mondays. Further information on many of the sites listed below is given in the city tours later in the book. In the interests of completeness, the following list includes a number of historical sites that aren't strictly museums.

*Ashtown Castle Visitor Centre*, north end of Phoenix Park, telephone 01–6770089. A renovated castle, part of which dates back to the fifteenth century, which now serves as a heritage centre for the Phoenix Park. Open weekends 9.30 a.m.–3.45 p.m.

*Bewley's Museum*, upstairs in Bewley's of Grafton Street. Located in the old chocolate factory run by Bewley's, a small exhibition of chocolate-making, tea and coffee paraphernalia. Photographs and documents record the development of the business and the rise and fall of Bewley's Quaker founders. Admission is free, and the obligatory coffee and sticky buns are available. Open 10 a.m.–7 p.m. daily.

*Botanic Gardens*, Botanic Road, Glasnevin, telephone 01–8377596. About 20,000 varieties of plant on 50 acres/20 hectares. Open 9 a.m.–6 p.m. Monday to Saturday, 11 a.m.–6 p.m. Sunday.

*Drimnagh Castle*, The Long Mile Road, telephone 01–2802203. Dublin's only restored medieval castle, with a great hall, moat and gardens. Open 2–5 p.m. Sundays.

*Dublin Castle*, telephone 01–6777580/6777129. The centre of British power in Ireland for centuries. The oldest parts date back to the thirteenth century, but the magnificent buildings in the Upper Castle Yard were built in the mid-eighteenth century. Open 10 a.m.–12.15 p.m., 2–5 p.m. Monday–Friday, 2–5 p.m. Saturday/Sunday and bank holidays.

*Dublin Civic Museum*, 58 South William Street, telephone 01–6794260. Open 10 a.m.–6 p.m. Tuesday–Saturday, 11 a.m.–2 p.m. Sunday. Free admission. Agreeable collection of coins, prints and other knick-knacks to do with Dublin. There are also changing exhibitions dealing with specialist areas of the city's history.

*Dublin Writers' Museum,* 18 Parnell Square, telephone 01–8722077. A new (opened in 1991) museum which gathers together memorabilia relating to many famous Dublin writers, including three Nobel prize-winners: W.B. Yeats, George Bernard Shaw and Samuel Beckett. The Irish Writers' Centre is next door. There is also a library, café and shop. Open 10 a.m.–5 p.m. Tuesday–Saturday, 1–5 p.m. Sundays and public holidays, April–September (open Mondays in June–August). Closed Monday–Thursday from October to March.

*'Dublinia'*, Synod Hall, Christ Church. A multi-media exhibition portraying Dublin life in medieval times. The show, which spans nearly 400 years of Dublin history from the coming of the Normans in 1170, leads the visitor through a medieval maze and life-size reconstructions of the old buildings. There's also a scale model of the old city and a collection of artefacts on loan from the National Museum before the tour concludes with an audio-visual presentation and a visit to Christ Church Cathedral. Open 9 a.m.–5 p.m. daily (Sunday 10 a.m.–4 p.m.) May–October.

*ENFO*, 17 St Andrew Street, telephone 01–6793144. Colourful and high-tech displays on environmental matters. Free admission.

*Fry Model Railway*, Malahide Castle, Malahide, telephone 01–8452758. Model railway layout with many Dublin trams and trains — even the DART. Open 10 a.m.–1 p.m., 2–5 p.m. Monday–Thursday, 11 a.m.–1 p.m., 2–6 p.m. Saturday, 2–6 p.m. Sunday; open 10 a.m.–1 p.m., 2–5 p.m. Friday in July and August. Train from Connolly Station, bus 32A from Lower Abbey Street or bus 42 from Beresford Place.

*George Bernard Shaw House*, 33 Synge Street, telephone 01–8722077. Open Monday–Saturday 10 a.m.–5 p.m., Sunday 2–6 p.m. May–September. Newly restored birthplace of the writer, this small Victorian house has been turned into a museum devoted to Shaw's long life and many works. Worth a combined visit with the nearby Irish-Jewish Museum. Bus 16, 19, 22 from O'Connell Street.

*Guinness Hop Store*, Crane Street, telephone 01–4536700. The story of brewing at Guinness, told with exhibits, a video and — best of all — a bar serving the best pints in town. Also a venue for visiting art exhibitions. Open 10 a.m.–3.30 p.m. Monday–Friday. Bus 21A, 78, 78A, 78B from Fleet Street.

*Howth Transport Museum*, Howth Castle, Howth, telephone 01–8475623. Exhibition of double-decker buses, lorries, trucks, bread vans, fire engines, and the last tram to run in Dublin. Open 2–6 p.m. weekends.

*Irish-Jewish Museum*, 3/4 Walworth Road, Portobello, telephone 01–4531797. Small museum chronicling the history of the tiny Jewish community in Ireland through the display of memorabilia, documents and photographs. Located in a former synagogue situated in what was the Jewish quarter of the city (once known as 'Little Jerusalem'). Afterwards, be sure to visit one remnant of this era, the delicious Bretzel kosher bakery on nearby Lennox Place. Museum open 11 a.m.–3 p.m. Tuesday/Thursday/Sunday in April–September; Sundays only in October–April. Free admission. Bus 16, 16A, 19, 19A from O'Connell Street.

*Irish Whiskey Corner*, Bow Street (behind the Four Courts), telephone 01–8725566. Whiskey is no longer made in Dublin, but the country's leading manufacturers, Irish Distillers, have preserved the distilling equipment and placed it on display here. In addition, there's an audio-visual presentation, souvenir shop and, most interesting, whiskey-tasting. Tours at 3.30 p.m. Monday to Friday (also at 11 a.m. May–October) last for 75 minutes. Other times by appointment only.

*James Joyce Museum*, Joyce Tower, Sandycove, telephone 01–2809265. The opening pages of *Ulysses* are set in the interior and on the roof terrace of the Martello tower in Sandycove, where James Joyce lived for six days in 1904. Today, the tower is a sort of shrine to the writer, and is filled with personal memorabilia such as his cane, waistcoat and guitar, as well as Joyce's death-mask and a collection of first editions of his work. Open May–September, 10 a.m.–5 p.m. (closed 1–2 p.m.) Monday–Saturday, 2–6 p.m. Sunday. 10 a.m.–5 p.m. Monday–Friday, April and October. Bus 8 from Eden Quay or DART to Sandycove.

*Kilmainham Gaol*, Inchicore Road, Kilmainham, telephone 01–4535984. A guided tour of the gaol and an audio-visual presentation covering the period of the prison's grim use (1798–1924) is included in the admission price. Charles Stewart Parnell was incarcerated here, as was Patrick Pearse and the other 1916 leaders. Open 11 a.m.–6 p.m. daily June to September, 2–6 p.m. Wednesday/Sunday, October to May. Buses 24 from the quays, 51, 51B, 78, 79 from Fleet Street.

*Malahide Castle*, Malahide, telephone 01–8452655/8452371. Home of the Talbot family from 1185 until 1976, when it was bought by the State. The tower house dates from the twelfth century, while other buildings are more recent. Fine collection of paintings and extensive grounds. Restaurant and craft shop. Open 10 a.m.–5 p.m. Monday–Friday and Saturday/Sunday afternoons all year round. Model railway system (see Fry Model Railway above). Open from 11.30 a.m. on Saturday/Sunday between May and October. To get there, take a train from Connolly Station to Malahide or take bus 42 from Beresford Place.

*Marsh's Library*, St Patrick's Close, telephone 01–4543511. The first public library in Ireland, located at the side of St Patrick's Cathedral. Furnished with tall rows of dark oak bookcases, it contains about 25,000 volumes of history, classics, religion and philosophy dating from the sixteenth to the eighteenth centuries. Open 10 a.m.–12.45 p.m., 2–5 p.m. Monday, Wednesday–Friday, 10.30 a.m.–12.45 p.m. Saturday.

*Museum of Childhood*, The Palms, 20 Palmerston Park, telephone 01–4973223. Private collection of antique dolls and toys from the eighteenth century onwards. Open 2–5.30 p.m. Sunday. Bus 13 from O'Connell Street, 14 or 14A from Burgh Quay.

*Natural History Museum*, Merrion Street, telephone 01–6618811. Stuffed birds and fish, skeletons of mammals, including that of the enormous Irish elk. The exhibition seems as fossilised as the items it contains, which adds to its curiosity value. Open 10 a.m.–5 p.m. Tuesday–Saturday, 2–5 p.m. Sunday. Free admission.

*National Maritime Museum*, Haigh Terrace, Dún Laoghaire (turn left off George's Street after the shopping centre), telephone 01–2800969. Housed in the old Mariners' Church, an exhibition dedicated to the sea and those who sail upon it. Highlights include the lens formerly in the Baily Lighthouse in Howth, and a longboat from the ill-fated French expedition in 1796, of which Wolfe Tone was a member. Open 2.30–5.30 p.m. Tuesday–Saturday, May–September. Bus 8 from Eden Quay or DART to Sandycove.

*National Museum*, Kildare Street, telephone 01–6618811. A magnificent museum featuring two permanent exhibitions: 'Ór/Irish Gold', the museum's famous collection of Bronze Age gold jewellery and other artefacts; and the history of Irish artworks up to the Middle Ages, including the Tara Brooch and the Ardagh Chalice. Open 10 a.m.–5 p.m. Tuesday–Saturday, 2–5 p.m. Sunday. Free admission. An annexe to the National Museum, located nearby on Merrion Row, is home to the museum's folklife and geology collections, and shows diverse exhibitions on other themes.

*National Wax Museum*, Granby Row, telephone 01–8726340. Life-size wax figures of pop stars, politicians and others, as well as a Chamber of Horrors. Not a national institution, in spite of the name; there is an admission charge. Open 10 a.m.–5.30 p.m. Monday–Saturday, 1–5.30 p.m. Sunday.

*Newbridge House and Demesne*, Donabate, telephone 01–8436534. Restored eighteenth-century house with original paintings, furniture, and a fourteen-roomed doll's house. Open 10 a.m.–5 p.m. Tuesday–Friday, 11 a.m.–6 p.m. Saturday, 2–6 p.m. Sunday April–October, Saturday/Sunday 2–5 p.m. November–March. Bus 33B or suburban rail.

*Newman House*, 85/86 St Stephen's Green South, telephone 01–4757255/4751752. The former home of the University College, James Joyce's alma mater, which has been magnificently restored in recent years. The spartan room in which the English poet Gerard Manley Hopkins lived, wrote and died in 1889 is maintained exactly the way it was a century ago. Open June–September, Tuesday–Friday 10 a.m.–4.30 p.m., Saturday 2–4.30 p.m., Sunday 11 a.m.–2 p.m., closed rest of year except for guided groups, by appointment only.

*Number 29 Fitzwilliam Street*, telephone 01–7026165. A re-creation of home life in Georgian Dublin 1790–1820 in a renovated eighteenth-century building. The opening of the exhibit amounts to an act of atonement by the ESB, the State electricity company, which flattened a block of Georgian houses on this street in the 1960s to build its headquarters, before completely restoring this house thirty years later. Free admission. Open 10 a.m.–5 p.m. Tuesday–Saturday, 2–5 p.m. Sunday.

*Old Library, Trinity College*, telephone 01–7022320. A beautiful building in its own right, but most famous as home to the Book of Kells, an intricately crafted Latin version of the Four Gospels dating from the early ninth century. Open Monday–Saturday 9.30 a.m to 4.30 p.m., Sunday 12 noon to 5 p.m.

*Pearse Museum*, St Enda's Park, Rathfarnham, telephone 01–4934208. The site of Scoil Éanna, the school founded by Irish patriot, poet and educationalist Patrick Pearse, 5 miles/8 km south of the city centre. Contains documents and artefacts on Pearse and his family, as well as an audio-visual presentation on his life and educational ideas. Open 10 a.m.–1 p.m., 2–5.30 p.m. May–August. Closes earlier in other months. Bus 16 from O'Connell Street.

*St Audoen's*, High Street, telephone 01–6791855. 'Flame on the Hill', a multi-media presentation about Ireland before the Vikings. Performances at 11.30 a.m., 2/3/4 p.m. Monday–Friday.

*State Heraldic Museum*, Kildare Street, telephone 01–6618811. An exhibition tracing the use of heraldic devices in various forms such as suits of armour or domestic china. Home to the State's collection of heraldic specimens, the museum is located in the former coffee room of the old Kildare Street Club. The Genealogical Office operates a consultancy service for those trying to trace their family origins. Open 10 a.m.–12.45 p.m., 2–4.30 p.m. Monday–Friday. Free admission.

## Art galleries

Most of Dublin's historic art is held in State institutions located on the south side of the Liffey. The National Gallery houses works by the great Irish painters and a modest selection of international masters. The Chester Beatty Library contains one of the world's finest oriental collections, and contemporary art has finally found an appropriate showcase in the new Irish Museum of Modern Art, established in 1989 at the Royal

Hospital, Kilmainham. On the north side there is the Hugh Lane Municipal Gallery, which houses the magnificent Lane bequest, including a number of impressionist masterpieces, as well as twentieth-century works by Irish and international artists. Other important galleries are the Douglas Hyde Gallery, in Trinity College's arts building, and the RHA Gallagher Gallery on Ely Place.

*Chester Beatty Library*, 20 Shrewsbury Road, Ballsbridge, telephone 01–2692386. One of Dublin's hidden treasures. A leading international collection of oriental manuscripts and artefacts. Open 10 a.m.–5 p.m Tuesday–Friday, 2–5 p.m. Saturday.

*Crafts Council Gallery*, Powerscourt Townhouse, South William Street, telephone 01–6797368. Visiting crafts and the best of Irish design, traditional and modern. Open 10 a.m.–5 p.m. Monday, 11 a.m.–5 p.m. Tuesday–Saturday.

*Douglas Hyde Gallery*, Trinity College, Nassau Street, telephone 01–7021116. High-profile painting, sculpture and photography exhibitions. Accompanying lectures and talks. Open 11 a.m.–6 p.m. Monday–Saturday (closes at 7 p.m. on Thursday, 4.45 p.m. on Saturday).

*Gallery of Photography*, 33 East Essex Street, telephone 01–6714654. Sadly, Dublin's only permanent photographic gallery. Interesting visiting exhibitions in a newly-renovated building. Open 11 a.m.–6 p.m. Monday–Saturday. Free admission.

*Guinness Hop Store*, see page 55.

*Hugh Lane Municipal Gallery of Modern Art*, Parnell Square, telephone 01–8741903. Excellent permanent collection of Irish and international art from mid-nineteenth century to present day. Coffee shop. Open 9.30 a.m.–6 p.m. Tuesday–Friday, 9.30 a.m.–5 p.m. Saturday, 11 a.m.–5 p.m. Sunday. Free admission.

*Irish Museum of Modern Art*, Royal Hospital, Kilmainham, telephone 01–6718666. Permanent and visiting exhibitions of modern painting, sculpture and photography. Coffee shop/restaurant. Open 10 a.m.–5.30 p.m. Tuesday–Saturday, 12 noon–5.30 p.m. Sundays and bank holidays. Free admission to some exhibitions.

*National Gallery*, Merrion Square, telephone 01–6615133. A recent renovation finally does justice to the Irish and international masters on display. Collection includes 'The Taking of Christ', which has only recently been identified as an authentic Caravaggio. Restaurant. Open 10 a.m.–6 p.m. Monday–Saturday (open until 9 p.m. on Thursday), 2–5 p.m. Sunday. Free admission.

*Project Arts Centre*, 39 East Essex Street, telephone 01–6712321. Visiting modern art exhibitions. Theatre, dance and performance art at the same venue. Open 11 a.m.–6 p.m. Monday–Saturday. Free admission.

*RHA Gallagher Gallery*, Ely Place, telephone 01–6610762. Large but underused exhibition space. Home of the Royal Hibernian Academy of Arts and venue for its exhibitions. Also visiting exhibitions. 11 a.m.–5 p.m. Monday–Saturday (Thursday until 9 p.m.), 2–5 p.m. Sunday. Free admission.

As well as the above, there are a number of smaller, commercial art galleries around town; see page 40 for details of some of the most interesting ones.

# DAYTIME ACTIVITIES AND SPORT

With parks, mountains, lakes, rivers and the sea available in such plentiful supply nearby, Dubliners are lucky in the choice of sports and outdoor activities open to them. Bad weather can be a bother, especially in winter, but it is never so severe as to prevent enthusiasts from enjoying their favourite leisure activities. The trick is to come prepared for extremes of weather by bringing waterproof and warm clothing. In one of the poorer countries of Western Europe, 50-metre (165-foot) swimming pools and all-seater football stadiums are notable only by their absence. In general, sports facilities in Dublin are inferior to those found in other European cities. However, the basic facilities — and they are often basic — are there, so make the most of them.

And remember that, in compensation, Dublin was granted a healthy excess of the Great Outdoors.

Up-to-date information on competitive matches and other sporting activities is available in the daily papers or *In Dublin*.

## ADVENTURE SPORTS

For information on boardsailing, caving, hang-gliding, mountaineering, orienteering, scuba diving, etc., contact AFAS (Association for Adventure Sports), House of Sport, Long Mile Road, telephone 01–4509845.

## ANGLING

Bord Fáilte publishes a number of booklets on sea, coarse and game angling in Ireland. In Dublin, sea angling is an all-year-round sport, with Skerries, Howth and Dún Laoghaire the main centres. Game anglers need a (single) licence for both salmon and sea trout fishing. Licences are issued by the Central Fisheries Board, Balnagowan House, Mobhi Road, Glasnevin, telephone 01–8379206, and by various tackle stores. For more information contact the Irish Federation of Sea Angling, telephone 01–2806873. The season for sea trout runs from about May to October; brown trout fishing begins in mid-February and ends in September; and the salmon season opens on New Year's Day on some rivers and continues until the end of August.

Salmon, trout, pike and perch are all to be found in the River Liffey. The best stretches for brown trout lie between Celbridge and Millicent Bridge, near Clane in Co. Kildare; spring salmon fishing is best from February to May. Buy a salmon licence from any good anglers' store, such as Watts Bros, 18 Ormond Quay, telephone 01–6788574, or Rory's Fishing Tackle, 17a Temple Bar, telephone 01–6772351. There is some coarse fishing in Dublin's two canals, on a year-round basis. The River Tolka also has brown trout.

## BOWLING

The biggest and best-known bowling alley in Dublin is the Stillorgan Bowl, which has 24 ten-pin bowling lanes. Open daily from 10 a.m. until late. Take the 46A, 84 or 63 buses from the city centre to Stillorgan village.

The Crumlin Super Bowl, Crumlin Road, telephone 01–4559659 has 16 bowling lanes and Laserworld, a live-action indoor space game.

## GAELIC GAMES

Gaelic football and hurling, Ireland's two great national sports, have their headquarters in Dublin's Croke Park (near the North Circular Road, telephone 01–8363222), the largest sports stadium in the country. All the major inter-county games are played here on Sundays, most importantly the two All-Ireland finals in hurling and Gaelic football, held on the first and third Sundays of September. Croke Park has two stands and of the terraced areas, Hill 16 is the liveliest. However, 'the Hill' is set to disappear shortly in a massive redevelopment plan which has begun at the ground. Hurling matches, often played at breakneck speed and with scant regard for player safety, are especially worth seeing.

## GOLF

Ireland boasts some of the best golfing in the world and Dublin is no exception. Several championship courses and many more top-level courses lie within thirty minutes' drive from the city centre. Green fees range from £10 to £45 a day, depending on the ranking of the course. The links courses at Royal Dublin and Portmarnock are arguably the most renowned, and visitors are not always welcomed, especially at peak times, unless accompanied by a member. Bord Fáilte has published a special brochure featuring the country's finest courses, available from any tourist office.

The following clubs lie within 10 miles/16 km of the city centre:

18-hole courses: Castle Golf Club, Rathfarnham; Clontarf Golf Club; Dún Laoghaire; Elm Park; Grange, Rathfarnham; Hermitage, Lucan; Howth; Island, Malahide; Milltown; Newlands, Clondalkin; Portmarnock; Royal Dublin, Dollymount; Slade Valley, Saggart. 9-hole courses: Carrickmines; Foxrock; Killiney; Lucan; Malahide; Rathfarnham; Sutton. In addition, there are numerous par 3 and pitch & putt courses in the Dublin area. Details from any tourist information office. More information too from the Golfing Union of Ireland, 81 Eglinton Road, telephone 01–2694111.

## GREYHOUND-RACING

Greyhound-racing is a popular spectator and gambling sport in Dublin. Races are held at the Shelbourne Park Stadium in Ringsend, on Mondays, Wednesdays and Saturdays at 8 p.m., and at Harold's Cross on Tuesdays and Thursdays at 8 p.m.

## GYMS AND EXERCISE CENTRES

Digges Lane Dance Studios, Digges Lane (off Aungier Street), telephone 01–4784288
Litton Lane Dance Studio, 2 Litton Lane (off Bachelor's Walk), telephone 01–8728044
Orwell Squash and Health Club, Orwell Road, telephone 01–4923146
Pulse Health and Fitness, 1 Temple Bar, telephone 01–6799620
YMCA, Aungier Street, telephone 01–4782607

## HILL-WALKING AND ROCK-CLIMBING

The Dublin Mountains, though modest in altitude, offer numerous pretty walks, many of which pass over into Wicklow and are dealt with in a later chapter. The best-known long-distance walk is the Wicklow Way, which starts in south County Dublin and extends the length of County Wicklow. (See 'Hill walks in the Dublin Mountains', page 114, and 'The Wicklow Way', page 149.)

## HORSE-RACING

Racing is one of the great Irish sports, embracing all classes. As Dublin has grown in size, some of the old racetracks in the county area have been swallowed up by housing developments, but there are still a number of top-class tracks within an hour of the city. For fans of National Hunt (racing over jumps, held in the winter months), these include Leopardstown, 6 miles/10 km south of the city centre, Fairyhouse, County Meath (home of the Irish Grand National, run on Easter Monday), Naas and Punchestown in County Kildare, and Navan in County Meath.

There is less passion, but more money, associated with the flat season which runs for the summer months. The Curragh in County Kildare is the headquarters of Irish racing. Race meetings there, especially the Irish Derby and Oaks, are always a big social draw.

All the national newspapers carry details of the day's race meetings. At the meeting, racegoers can place their bets either with the course bookmakers or with the State-run Tote. Back in the city, you can bet with one of the many bookmakers (sometimes called turf accountants) around town. Special buses usually run on race days, contact Bus Éireann for more details.

# HORSE-RIDING

There are several riding schools within easy reach of Dublin (by car):
Ashton Equestrian Centre, Castleknock, telephone 01–8387611
Brennanstown Riding School, Kilmacanogue, Co. Wicklow, telephone 01–2863778
Brooke Lodge Riding Centre, Stepaside, telephone 01–2952153
Broadmeadows Equestrian Centre, Swords, telephone 01–8401635
Carrickmines Equestrian Centre, Foxrock, telephone 01–2955990
Pine View Riding Stables, Rockbrook, Rathfarnham, telephone 01–4944433.
For more information contact the Equestrian Federation of Ireland, Ashton House,
Castleknock, telephone 01–8387611.

# ICE-SKATING

Dublin Ice Rink, Dolphin's Barn, telephone 01–4534153
Silver Skate Ice Rink, 372b North Circular Road, telephone 01–8301263

# RACQUET SPORTS

Badminton Hall, Whitehall Road, telephone 01–4580101/4505966
Badminton Clinic, 64 Ailesbury Grove, Dublin 16, telephone 01–4980349
The Badminton Union of Ireland is based at the Badminton Hall above.
Squash Ireland charges visitors fees to play at its centres in Clontarf, telephone
01–8331656, Dalkey, telephone 01–2801515, Dartry, telephone 01–4963910 and
Phoenix Park, telephone 01–8385850. Full gym facilities and sauna are also open to
visitors.
The Irish Squash Raquets Association, House of Sport, Long Mile Road, telephone
01–4501564, can provide more information on squash facilities.
There are public tennis courts (tarmac surface, but very cheap) in the following parks:
Bushy Park, Terenure, telephone 01–4900320
Herbert Park, Ballsbridge, telephone 01–6684364
St Anne's Park, Raheny, telephone 01–8331859.
Fitzwilliam Lawn Tennis Club, Appian Way, is a long-established male-only club with
tennis and squash facilities available to visitors (women are tolerated, no more),
telephone 01–6603988.
For more information contact Tennis Ireland, 105 Morehampton Road, telephone
01–6681841.

# RUGBY UNION

Rugby is played in the more exclusive and expensive schools in Dublin and
consequently has an elitist air about it. Nonetheless, when Ireland plays its internationals,
the whole country unites behind the men in the green jerseys.
Ireland plays its rugby internationals at Lansdowne Road in Ballsbridge. Home games
in the Five Nations Championship are played there on Saturday afternoons in
January–March. Stand tickets are hard to get, but there are sometimes terrace tickets
available.

# SAILING

Dublin Bay is home to many venerable sailing clubs, including the Royal Irish Yacht
Club, the National Yacht Club and the Royal St George Yacht Club. There are also
yacht clubs at Howth, Sutton, Malahide, Swords, Rush, Skerries and Clontarf. Visiting
yachting enthusiasts, or prospective sailors, should contact the Irish Yachting Association,
3 Park Road, Dún Laoghaire, telephone 01–2800239, for more information.

## SOCCER

As sports go, soccer is THE consuming passion in Dublin. Ironically, though, attendances at local matches in the League of Ireland are tiny and Ireland's big international games are played in the rugby stadium at Lansdowne Road (where the frequently bumpy terrain works to the home side's advantage).

League of Ireland matches are played on Sunday afternoons during the season (September to April) on various grounds around the city. The most popular clubs are Shamrock Rovers, which play at the RDS grounds in Ballsbridge, and Bohemians (Bohs), whose home ground is at Dalymount Park in Phibsborough. In the off-season, the Dublin teams often arrange attractive fixtures against the top English league sides.

## SWIMMING

There are numerous sandy beaches near Dublin. The most popular are: Dollymount (3.5 miles/6 km from Dublin), Sutton (7 miles/11 km), Howth (9 miles/14.5 km), Portmarnock (9 miles/14.5 km), Donabate (13 miles/21 km), Skerries (18 miles/29 km) and Malahide (9 miles/14.5 km) to the north; and Sandycove (9 miles/14.5 km) to the south.

There are also a number of stony beaches. The most popular is probably Killiney (8 miles/13 km south of the city centre). The Forty Foot, by the Joyce Tower (DART stop: Sandycove or bus 8. See page 110) is an artificially created bathing-place that has long been a favourite with Dubliners, in particular those souls who 'take the plunge' all year round. Go there especially on Christmas morning.

However, only four of the above beaches currently qualify for the Blue Flag awarded by the EC to beaches with high standards of water quality and beach management. These are Skerries South, Portrane, Donabate and Malahide.

## SWIMMING POOLS

Dublin Corporation operates the following public swimming pools:
Markievicz Pool, Townsend Street, telephone 01–6770503
Rathmines Pool, Lower Rathmines Road, telephone 01–4961275
Seán MacDermott Street Pool (off O'Connell Street), telephone 01–8720752.
There are also municipal pools in the suburbs of Ballyfermot, Ballymun, Coolock, Crumlin and Finglas.
Open Sea Baths, Dún Laoghaire, telephone 01–2841690 and at Blackrock and Clontarf (June–September)

# CHILDREN'S ACTIVITIES

*ENFO*, the Government environmental information centre on St Andrew Street, has a variety of activities for children, including videos and computer games as well as lots of printed information on all things to do with the environment.

The *Museum of Modern Art* in Kilmainham organises regular workshops for children, telephone 01–6718666.

The multiplex cinemas in Tallaght, Coolock and Santry run regular cinema clubs on Saturday mornings for children.

The *Fun Factory* in Dún Laoghaire and Blanchardstown is a sort of indoor playground with equipment suitable for babies. Open 10 a.m.–7 p.m. Monday–Thursday, 10 a.m.– 9 p.m. Friday–Sunday.

*Dr Quirkey's Good Time Emporium*, 55/56 O'Connell Street, has video games, a virtual reality machine and other noisy amusements.

The *National Wax Museum* features a Chamber of Horrors and a Children's World of Fairytales and Fantasy. There's also Bart Simpson, the turtles and other modern-day cartoon favourites. For more information see page 57.

The *Museum of Childhood*, 20 Palmerston Park, houses an unusual collection of antique dolls and toys. Open 2–5.30 p.m. Sunday only. See page 56.

*Dublin Zoo*, Phoenix Park, telephone 01–6771425, is one of the oldest in the world, and has lots to offer to children of all ages. There are almost a thousand animals, many of them rare, as well as a Children's Corner and a restaurant. Open 9.30 a.m.– 6 p.m. Monday–Saturday, 10.30 a.m.–6 p.m. Sunday. October–March 9.30 a.m.–4 p.m. Monday–Friday, 9.30 a.m.–5 p.m. Saturday, 10.30 a.m.–5 p.m. Sunday.

The *Fry Model Railway* in the grounds of Malahide Castle is an old-world re-creation of the Dublin system in model form, complete with trams, trains and the DART. See page 55.

The *Early Learning Centre*, Henry Street, telephone 01–8731945, holds weekly activity mornings involving playdough, face-painting, etc.

The *Dublin Writers' Museum*, 18/19 Parnell Square, telephone 01–8722077, has an interactive exhibition celebrating children's literature.

There are numerous fun parks and open farms in County Wicklow, which are detailed in the appropriate section.

There are baby sessions in most swimming pools at regular times. Contact one of the pools listed above for more information.

# BICYCLE TOURS

Heavy traffic, bumpy roads, narrow streets and the paucity of cycle lanes all make cycling in Dublin a hazardous experience. Yet thousands of Dubliners commute daily by bicycle, and travelling on two wheels is often the quickest way of getting around, as well as providing the ideal means of seeing the city and its environs.

Sundays, when traffic is lightest, offer the best opportunities for touring the city centre by bicycle; long summer evenings are also good times. For those undaunted by the traffic, the following itineraries are sketched out. More information on the individual attractions mentioned is available in 'Dublin Tours', page 65.

**Phoenix Park** (9.5 mile/15 km round trip from city centre)

Ride upriver on the south quays, crossing the Liffey at the bridge just before Heuston Station. Turn left up Parkgate Street, passing Ryan's pub on the right, and enter the Park by the main gate on the right. Turn left at the obelisk of the Wellington monument and follow a clockwise route around the perimeter of the park. See 'Dublin Tours' for information on the sights visited. This circular route ends back at the Wellington monument, from where Parkgate Street and the north quays lead in to the city centre.

**Pine Forest** (Round trip 19.5 miles/31 km)

This route involves some steep climbing, and offers in return fine views of the city and bay from the Dublin Mountains. Cycle south through Terenure to Rathfarnham. Shortly after passing Rathfarnham Castle on the left, turn right at the Yellow House pub. Keep to the main road for over a mile, and turn first right over the River Owendoher after passing through two traffic lights. Then turn left, from where the road rises steeply into the hills. After Rockbrook, the car park in the forest to the right is the starting-point for the quick but steep climb to the Hellfire Club (see pages 114–15).

Continue straight on until you come to Killakee, with its few parking spaces, ice-cream vendors and wonderful views of Dublin Bay. The road left descends to Cruagh Forest on the right. Further down, just after the bridge, is Pine Forest, which offers other walks and a pleasant picnic spot beside the babbling brook (the Owendoher again). From here, it's downhill all the way to Rathfarnham.

### South Wall (Round trip 9 miles/14 km)

A short and flat journey out to Dublin Bay. Start at Townsend Street, by the Screen Cinema, opposite Trinity College. Follow this street to the end, then turn right and left onto Pearse Street, which leads east to the pleasant suburb of Ringsend. Pass over the bridge where the River Dodder meets the Liffey. Veer right through Irishtown until the corner of Seán Moore Park is reached. Turn left onto Seán Moore Road. Turn right at the main roundabout and left shortly afterwards. The road leads out through the port area, passing coal depots and a small sewage-treatment plant, then passes around the Pigeon House electricity-generating station with its distinctive twin red-and-white-striped towers. At the end of the road, the South Wall extends for 5,592 feet/1,700 m out to the Poolbeg Lighthouse. The Wall is too bumpy for bicycles so walk out to the lighthouse, from where there are magnificent views of the Howth peninsula to the north and Dún Laoghaire and the Wicklow Mountains to the south. Return by the same route to the city centre.

### Howth (Round trip 22 miles/35 km)

Travel north from the city centre by Amiens Street and Fairview. Follow the coast road, passing through Raheny and Sutton. At Sutton Cross, go straight on for Howth village and the nearby Howth Castle demesne. Take the steep hill past the Abbey ruins and head for the Baily Lighthouse. From there, proceed to the eastern and southern sides of the Head. Return by the coast road.

### Dalkey (Round trip 12.5 miles/20 km)

Coming from the Screen Cinema, go down Townsend Street, turn right at the end and then left onto Pearse Street. From here, it's straight on all the way, following the coast road past Sandymount Strand and Blackrock. After Blackrock, turn left at the Car Ferry signpost to regain the coast and reach Dún Laoghaire. Visit the town, or take a stroll on the pier, and continue along the coast. The Joyce tower becomes visible across the bay, and just below, the Forty Foot bathing-place. Turn right and then left to return to the main road leading to Dalkey, a charming village with several castles. Follow the signpost for the scenic coastal route, passing Coliemore Harbour and looking over onto Dalkey Island. Loop back towards Dalkey and return by Dún Laoghaire. It is also possible to continue from Coliemore along the Vico Road; this route is very hilly but rewards the cyclist with splendid views of Killiney Bay and its stony beach.

# DUBLIN TOURS

## TOUR 1: HISTORIC DUBLIN: THE OLD CITY

The best and most appropriate place to begin a tour of medieval Dublin is Dublin Castle, for centuries the military and administrative centre of British power in Ireland. You can approach it by walking up Dame Street from College Green. Alternatively, walk along the quays until you reach Capel Street Bridge (officially, Grattan Bridge, but no one can remember this name) and then turn left onto Parliament Street. The attractive building on the corner is the Sunlight Chambers, and its tiled exterior recounts various episodes in the story of the manufacture of soap. Ironically for a property which was originally occupied by a soap manufacturer, today it stands badly neglected and in need of a good wash.

Capel Street Bridge is on the spot where the Liffey and Poddle (now underground) meet, and where Dublin was founded over a thousand years ago. This area was the site of the old harbour until a new port was built further east in the eighteenth century.

The **City Hall** (Lord Edward Street, telephone 01–6796111. Open 9 a.m.–1 p.m., 2.15–5 p.m., Monday–Friday, visits to the Council Chamber by appointment only) occupies an impressive site at the top of Parliament Street. Thomas Cooley won £100 for his design of the building, then used as the Royal Exchange, in an architectural competition organised in 1769. Cooley made his name as an architect with his design (despite the fact that it faces north and has been described as 'entirely useless' by a leading architectural historian), but died only five years later. The building was notorious as the site of repression and violence in its early years; for example, the rebels of 1798 were tortured here, and in 1824 three people were killed when the iron railings collapsed under the weight of people watching a public whipping. However, it acquired a more peaceful purpose when Dublin Corporation moved here in 1852.

Inside, the ancient regalia of the city and charters dating back to 1172 are on view in the Muniment Room. Look out, too, for some fine statues of nineteenth-century Irish patriots, including Thomas Davis and Daniel O'Connell, both of whom are commemorated elsewhere in the city. The interior is dominated by the spectacular dome. The city crest, three burning castles depicting a city under siege, is prominently displayed, together with its Latin legend meaning 'Happy the city where citizens obey'.

Just above the City Hall are the Municipal Buildings, formerly the Newcomen Bank, which was built by Thomas Ivory, the only native-born architect to leave his mark on eighteenth-century Dublin. Ivory lost out in the competition to build the City Hall, but many consider his building, which dates from 1781, more elegant than its neighbour. Unfortunately, it is not open to the public.

## Dublin Castle

Half-castle, half-palace, Dublin Castle (for details of opening hours see page 55) served as the military and administrative heart of foreign power in Ireland for seven centuries. Originally, the Castle was a military fortification in the classical sense, and its name was synonymous with British power and terror for most Irish people. Gradually, however, as the military threat to Dublin and the surrounding area receded, Dublin Castle evolved into the palace used as the administrative centre of British rule in Ireland and the venue for all occasions of State and high society. Even today, the Presidents of Ireland are invested in Dublin Castle and part of the site has recently been redeveloped as a major centre for EC conferences and summits.

Perhaps because of its historical associations, few Irish people stray into the Castle unless they have business there. However, it's a destination that no visitor to Dublin can afford to miss, containing as it does a treasure trove of architecture and artefacts dating from each of the last seven centuries. Quite apart from its contents, Dublin Castle, and especially the Upper Castle Yard, is a beautiful, finely proportioned architectural space, providing a welcome break from the bustle beyond the Castle walls.

It was King John who gave the order to build Dublin Castle in 1204, and work began about four years later on a site where the Danes are believed to have erected a fortress four centuries before. This was the great period of Norman expansion in Dublin; construction of the nave of Christ Church began about 1212, while the first bridge to cross the Liffey dates from 1215.

Located strategically near the Liffey, Dublin Castle became the nucleus around which the city built up, and those parts of the original building still in existence are, with the cathedrals, the oldest surviving architecture in Dublin. The original castle was rectangular in shape, with a tower at each corner, but only two of the large towers and a portion of the wall remain.

The entrance to the **Upper Castle Yard** lies directly west of the City Hall. The gate is surmounted by a statue of the figure of Justice which has, as every Dubliner knows, its back to the city.

A disastrous fire and series of gunpowder explosions destroyed much of the Castle in 1684. Rebuilding of the Great Courtyard began almost immediately, but continued until 1760. Today, the Upper Castle Yard is an elegant courtyard built in the Palladian style. The oldest buildings date from about 1740, while some of the others are twentieth-century reproductions, made necessary after another fire in 1941 ruined the eighteenth-century blocks.

Along the southern side are the **State Apartments**, the starting-point for guided tours (well worth doing, but sometimes the Apartments are closed for Government functions, so be prepared for a disappointment or ring in advance to check). Formerly the home of the English viceroys, the State Apartments are luxurious throughout, the most impressive room being St Patrick's Hall, 82 feet/25 m long and 39 feet/12 m wide, with its lofty panelled ceiling decorated with paintings of George III (in the centre), the conversion of the Irish by St Patrick, and Henry II receiving the homage of the Irish chieftains. Today, the Hall is used for the installation of modern Irish Presidents.

Throughout the tour, there are few reminders of the original role of the Castle in maintaining British domination of a rebellious people. The only exception here is the room dedicated to James Connolly, which is visited early on in the tour. Connolly, a republican socialist who was one of the leaders of the 1916 Rising, lay injured here for a week after the failure of the revolt. Finally, he was taken to Kilmainham Gaol, where he was strapped to a chair and shot by a firing squad.

The tour then passes from one splendid room to another, beginning with the Granard Room with its portrait of Lady Elizabeth, Countess of Southampton by Van Dyck and its beautiful ceiling, which was originally in Mespil House, a fine Georgian house demolished by developers. After the King's Bedroom, the Arts and Crafts Room also features a ceiling and stucco work transported from Mespil House. The Queen's Bedroom was where Queen Victoria slept on the three occasions she visited Ireland. Unhappy with the view from her window of the city's teeming slums, she ordered a special wall built to hide the sight. The wall, complete with false gate, is still there today and is known as Victoria's Folly, as it serves no other purpose.

The charming State Corridor is identical to one designed in the Bank of Ireland by the same architect, Edward Lovett Pearce. The Apollo Room was where the ladies retired for musical entertainment in the evenings. The ceiling here comes from Tracton House, another demolished Dublin mansion which once stood on the corner of St Stephen's Green and Merrion Row. The Drawing Room suffered badly in the 1941 fire, which started when a piece of turf fell out of the hearth, burned through the floor and set fire to some papier mâché ceiling work. However, it has been creditably redecorated, using paintings on loan from the National Gallery.

The Throne Room was where the British kings and queens received their subjects on their visits to Dublin, while the Portrait Gallery contains pictures of the British Viceroys, many of whom are commemorated in the names of familiar Dublin streets.

The Wedgwood Room is an oval room elegantly decorated with paintings by Angelica Kauffmann. The Bermingham Tower was where many Irish rebels were imprisoned in earlier centuries and from where Red Hugh O'Donnell, son of one of the great northern chieftains, made his dramatic escape to the Wicklow Mountains on a snowy Christmas Eve, 1592. The original room was destroyed in an explosion in 1775 and was restored in neo-Gothic style in the early nineteenth century. Today, it is dedicated to the signatories of the 1916 Rising.

From the State Apartments, the visitor is taken back in time and across the square to the **Viking and Norman Defences Exhibition**, to see the only visible remnants of the Viking town defences. The remains of the Powder Tower were discovered almost by accident here in 1986 and have been magnificently arranged for viewing. The fragment of tenth-century Viking wall here is the oldest part of Dublin still visible today. At the very bottom, the River Poddle, so central to the history of the city, still trickles by.

Across the Lower Castle Yard is the **Church of the Most Holy Trinity**, known as the Chapel Royal until it was taken over by the Catholic Church in 1943. This Church was built between 1807and 1814 in the Gothic Revival style to the design of Francis Johnston, one of the most famous Dublin architects. The exterior is decorated with over ninety heads of British monarchs and other historical figures; look out for St Peter above the main door and Jonathan Swift above one of the windows. By the chapel is another of the original towers, the **Record Tower**, which is being restored as a museum of the Castle's history. Observe the difference in the stonework between the base of the tower, which dates from the twelfth century, the middle, which is several hundred years younger, and the castellated top, which dates from the nineteenth century.

Sadly, the peace of the Castle has been partially destroyed by the construction in the Lower Castle Yard of several modern office-blocks which are used by Government departments. Of the other buildings on the site, the Genealogical Office, built between 1750 and 1761, is one of the prettiest. The Bedford Tower in the Upper Castle Yard was the scene of an astonishing theft in 1907 when the Irish Crown Jewels were stolen; they have never been recovered. The Treasury in the Lower Castle Yard has been tastefully restored and houses a bookshop and a café serving excellent meals and snacks.

Leave Dublin Castle by the Justice Gate and proceed via Lord Edward Street up the hill to Christ Church.

## Christ Church Cathedral

The Cathedral of the Holy Trinity, known to everyone as Christ Church Cathedral (open 10 a.m.–5 p.m. except during services. Sung Eucharist at 11 a.m., Choral Evensong 3.30 p.m.), is Dublin's oldest (Anglican) cathedral and occupies the high ground where the city had its beginnings. Because the cathedral sits squat in the hill, it gives the impression of being smaller than it is.

Christ Church was founded by the Norse King Sitric in 1038. The original wooden structure was rebuilt in stone by the Normans between 1173 and 1220 and thereafter the cathedral became the place of worship of the British establishment in Ireland. Four Irish kings were crowned in the church and it was here that the pretender Lambert Simnel was crowned Edward VI of England in May 1487. It became a Protestant cathedral after the Reformation but briefly reverted to Catholicism when troops loyal to King James II seized it in 1689. After the roof and south side collapsed in 1562, the cathedral fell on hard times, but survived until 1875 when a wealthy whiskey distiller paid for a lavish restoration (costing the equivalent of today's £23 million!) in the Gothic style.

Only the north wall of the nave, the transepts and the west bay of the choir remain of the original stone building. While the interior is crammed with various artefacts, probably the most interesting item is the strange monument which is reputed to be the tomb of Strongbow, the first Norman conqueror of Dublin, who died in 1176. The original tomb was destroyed when the wall above and roof collapsed in 1562, but a replacement figure dating from the fourteenth century was found.

The heart of St Laurence O'Toole, who was Archbishop of Dublin in Strongbow's time, is preserved in a metal casket located in a chapel at the east end of the cathedral. Look out here, at the Peace Chapel of St Laud, for the superb medieval floor tiles, which the Victorians copied throughout the cathedral. The adjacent Lady Chapel, which is dedicated to the Virgin Mary, has a lovely modern statue of the Virgin and Child by Imogen Stuart.

One can see the differing Romanesque and Gothic styles employed at various stages in the construction of the cathedral. Half-way down the left-hand side, in the north transept, there are some fine medieval stone carvings dating from about 1200. The observant visitor who looks back on the nave will also spot the leaning wall of Dublin — out of perpendicular since 1562 by about 18 inches/0.5 m.

Under the cathedral is the vaulted crypt, believed to be Dublin's oldest building. Dating from the years after 1171, this forest of heavy rough-stone pillars is one of the largest medieval crypts in these islands. A mummified cat, several statues of former kings, and the official ancient stocks used to punish offenders in medieval times are among the curious exhibits of Viking Dublin gathered here.

A picturesque bridge, added during restoration work in the last century, links Christ Church with the **Synod Hall** opposite. In recent years, the Hall has been used for corporate hospitality and even a discothèque, but it is now the venue for 'Dublinia', an exhibition portraying Dublin life in medieval times. The exhibition spans nearly 400

Dublins two cathedrals, within a few hundred yards of each other. Christ Church (*above*) and St Patrick's (*right*) were originally medieval but both were heavily restored in the nineteenth century.

years from the coming of the Normans in 1170 to the Reformation and the closing of the monasteries in 1540. There is a medieval maze, a scale model of the old city, life-size reconstructions of the old docks buildings and a collection of artefacts on loan from the National Museum. The tour concludes with an audio-visual presentation before the visitor crosses the bridge to see Christ Church.

In essence, **'Dublinia'** is a brave attempt to use modern means of communication — the visitor is provided with a headset and accompanying cassette in any of five languages — to re-create the great heritage of medieval Dublin, much of which has been lost and destroyed in the distant and not-so-distant past. (For details see page 55.)

Cross back towards Dublin Castle again and pass down Werburgh Street, immediately to the left of the newly built Jury's Hotel. Burdock's fish and chip shop (open until 11 p.m. daily except Sunday) on the right-hand side is generally considered the best in Dublin and is certainly one of the most traditional. **Saint Werburgh's Church** on the left is of Anglo-Norman origin, and lies on the site of an earlier Viking construction. It was rebuilt twice in the eighteenth century and boasted a magnificent 160-foot (49 m) spire until this was removed in 1810. Lord Edward Fitzgerald, one of the principal leaders of the 1798 Rising, is buried in the vaults. John Field, the composer and pianist credited with the creation of the nocturne, was baptised here in 1782. He died in Moscow in 1837. Unfortunately, the church is usually closed; Sunday morning is a good time to visit.

Hoey's Court, a small lane to the left, is where Jonathan Swift was born in 1667, although the house no longer exists. (Ironically, the ugly building occupying the site is used as an unemployment exchange.) Continuing down Werburgh Street and onto Bride Street, one comes firmly into the area historically known as the Liberties, which lay just outside the medieval walls and were exempt from city jurisdiction and taxes, hence the name. The area's special character lent itself to commerce, trades and crafts, and attracted French, Dutch and particularly Huguenot immigrants. Amid the industry, an anarchic, bohemian

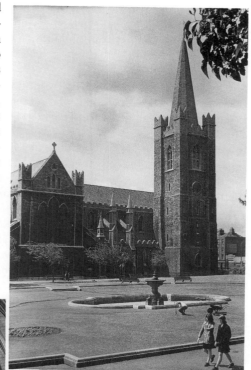

atmosphere prevailed, whose reputation lives on to this day.

However, the punitive Trade Laws introduced in the nineteenth century ruined the area financially, and the Liberties quickly developed into a dangerous and disease-ridden slum. Today, the area is a mixture of the run-down and the newly developed, whose remaining inhabitants enjoy the reputation of being the 'real Dubs'. Cruelly, too, the Liberties of today is bisected by a new six-lane highway which passes right in front of historic buildings and is designed to transport suburban car-drivers to and from their homes.

From Bride Street the rear of St Patrick's Cathedral (telephone 01–4475817, open daily) looms into view, with its attractively landscaped park to the side. Cross the park, reputedly the location of St Patrick's Well, one of the ancient wells of Dublin. This is the oldest Christian site in Dublin — St Patrick is said to have baptised the local inhabitants at this well in the fifth century — though Christ Church is the older building.

### St Patrick's Cathedral

St Patrick's was founded in 1190 by John Comyn, the first Englishman to become Archbishop of Dublin, who rebuilt the existing church in stone. It became a cathedral in 1213 and was rebuilt in its present form in an early English style between 1220 and 1250. When a fire destroyed the west tower, Archbishop Minot rebuilt this in 1370 and installed the largest peal of bells in Ireland. Indeed, St Patrick's is a superlative cathedral, arguably the most impressive church in Dublin; it is the biggest church in Ireland with its 141-foot (43 m) tower, which is surmounted by a 105-foot (32 m) spire, added in 1749. Ireland's largest remaining public clock was first mounted here in 1560.

St Patrick's, which today is the national cathedral of the Church of Ireland, was the seat of the first and only university in Ireland from 1320 until Trinity was founded in 1592, and the Grammar School associated with the Cathedral is still in existence nearby. The Chapter of St Patrick's staunchly resisted the Reformation and as a result its revenues and valuables were confiscated. During the wars of the seventeenth century Cromwellian troopers stabled their horses in the aisles. Like Christ Church, St Patrick's fell into disrepair until extensively renovated in the mid-nineteenth century by drink merchants — in this case, the Guinness brewing family.

Although less elaborate than Christ Church, the interior of St Patrick's is extraordinarily impressive. Opposite the entrance is the medieval Chapter House, which has a door with a hole in it dating from 1492. The expression 'to chance your arm' is said to have its origins here. The story goes that Lord Kildare cut the hole and put his arm through it in order to shake hands and secure a peace with his enemy, Lord Ormonde, who was under siege in the Chapter House.

The atmosphere inside St Patrick's lies heavy with memories of the Anglo-Irish, for on all sides relics and monuments recall seven centuries of their history. The great length of the nave, the heraldic banners around the choir stalls and the stained-glass windows in the Lady Chapel all combine to produce an effect of dignity and splendour. Those fallen in the battles of the past, including the 50,000 Irish who died fighting for Britain in the First World War, are commemorated on the walls and tombs. The largest monument is the one erected in 1631 by Richard Boyle, which memorialises that family of English settlers, including Robert Boyle, the famous chemist and originator of Boyle's Law, who is depicted in the centre of the lowest tier of the monument.

Many famous people have been associated with St Patrick's, but the name of one man, Jonathan Swift, is inextricably linked with the cathedral. The author of *Gulliver's Travels, A Tale of a Tub, A Modest Proposal* and other satires, Swift returned to his native Dublin in 1713 to become Dean of St Patrick's, which he remained until his death in 1745. As Dean, he was responsible for justice and administration in the Liberties, and his work with the teeming, destitute masses living all about St Patrick's led him first to promote Irish industry and later to promote eloquently the view that English misrule was the cause of Ireland's woes. A complex, melancholy man possessed of deep reservoirs of savage indignation and acid but lucid prose, Swift almost single-handedly forged a new consciousness for the Anglo-Irish, one which formed a blueprint for later patriots to act upon.

The great Dean is buried in his beloved St Patrick's. His tomb lies to the right of the entrance porch, and nearby is the grave of 'Stella' (Esther Johnson), Swift's partner in one of the most enigmatic and tragic love stories of history. There is also a fine marble bust of Swift, and his bitter and immortal epitaph is to be read over the door of the robing-room: 'He lies where furious indignation can no longer rend his heart. Go traveller and imitate if you can one who was, to the best of his powers, a defender of Liberty.'

Leave St Patrick's and turn left into St Patrick's Close. A statue of Sir Benjamin Lee Guinness, benefactor to the Cathedral, sits behind the railings. Opposite is the choir school attached to St Patrick's, which was founded in 1432.

Further down St Patrick's Close is the gem of **Marsh's Library** (for details see page 56). Established by Narcissus Marsh, Archbishop of Dublin, in 1707, this charming building is the oldest public library in Ireland. The interior of the library, with its oak stalls and bookcases and three wire cages into which readers are locked with rare books, has changed little since its foundation. Many of the books were exceptionally rare and valuable even in Marsh's time and some of them were actually chained to the shelves. Today, the collection numbers about 25,000 volumes from the sixteenth, seventeenth and early eighteenth centuries. Dean Swift often read here — even though he heartily detested Marsh — and his scribbles are still to be seen on some of the books.

Leaving the Library turn left, and at the end of St Patrick's Close turn right onto Kevin Street. The alleyway opposite, Cathedral Lane, leads through blocks of flats to a small park known as the Cabbage Patch because Swift's gardens were near here. This was once a Huguenot graveyard and although the remains have been moved, the tombstones are still here, stacked up on one side of the park.

Go straight on, passing the Deanery of St Patrick's on your right. Number 35 is a modest enough building with a gabled top which is notable for being the only surviving example of Dutch Billy architecture in the Liberties.

Cross Patrick Street onto Dean Street. Ahead lies the Coombe, the heart of the Liberties and of the weaving trade that once thrived in the area. Then turn right onto Francis Street, a quiet street that is home to an enormous variety of antiques and craft shops. **Saint Nicholas of Myra** is a handsome enough church on the right that was built in the 1830s to celebrate Catholic emancipation in Ireland. There is a stained-glass window in the wedding chapel by the celebrated Irish artist Harry Clarke. Cooke's Bakery at No. 31 sells excellent breads and confectionery. Further up the street is the **Iveagh Market**, a Victorian building of some beauty. Note the carved heads of Moors and oriental traders which adorn the keystones of the arches. The market itself — mostly clothes, bric-à-brac and fish — has been in sad decline since many of the local families who lived for generations in the Liberties were rehoused in the suburbs. There are plans for its redevelopment, but it is doubtful if the original working-class character of the market can be maintained as more affluent young people buy small houses and new apartments in the area.

At the top of Francis Street the tour turns right, but the visitor may wish to turn left onto Thomas Street in order to see the **Guinness Brewery**. If this option is chosen continue up Thomas Street, passing St John's Lane Church (officially the church of SS Augustine and John but, as the visitor may already realise, nearly every building in Dublin has at least two versions of its name — the official and the familiar), which was built between 1862 and 1895. Further up on the right the National College of Art and Design occupies the former Power's Distillery which was founded here in 1791. This part of Thomas Street is a bustling shopping area well known for good value; it also suffers from an above-average level of petty crime such as handbag-snatching, so beware. The once-beautiful St Catherine's Church, on the corner of Thomas Street and Meath Street, now lies severely dilapidated, a cruel case of official neglect. The church was built between 1760 and 1769, and Robert Emmet was executed in front of the building in 1803 after his ill-conceived rebellion ended in failure.

Continue along Thomas Street towards St James's Gate. By the time you turn left into Crane Street, the unmistakable aroma of the Guinness Brewery should be growing ever stronger. This spot, which marked the edge of the outer city in medieval times, has been a brewing centre for hundreds of years. In 1759 Arthur Guinness bought a disused brewery here and began brewing porter, a dark beer made from roasted barley. When this was a success in Ireland and Britain, Guinness came up with a stronger brew called extra stout — or 'stout' as it became known throughout the world. By the start of this century, St James's Gate was the largest brewery in the world and the mysterious black liquid with the creamy head had already become synonymous with Dublin. Today, the factory, which covers 40 acres/16 hectares, is the biggest brewery in Europe, and exports more beer than any other factory anywhere.

The company stopped bringing visitors around the factory some years ago, but the Guinness Hop Store in Crane Street is a tastefully restored warehouse which contains the 'World of Guinness' exhibition, as well as a bar and shop. Open 10 a.m.–4.30 p.m. Monday to Friday; last programme starts 3.30 p.m. Buses 21A, 78, 78A from Fleet Street. Be sure to try the free samples; the connoisseurs say that stout doesn't travel well, so it follows that the best Guinness is to be had in Dublin, and the best Guinness in Dublin is to be had in the factory itself.

Return by foot or bus to the route of the original tour, to the junction of Thomas Street and Francis Street. Continue along Thomas Street; Bridge Street to the left goes down to the Liffey and the Brazen Head, Dublin's oldest pub. This inn, which today is a good spot to hear traditional Irish music, almost certainly dates from before 1600 and was the meeting-place for the leaders of the United Irishmen who planned the rebellion of 1798.

**St Audoen's Church of Ireland church** (open 2.30–5 p.m. Saturday/ Sunday), on Cornmarket, is one of the most ancient in Dublin. It was founded by the Normans shortly after their arrival in the city. Dedicated to St Ouen of Rouen, it was probably built on the site of an earlier church dedicated to St Columba. The tower at the back hangs three bells made in 1423 that are said to be the oldest in Ireland. Look out for the Norman font, a good specimen of an early square-bowl font, dated 1192. The 'Lucky Stone' in the porch is an early Christian gravestone which has been the subject of many stories over the centuries. Walk down the steps to St Audoen's Arch, the only surviving gate of the walled city of Dublin. It was built in 1215 with stones taken from the old Dominican monastery across the river. A small park by the entrance to the church offers access to the ramparts of the city walls, but there isn't much of a view, apart from the green domes of the Four Courts, the nearby Adam and Eve's Church and Liberty Hall in the distance to the right.

Beside the ancient church, there is another St Audoen's on High Street, a brasher Catholic church built in the nineteenth century and home to 'Flame on the Hill', an audio-visual presentation which tells the story of Ireland before the coming of the Vikings (for details see page 57).

Across High Street, on Back Lane, is **Tailors' Hall** (telephone 01–4544794. Open 9.30 a.m.–4 p.m.), Dublin's only surviving guild-hall. It was built for the Guild of Tailors about 1706 but was also used by other guilds, such as Hosiers, Tanners and Saddlers. The Hall was closed in 1960 and came within a hair's breadth of demolition in the 1970s but was saved by conservationists and today houses the headquarters of An Taisce, the Irish National Trust. The building has an honourable place in Irish history as the venue of the Back Lane parliament of 1792, where the Catholic Committee met to secure relief against the Penal Laws and the United Irishmen planned to free the country from English domination.

**Mother Redcap's Market**, a pleasant haunt for antiques hunters and lovers of food and cheese, is also located in Back Lane and is open Friday–Sunday, 10.30 a.m.–5.30 p.m.

To return to the city centre, recross the road and walk past Christ Church Cathedral once more. Turn left immediately after the cathedral and walk down Fishamble (from fish shamble or market) Street. The Civic Offices, a horrendous bunker-like office-block built in the face of massive street protest, looms unavoidably on the horizon. Excavations on this site in the 1970s uncovered hundreds of fascinating artefacts — coins, bone combs, swords, pottery, household implements and leatherwork — dating from Viking times, which are now displayed in the National Museum and 'Dublinia'. Despite the widespread belief that an even greater archaeological treasure trove lay still buried on the site, the building of Dublin Corporation's new offices was allowed to proceed. The same misguided planners have since widened the roads in the area, so Christ Church lies marooned on the wrong side of a busy street that is difficult and dangerous to cross.

Although there is little left of **Fishamble Street**, the location is famous as the venue for the first ever performance of Handel's *Messiah*, conducted by the composer himself, in the Musick Rooms (long since disappeared) on 13 April 1742. Because the hall was so small and a large attendance was expected, the ladies were asked not to wear hooped skirts and the gentlemen not to wear their swords. The event is commemorated on a wall-plaque nearby; the site itself is now an iron foundry. On the right-hand corner with Essex Street West stands the oldest surviving private residence in Dublin, believed to date from the seventeenth century. However, the house had to be shored up with timber supports after the demolition of neighbouring buildings in the 1980s.

## Temple Bar

From Essex Street, it's a straight walk back into the city centre, to Westmoreland Street. This route also cuts through the heart of Temple Bar, a veritable rabbit-warren of side-streets which is currently being touted as Dublin's version of the Left Bank. The area owes its name to Sir William Temple, a seventeenth-century Provost of Trinity, whose back-garden this was. In this century it was neglected by everyone except the planners, who thought of demolishing buildings to put up a bus station, and a motley collection of hippies, punks and other entrepreneurs who availed of the low rents available to open numerous now-thriving crafts and retail businesses.

Today, Temple Bar boasts cooperatives, alternative music stores, a new-age shop, a Communist bookshop, a Hare Krishna centre, the magnificent Irish Film Centre, a condom shop, and much, much more. The Government has belatedly come on side and investment funds are being pumped into the area with great abandon. Whether this will have a totally beneficial effect remains to be seen. The best way to have a look at the area is to walk around and dip at random, but the Temple Bar Information Centre, 18 Eustace Street, can provide information on specific activities.

Off Temple Bar, the picturesque Merchant's Arch in Temple Bar leads to the river and the Ha'penny Bridge, whose looping, graceful arc is widely used as a symbol of Dublin. Also known to the powers that be as Wellington, Metal and Liffey Bridge, it was designed in cast iron in 1816 and has endeared itself to Dubliners ever since for its elegance and convenience. The curious popular name stems from the fact that it operated as a toll bridge from 1816 to 1918, when it could be crossed for the princely sum of one halfpenny.

The tour passes down Fleet Street to end in Westmoreland Street, where Bewley's is a good spot to enjoy some well-earned sustenance.

---

### Street-names

Dublin street-names are derived from English, Irish, Norse and even French words. The larger streets were named after big land-owners or members of the aristocracy in the Georgian period, and some of these were renamed in honour of Irish statesmen and politicians when nationalists took control of the city corporation in the last century (for example, Sackville Street was renamed O'Connell Street).

The smaller streets and alleyways were left with their original names in many cases, at least until they were replanned out of existence. These names were often taken from the trades traditionally associated with a particular area, such as Fishamble Street or Winetavern Street. While many of the tiniest alleyways have disappeared, a surprising number of these charmingly named backwaters survive off the main streets. There are Copper, Smock and Thundercut Alleys; Bumbailif, Cuckoo, Cut Throat, Fumbally, Marrowbone, Mutton and Pinchgut Lanes; and Cuckold, Cut Purse, Pudding and Skinners Rows, and probably many more to look out for in the course of your travels.

---

## TOUR 2: GEORGIAN DUBLIN AND THE SOUTH CITY

This tour starts in College Green, in many ways the centre of Dublin. After a visit to Trinity College, it proceeds via Grafton Street, Dublin's most fashionable shopping district, to St Stephen's Green. From there, the tour continues through the most elegant streets and squares of Georgian Dublin, before returning to College Green. The whole tour can be covered in three to four hours.

## Trinity College

The entrance to Trinity College is modest enough, especially compared to the curving grandeur of the Bank of Ireland opposite — James Joyce in *A Portrait of the Artist as a Young Man* described the college as 'set heavily in the city's ignorance like a dull stone set in a cumbrous ring'.

While outside on College Green, the traffic squeezes by unrelentingly and the pace of the city is at its most extreme, a few short steps take the visitor through the college entrance and into an altogether different environment. Entering the stately, geometrical elegance of the college's Front Square, the clamour of the city is left behind, the din of traffic subsides and another, impossibly superior world reveals itself. The architectural grandeur of the setting is perfectly complemented by the absence of cars or any other trappings of twentieth-century life and is further improved on by the bustle of students living university life to the full.

Yet if Trinity is the jewel in the crown of Dublin — and it undoubtedly is — the college sits somewhat uneasily in its location. Trinity was established in 1592 as an exclusively Protestant university in a mainly Catholic country. It excluded Catholics for much of its history and then found that when it relented, these same Catholics were largely forbidden by their bishops to attend the university until as late as 1970. It is only in the last twenty years that Catholics have begun going to Trinity in great numbers, and they now account for over three-quarters of the student body. Even so, many Dubliners have never set foot inside the college and the feeling that it is a 'foreign' institution persists in some quarters.

Nonetheless, few cities are so lucky as to have a beautiful university right in the centre. The college's 10,000 students, many of whom live on campus, add immeasurably to the life of the city, while Trinity's squares, buildings and parks are an oasis of calm and seclusion for office-workers and inner-city dwellers from the surrounding area. In addition, few universities can claim so many illustrious graduates; in literature alone, Oscar Wilde, Samuel Beckett, Thomas Moore, John Millington Synge, Oliver St John Gogarty, Bram Stoker and Sheridan Le Fanu were all educated here.

Trinity was founded on foot of a charter from England's Queen Elizabeth I on the site of the former Augustinian Priory of All Hallows, which had been suppressed and confiscated during the Reformation in 1538. The original charter called for a college where 'Knowledge, Learning and Civiltie may be increased, to the banishment of barbarism, tumult and disorderly living'. This worthy aim, it must be said, was not always achieved.

Set up specifically to provide an education for the Anglo-Irish, Trinity shares in the glory of the great achievements of this class. By sending their sons and (from this century) daughters here, rather than to university in England, the Anglo-Irish gradually developed the sense of a separate identity, not English, yet not thoroughly Irish either. Statues of the most illustrious graduates pepper the campus; most prominent are the statues of the philosopher and statesman Edmund Burke (1729–97) and the poet Oliver Goldsmith (1728–74) in front of the college.

The best way to see Trinity is simply to browse around, picking up a little of the atmosphere and stopping before the buildings of greatest interest. In the summer months, students from the college offer tours; the price of the tour includes admission to see the Book of Kells. The guides, with their plummy accents and imaginative story-lines, are entertaining in their own right.

Trinity is built on 40 acres/16 hectares of land reclaimed from the Liffey estuary. No trace of the original Elizabethan structure remains

today. The Rubrics, a residential red-brick block on the east side of Library Square (straight ahead when viewing from Front Arch), is the oldest surviving building, dating from 1722. Most of the older buildings were constructed in the eighteenth century and extended in the nineteenth. The façade of the college, for example, was completed in 1759.

The **Examination Hall** (1779–91), on the right side of Front Square, is frequently the venue for classical concerts and is decorated with portraits of renowned Trinity graduates such as Bishop Berkeley, Dean Swift and Burke. Opposite this building stands the finely proportioned Chapel, which today is shared between all the main Christian denominations.

*The Campanile in Trinity College*

The **Campanile** or bell tower facing the visitor is a curiosity which was erected in the middle of the square in 1853. It is believed to stand on the site of the priory that pre-dated the university. The 100-foot (30 m) tower houses a peal of bells and has long provided an irresistible temptation for the climbing talents of the college mountaineering club. To the left steps lead up to the **Dining Hall**, which was finished in the mid-1740s but badly damaged by a fire in 1984. Happily, it has since been restored and the great hall upstairs again serves as a dining-room for staff and students alike. It is also the site of Commons, one of the oldest college traditions, when the scholars and fellows of Trinity gather daily in traditional black gowns and recite prayers in Latin before commencing their evening meal. After the fire in 1984, a new Atrium and a Fellows' Bar, modelled on Adolf Loos' bar in Vienna's Kärtnerstrasse (not open to the public), were added at the back of the building. The vaulted Buttery below (entrance by the side) is the main students' bar and cafeteria and serves cheap food and snacks.

Beyond the Dining Hall lie the **Graduates' Memorial Building** and, further down on the left, the charming **Printing House**, a little Doric temple between the two main squares of the college which is now used by the Department of Microelectronics and Electrical Engineering.

Trinity's library is one of only four copyright libraries in the British Isles, meaning that it receives (or is supposed to receive) automatically a copy of every book published in the region. In all, the college's collection amounts to nearly three million volumes, most of them stored off-site, where a half-mile or kilometre of new shelving is needed each year to accommodate new volumes. On the campus, the busiest library is the Berkeley, a stark modernist creation dating from the 1960s and claimed by some as Ireland's best example of modern architecture. The spherical sculpture in front of this library is by Pomodoro.

The Long Room of the **Old Library**, on the right-hand side of Library Square, is the main focus of visitor interest. This building is not only beautiful in its own right, but also houses Ireland's largest collection of books and manuscripts, including the world-famous Book of Kells. There is an admission charge for entry to the Library, but it's well worth the visit. The opening hours are Monday–Saturday 9.30 a.m to 5.30 p.m., Sunday 12 noon to 5 p.m. (last admissions half an hour earlier).

A masterpiece of symmetry and proportion, the Old Library was completed at a cost of £15,000 in 1732, but was altered considerably by Deane and Woodward in 1860. The Long Room, with its barrel-vaulted ceiling lit by 100 windows, is 209 feet/64 m long and lined with two floors of books on each side. The room exudes tranquillity and learning and is adorned by white marble busts of famous scholars and writers; watch out for Homer, Socrates, Plato, Shakespeare, Milton, Bacon and, of course, Swift. Notwithstanding the constant stream of tourists, this is a place of near-religious beauty.

Among the treasures of the library are a copy of the first German Bible, some early folios from Shakespeare, hundreds of Greek, Latin and Irish manuscripts, as well as the Book of Armagh and Book of Durrow. However, the most famous manuscript is undoubtedly the celebrated Book of Kells, which dates from the early ninth century. A reminder of the golden era of the Irish monastic tradition, when monks carried the Christian faith from Ireland to continental Europe, the Book of Kells is an intricately illustrated version of the Four Gospels. The book was saved from destruction with the dissolution of the monasteries during the Reformation, and was presented to Trinity in 1660. Armed with dextrous draughtsmanship and vivid inks, the monks who created this unparalleled document were expressing the depth of their veneration for God. The success of their endeavours is evidenced by the massive interest shown today in the world's most renowned illuminated manuscript. Because the book is so old and fragile, it is carefully exhibited under a glass case and only two pages can be viewed at any one time. The library bookshop is well stocked with books, posters and postcards detailing the most decorative pages.

At the far end of the library are two early Irish harps, one of them traditionally known as Brian Boru's harp, after the medieval Irish chieftain of that name. The harp actually dates from the fifteenth or sixteenth century, which still makes it the oldest known Irish harp in existence. The library also houses the 'Dublin Experience', a multi-media reconstruction of the city's history from the earliest times, which runs between May and September. The show, which makes use of archive and new material, is on daily every hour, 10 a.m.–5 p.m.

There are many other fine buildings in Trinity, most of them open to the public during the daytime. The Museum Building on New Square (just beyond the Old Library), a mock Venetian-Byzantine edifice designed by Deane and Woodward in 1853, is a personal favourite, not least because the author spent many hours at lectures there. The Arts Building, which fronts unassumingly onto Nassau Street, is the focus of student life on the campus by day and houses the Douglas Hyde Gallery (see page 58). In contrast to the established architecture in the front half of the college grounds, the back end of the university, with its playing-fields and science buildings, is expanding most rapidly these days. On sunny summer afternoons, there is no better place to lounge about than College Park (behind the Berkeley Library), preferably by ordering a drink in the Pavilion Bar and watching the cricketers at play.

Leave Trinity College by the front gate. Statues commemorating two of Ireland's greatest patriots (both of them Protestant), Henry Grattan and Thomas Davis, stand on the traffic island straight ahead. The other fine building dominating College Green, the **Bank of Ireland**, is opposite. Begun in 1729 and originally known as Parliament House, the bank is the work of at least four different architects, though its curved — if windowless — beauty is seamless. The parliament was at the centre of Irish political life in the eighteenth century, until the Act of Union abolished the two houses of the Irish parliament in 1800. In 1803 the building was sold to the Bank of Ireland for £40,000 on the condition that it never again be used for public debate. There were plans to restore it to its former use when Ireland gained her independence in the 1920s, but these were never followed up.

Today, the bank is heavily used by workers and students in the vicinity, who scurry around its labyrinthine interior and pass through the former House of Commons in great numbers. Guides give free tours of the old House of Lords, whose appearance has changed little from the eighteenth century. With its panelled walls, lavish furnishings and hung tapestries, the hall accurately conveys a sense of the power and privilege attaching to its members in the heyday of Henry Grattan's parliament from 1782 on. The hall can be viewed any day during normal banking hours, but guided tours are given on Tuesdays only, at 10.30 and 11.30 a.m. and 1.45 p.m.; telephone 01–6615933 for more information.

In Foster Place, a small cul-de-sac behind the bank, is the Bank of Ireland Arts Centre (telephone 01–6711488. Open 10 a.m.–5 p.m. Monday–Saturday, noon–5 p.m. Sunday). This was traditionally the Armoury and is now the venue for exhibitions and occasional concerts.

Recross the road to face Trinity and turn right towards Grafton Street. On the left, set back from the large gate, is the Provost's House, home to Trinity's chief administrator. Started in 1759, this is one of the grandest of Dublin's Georgian mansions and is considered the city's most exclusive address (No. 1 Grafton Street).

Across the road, near the corner with Suffolk Street, is a statue of Molly Malone, the Dublin street trader celebrated in the famous ballad which starts:

> In Dublin's fair city
> Where the girls are so pretty
> I first set my eyes on sweet Molly Malone
> As she wheeled her wheelbarrow
> Through streets broad and narrow,
> Crying, 'Cockles and mussels, alive, alive, oh!'

Molly dies tragically of a 'fever' at the end of the song, but curiously, the buxom girl of the statue appears to be in the full flush of health.

Continue along Grafton Street, now pedestrianised. This is Dublin's most chic shopping area, and it has a lot in common with shopping streets anywhere. But what usually strikes the visitor as different here is the density of people out on the streets, most of them young, as well as the enormous number of buskers or street musicians. At the bottom of the street the two main department stores, Brown Thomas and Switzers, face each other in friendly rivalry — they share the same owner. Grafton Street is dealt with in detail in 'Shopping', but the one obligatory stop on the street is Bewley's Oriental Café, half-way up on the right. Bewley's is quintessential Dublin, a noisy but intimate meeting-place decorated in dark panelling, deep seats and stained glass. The food is cheap but unremarkable — except for the Irish breakfasts — but the tea, coffee and sticky buns are great, and the atmosphere is unbeatable. Punks, grannies, local office-workers — everyone meets in Bewley's, or reads the paper there. Waitress service, fondly remembered by older Dubliners, has given way to self-service, except on the first floor of the Grafton Street café.

There's a small museum on the second floor which tells how Bewley's was established in the 1840s by the descendants of Quaker immigrants into Ireland. It became a workers' cooperative in 1971, but almost closed in 1986 and caused a national crisis until a buyer was found, who has since put the enterprise on a firmer if more commercial footing. Two other city-centre branches of Bewley's, in Westmoreland Street and South Great George's Street, are worth visiting.

Johnson's Court, a small laneway to the right near Bewley's, leads directly to the Powerscourt Townhouse Centre, a tastefully designed upmarket shopping centre on three floors. The building itself dates from 1774 and was formerly the town residence of Lord Powerscourt.

Return to Grafton Street and continue straight on until **St Stephen's Green**, Dubliners' favourite park, is reached at the top of the street. This space was an open common until 1663, when it was enclosed and quickly became the focus of town planning and of fashionable life in the city. The Green was finally ringed by a variety of townhouses and other fine buildings by the late eighteenth century, though sadly a number of these were destroyed by speculators in the 1960s and 1970s. The park, which covers 27 acres/11 hectares, was railed in in 1815 to commemorate the Battle of Waterloo, and the land was properly laid out with flower gardens and an artificial lake in 1880 by Lord Ardilaun, of the Guinness brewing family.

Today, the gardens are as beautiful as ever and the Green represents a haven of quiet in the commercial heart of Dublin for thousands of office-workers and shoppers. Particularly on sunny summer days, when there might be a band playing, it's a lovely place to laze about, feed the ducks or read a book. Architecturally, there isn't all that much to see in the park, which is dotted with statues of various luminaries such as James Joyce, whose bust is near Newman House (see below), Tom Kettle, the Irish poet who died in the First World War, and Wolfe Tone, the Irish nationalist (this piece, known locally as Tonehenge, is at the Merrion Row entrance). There is also a Yeats memorial garden with a Henry Moore sculpture and a garden for the blind located near the centre of the park.

Pass through to the south side of Stephen's Green to reach Newman House, or alternatively walk around the west perimeter of the Green. The modern shopping centre on the right stands on the site of the old Dandelion Market, where U2 first played. Walk past the Royal College of Surgeons building on the right, before turning left onto St Stephen's Green South. Harcourt Street, which extends up from the Green at this corner, is a pleasant Georgian street that was laid out in 1775. Edward Carson, the champion of Ulster Unionism, was born at No. 4; at the time of writing, the survival of this severely delapidated building is under threat. Bram Stoker, creator of Dracula, resided at No. 16; George Bernard Shaw lived at No. 61 (Shaw's birthplace, further out at 33 Synge Street, has been restored and turned into a museum; see page 55).

**Newman House**, 85/86 St Stephen's Green South, has recently been restored (for details see page 57). The house served for many years as home to the Catholic University, later University College, which moved out to the suburb of Belfield at the start of the 1970s. The college was founded by Dr (later Cardinal) John Henry Newman in 1850, and the English poet and Jesuit Gerard Manley Hopkins lived and taught here. Hopkins was miserable all the time he was in Dublin and died in 1889; the simply furnished room where he wrote his dark, brilliant sonnets can be visited as part of the tour of Newman House. James Joyce is the most famous graduate of the university, but Irish patriots such as Patrick Pearse and Éamon de Valera also studied here.

Newman House is comprised of two separate houses; one of them, No. 85, is among the oldest surviving buildings on the Green. Built in 1740, it boasts marvellous rococo ceilings with stucco work by the Italian Lafranchini brothers. Number 86 was built in 1765 for Richard 'Burnchapel' Whaley, a notorious anti-Catholic bigot whose son 'Buck' Whaley is the source of many stories. According to one tale, Whaley, an inveterate gambler and rake, wagered that he would walk to Jerusalem and back for a stake reputed to be £15,000. He won the bet.

Miraculously, Newman House has survived the wear and tear caused by thousands of students passing through it. As the informative and helpful guides explain, the Jesuits censored some of the more revealing figures on the ceilings by painting over them. Next door to the right is the University Church, built in a curious but charming Russian Orthodox style in 1856, using Irish marble.

**Iveagh House**, home of the Department of Foreign Affairs, occupies Nos. 80 and 81 St Stephen's Green. Number 80, originally built in 1736 as a town mansion for the Protestant Bishop of Cork and Ross, was acquired by a member of the Guinness family (the name Iveagh, to be found on so many Dublin buildings, always denotes the involvement of one of the branches of the philanthropic brewing family), who amalgamated it with the adjoining house. In 1939 the second Earl of Iveagh presented both buildings to the Government. The house has a magnificent interior but is not open to the public.

Turn left onto the east side of the Green, where several dubious 'mock Georgian' office buildings have been built. Then turn right into Hume Street, scene in 1969 of the first great architectural battle between developers and conservationists. When it was planned to demolish the Georgian buildings reaching onto St Stephen's Green on the right, architectural students moved into the houses in protest. The developers eventually got their way (the present buildings are pastiche) but the event marked the end of a period when developers had free rein to destroy historic Dublin.

The interior of Ely House, at the end of the street, is decorated with lovely plasterwork by Michael Stapleton, but gaining entry to the building is difficult. The house today is occupied by the Knights of St Columbanus, a home-grown Catholic version of the freemasons.

To the right, at the end of Ely Place Upper, is the Gallagher Gallery of the Royal Hibernian Academy of Arts (for details see page 58), a modern red-bricked affair built by a property speculator, perhaps as a penance for his misdeeds. The site once held the house of Oliver St John Gogarty (1878–1957), a Dublin surgeon, wit and writer whose own fame has been obscured by Joyce's depiction of him as stately, plump, Buck Mulligan in *Ulysses*. Another writer, George Moore, lived for ten years at No. 4.

Return to the end of Ely Place and turn left onto Merrion Row. On the left is an annexe to the National Museum (the main building is on Kildare Street), used to house diverse exhibitions, generally on geology or folk-life. Adjacent, behind some iron railings, is a small Huguenot graveyard dating from 1693. Further along here, on the north side of the Green itself, is the Shelbourne Hotel, Dublin's most traditional grand hotel and an ideal place to take a break for a drink or afternoon tea.

Many of the large houses on this side of the Green are clubs, excellently preserved but closed to the public. This stretch, where dandies and high society paraded themselves, used to be called the Beaux Walk in the eighteenth century.

Turn right after the Shelbourne, on to Kildare Street. Leinster House, half-way down on the right, is the seat of Ireland's parliament and is flanked by the National Museum and the National Library, two nearly symmetrical buildings designed by Sir Thomas Deane in 1890.

Before Leinster House was begun in 1745, the area north of the Liffey was the most fashionable part of Dublin. When commissioning the building, however, the Earl of Kildare confidently predicted that the fashionable classes would follow him across town — and his prophecy was duly borne out. In due course, the Earl of Kildare was upgraded to become Duke of Leinster: the house took the new name while the street retained the old. The building is open to the public when the Dáil (parliament) is not sitting; ask at the entrance.

On the left the **National Library** (telephone 01–6618811), with its dark panelling and green lampshades, has an appropriately scholarly atmosphere. Its collection is of mainly Irish interest. Ring ahead for information about gaining access to the reading room, for which tickets are required. Alternatively, linger awhile at the entrance, as James Joyce did for long hours during his student years at the turn of the century.

The **National Museum** (for details see page 57) is home to Ireland's greatest treasures, covering over 8,000 years of civilisation and crafts-manship in the country. The exhibitions on display trace crudely the history of Ireland's earliest inhabitants, and their use of stone, copper, bronze and then iron to make tools and weapons. Artefacts from the Iron and Bronze Ages are shown in astonishing quantity; of these, the highlight is arguably the outstanding collection of gold jewellery from 2000 BC on. Ireland produced and even exported large amounts of gold jewellery in the late Bronze Age, much of it executed with a high degree of skill. Many of the gold ornaments exhibited here were found in 1854, when they were unearthed during the construction of the West Clare Railway.

The Tara Brooch, which dates from the eighth century AD, is regarded as the greatest piece of Irish metalwork. Its intricate ornamentation — on the back as well as the front — is reminiscent of the swirls and flourishes in the designs seen in the Book of Kells. Such is the level of decoration, some of the elaborative work can be properly viewed only using a magnifying glass. The brooch was found in 1850 in material that collapsed from a cliff in Bettystown, Co. Meath. The name Tara was given to it by a dealer later for no good archaeological reason.

The beautifully designed Ardagh Chalice from the same period was found in a field near Limerick in 1867 by a boy digging potatoes. The cup, made of an alloy of copper and silver, is decorated with panels of fine gold filigree and settings of enamel, amber and crystal.

There are many more items worth viewing, including the twelfth-century Cross of Cong and St Patrick's Bell. A more recent find is the Derrynaflan hoard, which was discovered in February 1980 by amateur treasure-hunters using metal-detectors. The Museum also houses collections of silver, glass, ceramics, costumes, Irish lace and coins. A special room is devoted to the 1916 Rising.

At the bottom of Kildare Street, where it meets Nassau Street, the Kildare Street Club, formerly a central institution of Anglo-Irish life, is on the right. The building is High Victorian in style and was inspired by Venetian architecture. Its innards were ripped out in 1972 to make way for functional offices whose floors manage to bisect the windows to stunningly awful effect. The only detail left for the visitor to admire is the whimsical ornamentation on the window-sills; look out for monkeys playing billiards and dogs chasing rabbits. The building also houses the State Heraldic Museum (for details see page 57).

Turn right onto Nassau Street and walk straight on. The playing-fields of Trinity lie behind the railings on the left. Continue along Clare Street, location of Greene's new and second-hand bookshop, until Merrion Square is reached.

Georgian Dublin, of which Merrion Square is the heart, is the defining architectural glory of the city. The creation of an ascendant Anglo-Irish class, Georgian architecture is breathtaking in its appreciation of proportion. The houses in this part of Dublin simply feel the right height, the streets appear to possess a perfect width. Although all the houses, typically red-brick three- or four-storey affairs built over a basement, seem similar, they are all subtly different.

When touring this quarter, watch out for the typical features of the Georgian house; the pitched roof made of slate, granite steps leading up to the fanlighted doors, ironwork railings in front. The wide doorways come in all colours, and boast elaborate knockers and handles. Look for ornamentation and fine plasterwork in the ceiling cornices, and as much elegance in interior proportions as is visible outside in the streets.

Laid out in 1762 for Lord Fitzwilliam, Merrion Square has been home to many famous residents, among them Sir William and Lady 'Speranza' Wilde (No. 1 facing — their son Oscar was born nearby at No. 21 Westland Row in 1854), the politician Daniel O'Connell, the poet William Butler Yeats and the Nobel prize-winning physicist Erwin Schrödinger. The Duke of Wellington was born just off the square, at No. 24 Upper Merrion Street. During the Great Famine of the 1840s, soup kitchens were set up in the square to feed the starving population. The park in the centre belonged to the Catholic Church for some time, and there were plans to build a cathedral there. Happily, Dublin Corporation now owns the park and keeps it well planted with trees, shrubs and flowers. At weekends, amateur artists sell their wares by the railings around the square.

Turn right onto the west side of the square. Ireland's **National Gallery** lies on the right, opposite the unused Rutland fountain, which was design-ed in 1791. The National Gallery (for details see page 58) was opened to the public in 1864, and is considered one of the best small collections in Europe. The Gallery has benefited greatly from the generosity of the playwright George Bernard Shaw, who left one-third of his legacy to the institution where he says he received his education. Appropriately, a statue of the bearded Shaw stands in the garden in front of the building.

Today, the Gallery has over 7,000 paintings and 250 pieces of sculpture. Its manageable proportions and lack of crowds — not to mention an excellent restaurant — make it an enjoyable place to while away an hour or two. While there are paintings from seventeenth-century France, Italy and Spain (look out for 'The Taking of Christ' by Caravaggio), as well as a few Rembrandts and Turners, the real quality lies in the Irish section. These paintings, mostly by the Anglo-Irish, date from the seventeenth to the twentieth century. The colourful canvases of Jack B. Yeats are particularly well represented.

Beside the National Gallery is the generous lawn at the back of Leinster House, the Irish parliament, but this is not open to the public. **The Natural History Museum** (for details see page 56), a dusty col-lection of animals, birds and fish, is next door on Merrion Street. Further up this street are the newly restored **Government Buildings** housing the office of the Taoiseach (the Irish Prime Minister).

Turn left onto the south side of the square. A pleasant vista of Georgian Dublin opens up, extending to the end of Upper Mount Street, where the delightful St Stephen's Church with its pepper cannister tower can be seen framing the view. Plaques mark the residences of W.B. Yeats between 1922 and 1928 (No. 82) and Daniel O'Connell (No. 58), as well as the workplace from 1940 to 1956 of Erwin Schrödinger, the creator of wave mechanics (No. 65).

Turn right off the square onto Fitzwilliam Street, which was the longest unbroken Georgian street in Dublin until the 1960s when the Electricity Supply Board demolished sixteen townhouses and put a faceless office-block in their place (on the left). This act of vandalism by a State-owned company paved the way for many others over the succeeding twenty years. The ESB now appears to regret its misdeeds and has recently restored No. 29 Fitzwilliam Street, on the left, as a museum of Georgian Dublin (for details see page 57). The exhibit gives a fair idea of what life must have been like for an upper-middle-class family of the period 1790–1820.

From here, the views extend up to the Dublin Mountains and down to Holles Street Maternity Hospital, which features strongly in *Ulysses*. Continue up Fitzwilliam Street, crossing the busy intersection with Baggot Street, and turn right into Fitzwilliam Square. This was the last of Dublin's Georgian squares to be completed. The earliest buildings date from 1714, but the square was finished only in 1830. The houses are smaller but better preserved than in Merrion Square, and the park in the centre is reserved for local residents.

Walk around three sides of the square before turning right onto Fitzwilliam Place, the continuation of Fitzwilliam Street. The corner house, No. 18, was the home and studio of the artist Jack B. Yeats, brother of the poet W.B. Yeats.

Turn right onto Leeson Street, which was originally the main highway from Dublin to Donnybrook. The present street dates from 1758 and was formerly called Suesey Street; this is 'commemorated' in the name of a nightclub here. In fact, 'the strip' of tiny clubs in the cellars of buildings on this street is its main claim to fame with Dubliners today.

Leeson Street leads back to St Stephen's Green. Walk through the park and down Grafton Street in order to return to the city centre. Alternatively, pass down Dawson Street, the parallel street between Grafton Street and Kildare Street. The **Mansion House** at the top of this street was built in 1710 and is home to Dublin's Lord Mayor. The Round Room to the left saw the first sitting of Dáil Éireann, the Irish parliament, in January 1919, when the Declaration of Independence was adopted. Nowadays, it is the venue for dog shows, antique fairs and the occasional political meeting.

At No. 19, further down on the right, is the **Royal Irish Academy** (telephone 01–6762570. Library open 10.30 a.m.–5.30 p.m. Monday–Friday), one of Dublin's leading and least-known scholarly institutes. It was founded by the Royal Dublin Society in 1785 for the study of 'Science, Polite Literature and Antiquities'. Those manuscripts that aren't in the library at Trinity seem to have ended up here; perhaps the most precious is the Psalter of Saint Columcille.

Next door to the RIA is St Ann's, a Church of Ireland church that was given an ornate Italian-style façade in the nineteenth century. Beside the altar are wooden shelves built specially to take loaves of bread for distribution to the poor.

On Molesworth Street, a short street off to the right, is the **Masonic** (or Freemasons') **Hall** (telephone 01–6761337. Open June–August, Monday–Friday for a video show followed by a tour at noon/1/2/3 p.m.), home since 1865 to the Grand Lodge of Freemasons in Ireland. This body was established in 1725 and is the second oldest Grand Lodge in the world. Once enormously powerful in Dublin, the Freemasons have declined in influence since Ireland gained its independence. Their current strength is unknown. As for the building itself, the austere exterior hides a wealth of ornamentation inside. The four major rooms are decorated with classical, ancient Egyptian, medieval Gothic and Tudor designs, and there is a small museum.

To return to College Green, walk to the bottom of Dawson Street, and follow the curve of Trinity College around to the left.

## TOUR 3: NORTH CITY

A sense of place, of where one belongs and doesn't belong, is deeply engrained in the Irish psyche. Nowhere is this more evident than in Dublin, where an unremitting if undeclared war has been waged between northsiders and southsiders for almost as long as the city has existed. Each group claims its area of the city is superior, and swears it can identify someone from the other side at the drop of a phrase. The simple act of crossing the Liffey is never taken lightly, as every Dubliner immediately becomes aware of changes in mood and atmosphere, in taste and sensibility, on the other side.

The rivalry between the north and the south of the city is usually a friendly one, but it sometimes spills over into a nastiness that borders on the racist. Northsiders are frequently the butt of cheap jokes ('What do you call a northsider in court?' — 'The defendant'), the result of their area containing most (though by no means all) of the underprivileged quarters of Dublin.

The north side of Dublin has been out of favour for over 200 years, but it wasn't always so. The medieval city grew around Dublin Castle, just south of the river, but when Dublin began to expand significantly in the reign of Charles II, bridges were built across the Liffey and fashionable Dublin decamped to the then open spaces north of the river. The move was led by Luke Gardiner, who bought up large tracts of land for development. Three generations of the Gardiner family developed much of

Georgian northside Dublin, starting with Henrietta Street and culminating in the creation of Mountjoy Square between 1792 and 1818.

However, by this time, the rival Fitzwilliam family had set about developing the south side. They were greatly helped when the Earl of Kildare chose to build his townhouse south of the river. Many nobles followed the example set by this building, now known as Leinster House, and the surrounding area has been pre-eminent in fashionable circles ever since.

The battle joined, it seemed likely at the close of the eighteenth century that Dublin's two halves would continue to compete in the creation of beautiful squares and elegant streets (further out from the city, it must not be forgotten, lived the masses of poor). The rivalry is best exemplified by the construction of two canals, the Royal Canal on the north side and the Grand Canal on the south side, both starting from roughly the same area, both following a similar route through the Midlands and both now largely unused.

However, this golden age of development was not to last. The Act of Union abolished both houses of the Irish parliament, and turned Dublin from a capital city into a provincial backwater almost overnight. Many of the noble families moved to London, bringing the construction industry to a halt and pushing armies of craftspeople, artisans, professional people and servants into poverty. The north side, as the less fashionable part of Dublin at the time, was inevitably the harder hit.

Dublin's finest buildings — the Four Courts and the Custom House — lie on the north side, and this tour takes the visitor to these and other gems of architecture and history. But in between are vast swathes of shameful dereliction, both of buildings and of people. Yet for all that, the north side is without doubt the more authentic part of the city. It lacks the refinement and self-consciousness of the areas south of the Liffey, but more than compensates in charm, honesty and humour.

The tour is divided into two parts, covering the areas lying roughly east and west of O'Connell Street, Dublin's main thoroughfare.

### East of O'Connell Street

Start from College Green and head north towards the Liffey via Westmoreland Street. Stop if there is time for a coffee in Bewley's Oriental Café on the left; this branch of Bewley's, with its lofty ceiling, plush red seating and Art Nouveau detailing, is perhaps the prettiest and best preserved. Two doors down, Beshoff's is one of the finest fish and chip shops in Dublin.

Cross the river by O'Connell Bridge, the traditional centre of Dublin. To the left, where the quays extend upstream, it appears that no two buildings are of the same height, and the abundance of derelict sites gives the impression of teeth in bad repair. To the right are Liberty Hall, the Custom House and the looming mass of the modern International Financial Services Centre.

As long as it is broad, Carlisle Bridge, as it was originally known, was erected in 1790 after a design by James Gandon, Dublin's most famous architect.

There is a good view of O'Connell Street from the central island of the bridge. Straight ahead is the monument erected to the memory of Daniel O'Connell, known as 'the Liberator'. O'Connell (1775–1847) was a lawyer and nationalist politician famous for securing Catholic emancipation for Ireland in 1829. O'Connell himself stands atop the monument, above some thirty figures representing the Irish people. Around the base of the statue are four winged figures depicting Courage, Fidelity, Eloquence and Patriotism. Three of these figures and that of O'Connell still bear bullet-holes from the fighting in 1916.

Turn right onto Eden Quay, and look back at the keystone head representing Neptune on the side of the bridge. There is another head representing the Liffey, Anna Livia Plurabelle herself, on the other side of the bridge; both are by Edward Smyth. Continue down Eden Quay to **Liberty Hall**, Dublin's tallest building. Ireland's largest trade union has occupied this site since 1912, but the current building is a fairly brutal example of 1960s architecture. Apart from an interesting corrugated roof, there is little to be said in the building's favour.

Further along the quays, and partially obscured by the Loop Line railway bridge, the **Custom House** is widely considered to be Dublin's finest piece of architecture. To get the best view of this masterpiece by James Gandon, cross to the facing quay south of the river. Invited over from London in 1781 for the commission, Gandon was to spend the rest of his life in Dublin. He drew on French designs for inspiration and set his building on reclaimed land. There was tremendous opposition to the project from local business interests, but the Custom House was constructed on time within ten years, in spite of a fire, frequent mob attacks and the death of Gandon's wife.

For all its magnificence, the Custom House has had a chequered history. Soon after it was completed, the Act of Union led to a sharp decline in trade and made its construction unnecessary. It survived a fire in 1833 and another in 1921, when as the seat of local government it fell victim to the battles between rival sides in the War of Independence. After the fire, which lasted for five days, it at first seemed likely that the building would have to be demolished, but an extensive renovation programme was carried out successfully in the 1920s. In this, the original Portland stone of the dome was replaced by a native variety; this has darkened over the years and no longer matches the original colour of the rest of the building.

The 125-foot (38 m) central copper dome is topped by a statue of Commerce by Edward Smyth, who was also responsible for the decorative keystones above the window and entrance on the riverfront. The sculpted figures represent the Atlantic Ocean and the thirteen principal rivers of Ireland; the one female head, in the centre overlooking the river, is the Liffey herself.

As the result of a newly completed six-year renovation programme, the exterior today looks as pristine as it did in 1791. The building, which is used as Government offices, is not open to the public.

Beyond the Custom House lies the tinted-glass façade of the International Financial Services Centre, founded in 1987 as part of an ambitious plan to make Dublin an international centre for finance. For our tour, however, we turn our back on this building and on the beckoning mouth of the Liffey, and pass around the back of the Custom House. Busáras, opposite, is a 1950s bus station designed by Michael Scott. Like Liberty Hall, its chief virtue is a corrugated roof. The building has been considered good enough to be reproduced on a postage stamp, but the visitor may beg to differ.

Walk up Lower Abbey Street until the junction with Marlborough Street is reached. Another of Scott's modernist creations, the **Abbey Theatre**, is on the left. The bleak façade dating from 1966 was relieved only slightly by alterations made to the Marlborough Street side in 1989.

The Abbey is Ireland's national theatre, and these days seems weighed down by the burden of this responsibility. But then the theatre has never had it easy since its foundation in 1904. Established by W.B. Yeats, Edward Martyn and Lady Augusta Gregory to provide a forum where the Irish imagination could express itself on stage, it quickly found that the locals had a mind of their own and were quick to voice their disapproval of individual plays.

The most famous uproar of many was triggered by the première in 1907 of J.M. Synge's *The Playboy of the Western World*. The play, and especially its depiction of peasant life, was seen by nationalists as a denigration of the Irish character, and a riot ensued after the word 'shift' (petticoat) was used. Seán O'Casey's *The Plough and the Stars* met a similar fate in 1926, when the audience rioted at the appearance of a prostitute in the play. After this performance, Yeats walked onstage and uttered his famous admonishment to the protesters: 'You have disgraced yourselves again. Is this to be an ever-recurring celebration of the arrival of Irish genius?'

In 1951 the original Abbey was burned down after a performance of the same play, and the troupe was based south of the river for fifteen years until a new theatre was built. Downstairs from the Abbey, the Peacock is a smaller theatre used for experimental work. The ticket office for both theatres is entered from Marlborough Street; the foyer is hung with portraits of prominent people associated with the Abbey, including Yeats, Synge and Lady Gregory.

Turn right into Marlborough Street by the Flowing Tide pub, a popular theatrical haunt. Half-way up on the left is **St Mary's Pro-Cathedral**, built between 1816 and 1825. The city's leading Catholic place of worship was forced into this cramped site by religious prejudice at the time, and the results are suitably mean. The Doric front is cold, and even the interior is a little depressing. However, the Pro-Cathedral is home to the excellent Palestrina Choir, which sings at 11 a.m. mass on Sundays and on major holy days.

Ironically, these streets around the Pro-Cathedral were once the site of Dublin's red-light district, known as 'Monto'. At the beginning of this century, when large numbers of troops were stationed in the city, Monto was one of the biggest red-light districts in Europe, home to an estimated 1,600 prostitutes. You wouldn't know it now, as many of the streets have since been razed to the ground as a result of slum clearance.

However, the atmosphere and indeed the spirit of Monto lives on in Joyce's *A Portrait of the Artist as a Young Man* and *Ulysses*, where it is the location of the Nighttown chapter. The last prostitutes in the area were cleared in March 1925, when police and the Legion of Mary, a strident Catholic missionary group, raided the district. Over a hundred people were arrested, including a member of parliament who said he was only there for the drink. The brothels were blessed, holy pictures were pinned on the doors, and Monto was no more.

On the other side of the street is Tyrone House, designed by Richard Cassels (or Castle) for the Beresford family in 1740. The house is now the headquarters of the Department of Education and is not open to the public.

Monto may be no more, but the area to the east of Marlborough Street does have a modern-day reputation for being dangerous, so visitors are advised to secure valuables as they proceed to the top of the street.

Georgian splendour: The Custom House (*above*) and an interior in Belvedere House (*over*)

Cross the junction with Parnell Street and continue up the hill of North Great George's Street. In many ways, this quiet street gives hope for the rest of Dublin; a few of its Georgian buildings are in good shape, more are hanging on for dear life, though others are quite clearly doomed. At the same time, renovation projects are afoot in some houses, and latterly builders have put up modern infill apartment blocks that are passable if not pretty. Thus, a street that was a picture of desolation twenty years ago is slowly on the mend, and has become a fashionable address for the intelligentsia.

As with so much Georgian street architecture, the glories of North Great George's Street appear modest at first glance, but a closer examination of the details of the streetscape reveals a different picture. The houses here were built during the most brilliant period of the Ascendancy, and are adorned with beautiful plasterwork, fireplaces, fanlights and foot-scrapers. For example, on the right, the doorcase of No. 38, former home of the Trinity Provost and tutor of Oscar Wilde, Rev. Sir John Pentland Mahaffy, is well worth a look. Number 35 is being restored as the James Joyce Cultural Centre (telephone 01–8731984) by the writer's nephew.

At the top of the street is **Belvedere House**, now Belvedere College, which was built in 1786 and was one of the last great mansions to be put up north of the Liffey before the south side became fashionable. Michael

Stapleton, who was responsible for much of the finest plasterwork in Dublin, was both architect and stuccodore here. Multiple encrustations of plasterwork, painted in tasteful hues of pink, lime-green and blue, cover the ceilings on the staircase and in rooms dedicated to Diana, Apollo and Venus.

The decoration in the Venus Room was considered improper and removed when the house was converted into a Jesuit boys' school in 1841. Joyce attended here at the end of the last century and his schooldays are recounted in *A Portrait of the Artist as a Young Man*. Today, the building is still a Jesuit school and has a lovely lived-in feel about it. Visitors are welcome; just ring the bell and ask to have a look around the downstairs rooms and the study on the first floor.

Turn right onto Great Denmark Street, and left onto Temple Street. Just off Temple Street in Hardwicke Place is St George's Church, designed by Francis Johnston and built between 1802 and 1813. The bulky spire is modelled on the church of St Martin's in the Fields in London. The Duke of Wellington was married here in 1806. No longer in use as a church, St George's faces an uncertain future.

The continuation of Temple Street is Eccles Street, where at No. 7 Joyce's Leopold Bloom was supposed to have lived. However, No. 7 is no more (the original door stands in the Bailey pub off Grafton Street) and Eccles Street is a shadow of its former self, so go back to the junction with Gardiner Place and turn left, continuing until Mountjoy Square is reached. This square was the only one in Dublin to be built with all four sides the same size, but it is now sadly derelict. Actually, from this corner of the square on a summer's day, it doesn't look too bad, as the trees in the well-maintained park in the centre obscure the worst decay. The shell of an unfinished pastiche modern office-block stands bleakly over in the far corner.

Return along Gardiner Place and Great Denmark Street to Parnell Square, the second oldest of the city's squares. In the centre is the Garden of Remembrance, which was opened in 1966 on the fiftieth anniversary of the 1916 Rising and is dedicated to those who gave their lives in the cause of Irish freedom. A large bronze monument by Oisín Kelly depicts the three Children of Lir, who according to Irish legend were transformed into swans. With its rows of park benches facing the afternoon sun, this is a good place to take a breather.

On the north side of the square, past Findlater's Church, is the **Dublin Writers' Museum** (for details see page 55). This is a new museum which, together with the Irish Writers' Centre next door, provides a national centre for all strands of Irish literature and complements the smaller, more detailed museums in the city devoted to Joyce, Shaw and Pearse.

The first part of the exhibit covers the story of Irish literature from the earliest times up to the literary revival at the end of the nineteenth century. The latter half of the museum focuses on this century, starting with the development of the Abbey Theatre and ending with Brendan Behan. The building itself is richly decorated with plasterwork by Michael Stapleton, though the original fireplaces were pulled out while the house stood idle in the 1980s.

Further on is Charlemont House, now the **Hugh Lane Municipal Gallery of Modern Art** (for details see page 58), one of the finest galleries in the city. Built between 1762 and 1765 for Lord Charlemont, the house was among the most opulent in the city, though little of the detail of the interior remains.

The collection concentrates on paintings of the nineteenth and twentieth centuries, from both Ireland and the Continent. The core was bequeathed to Dublin Corporation by the art collector Sir Hugh Lane in 1905 on condition that the paintings be housed in a suitable building. When the Corporation was slow to find a gallery, Lane indignantly transferred his gift to London. Later, he changed his mind and added a codicil to his will, but before this could be legally witnessed, he drowned in the torpedoing of the liner *Lusitania* in 1915. After legal arguments lasting almost fifty years, the Gallery and the National Gallery in London worked out an agreement in 1959 to share the collection on a seven-year rotating basis. In 1979 a new agreement began, whereby thirty of the pictures, including such masterpieces as Manet's *Eva Gonzales*, Courbet's *Snowstorm* and Monet's *Vetheuil*, remain in Dublin and eight in London. The thirty-ninth and most famous painting, *Les Parapluies* by Renoir, goes to each city on a rota basis. However, this agreement is currently being renegotiated.

In addition to the Lane collection, there is a portrait collection with works by Mancini, Lavery and Orpen, and a sculpture hall which includes figures by Rodin, Degas and many Irish sculptors. Finally, there is a large collection of modern Irish works, by Robert Ballagh and others.

The **National Wax Museum** (for details see page 57), on the northwest corner of Parnell Square, is a completely different sort of institution. It features 200 wax exhibits of politicians, pop stars and the like, and charges an admission fee. A short walk up Granby Row and across Dorset Street is the **Black Church** — officially St Mary's Chapel of Ease — in St Mary's Place. This Gothic design was completed in 1830 and gets its popular name from the black limestone with which it was built. No longer used as a church, the building has been very stylishly renovated by an insurance broking firm.

Walk down the unremarkable west side of Parnell Square. The complex of buildings inside the square on the left is the Rotunda, the world's first lying-in, or maternity, hospital and also one of the most progressive. The Rotunda after which the hospital was named looks down O'Connell Street and has been the location for many historic events. It is currently disused.

The **Rotunda Hospital Chapel** deep inside the building is a remarkable sight. Located among the maternity wards which have resounded to the sounds of bawling baby Dubliners since the hospital opened in 1757, the chapel is a unique Baroque concoction created from stained glass, deep mahogany carving, fine ironwork and, most striking of all, a marvellous ceiling executed by Bartholomew Cramillion, of whom practically nothing is known.

The ceiling teems with baby-faced cherubs in whole relief, ribands of biblical text and bunches of grapes. The recesses are filled with groups emblematic of Faith, Hope and Charity, while two angels hang over the organ. The work cost £585, a massive amount for the time. It had been intended to fill the centre of the ceiling with scenes from the nativity, but this had to be left blank after the hospital's founder and principal fundraiser, Dr Bartholomew Mosse, died in 1759 at the age of forty-six.

Entry to the chapel is via the new reception area on the west side of the square; ask at the desk there for directions.

On the south-eastern corner of the square is the **Gate Theatre**, Dublin's most important playhouse after the Abbey. The Gate was founded in 1928 by Micheál MacLíammóir and his partner, Hilton Edwards, whose aim it was to bring to the city a repertoire of foreign masterpieces it wouldn't otherwise have an opportunity to see. The theatre witnessed the acting début of Orson Welles, who came to Dublin as a precocious sixteen-year-old and bluffed his age and his way onto the stage. James Mason, too, came here as an unknown. In recent years, the Gate has upstaged the Abbey with a series of commercial and, to a lesser extent, critical successes. The theatre itself is an attractive building; look out (or up) for the ornate blue and gold ceiling designed in 1785.

Dominating the top of O'Connell Street is Augustus Saint-Gaudens' memorial to the Irish politician Charles Stewart Parnell (1846–91). Known as 'the uncrowned King of Ireland', Parnell led the country to the brink of Home Rule (the restoration of a Dublin parliament), but his career came to an abrupt end when his adulterous relationship with Kitty O'Shea, the wife of another Irish politician, was discovered. Within a short time of this revelation, his career was destroyed and he was dead. Parnell's funeral was attended by one of the largest crowds ever seen on the streets of Dublin and the reverberations of his death ring on in the works of Joyce and other writers.

Walk down O'Connell Street, past the elegant façade of the Gresham Hotel and the tourist office on the left. The central island of the street is lined with a succession of statues commemorating a curious collection of people, including a priest, a socialist and, as has been frequently noted, several statesmen who doubled up as adulterers (Parnell and O'Connell; Lord Nelson also qualified under this category, but his pillar was blown up in 1966).

The first statue we come to is that of Father Mathew, a crusading temperance campaigner of the nineteenth century. The next piece, the Anna Livia fountain, is arguably the worst statue on the street and certainly the most controversial. Anna Livia was unveiled in 1988 and within weeks was rechristened 'the floozie in the jacuzzi'. To be fair to the sculptor, he wasn't to know that his symbolic personification of the Liffey and Irish womanhood would come to be used as a paddling pool and litter dump. The hapless fountain has even been blamed as a cause of crime by the city-centre business association.

Perhaps the best statue on O'Connell Street is the one of Jim Larkin beyond the General Post Office. Larkin was a committed socialist and leader of the 1913 Lockout and here he is depicted accurately in oratorical mode, his hands raised beseechingly to the heavens.

### West of O'Connell Street

The **General Post Office** is the most historic building of recent Irish history. This has less to do with its architecture, which is too forbidding for most Dubliners' taste, than with its having been the rebel headquarters in the 1916 Rising and the place where the Irish Republic was proclaimed in such proud terms on that Easter weekend.

The building with its imposing Ionic portico was completed to a design of Francis Johnston's in 1815. It was chosen by the 1916 insurgents as their headquarters for its solidity and central location. British forces responded by placing a cannon in front of Trinity College and pounding the GPO relentlessly for a week. Most of O'Connell Street was destroyed by

Oliver Sheppard's statue of the dying Cuchulainn in the GPO

the artillery-fire (it was rebuilt in the 1920s) and the GPO's pillars are still pock-marked by the bullet-holes. The building is open 8 a.m.–8 p.m. on weekdays, and 10.30 a.m.–6 p.m on Sundays and bank holidays.

Turn left off O'Connell Street into the pedestrianised stretch of Henry Street, remarkable only for being Dublin's busiest shopping area. To the right — just before the ILAC Shopping Centre, which houses the central library — is **Moore Street**, Dublin's best-known open-air fruit and vegetable market. Looked at on one level, this is a colourful street market run by robust and vociferous women; at another level, though, it's traditional Dublin fighting for its dear life against the encroachment of faceless shopping malls and discount stores selling cheap plastic imports. Nonetheless, Moore Street has survived Dublin Corporation's attempts to get the traders off the street, and the tourist board's efforts to present it as a sort of living museum full of 'characters' (Dublin-speak for eccentrics), so the chances are that it will continue to survive.

Keep going along Henry Street, with the sounds of illegal street hawkers selling tobacco, sweets and, near Hallowe'en, fireworks, ringing in your ears. Look out for Arnotts and Roches department stores and then continue into Mary Street, passing St Mary's Church on the left.

This disused church dates from 1697 and is the only surviving seventeenth-century church in Dublin. A small park behind is dedicated to Wolfe Tone. Walk to the end of Mary Street, turn left onto Capel Street, where the City Hall can be seen across the river. After about 100 feet/30 m, take the first turn right. On the right is an alleyway, Meetinghouse Lane, on which lies **St Mary's Abbey** (telephone 01–8721490. Open mid-June to mid-September 10 a.m.–5 p.m., Wednesday only). The Chapter House here is all that remains of the great Cistercian Abbey of St Mary's, founded originally by the Benedictines in 1139. After the Reformation, the Abbey was demolished and the stones used in a bridge over the Liffey. It was only at the end of the last century that the long-buried Chapter House was rediscovered under a bakery, 7 feet/2 m below the present street level. It was in the Chapter House in 1534 that Silken Thomas, on hearing rumours of his father's execution in London, flung down his sword of state and marched out to organise a rebellion. This revolt was short-lived and the young rebel met the same fate as his father.

Walk back to Capel Street and proceed to the quays. Turn right and travel upstream along Ormond Quay. Pass the Ormond Hotel, which was the setting for the Sirens episode in *Ulysses* (the present building wasn't actually around in 1904). Across the river, Christ Church Cathedral peeks out from behind the modern excrescence of the Civic Offices.

Eventually, the **Four Courts** (open 11 a.m.–1 p.m., 2–4 p.m., Monday–Friday) is reached. This is another of Gandon's masterpieces and was built between 1796 and 1802 at a cost of £200,000. The central block with its six Corinthian pillars is surmounted by the copper-covered lantern dome which makes the building so distinctive. This structure is flanked by two wings enclosing quadrangles. The Four Courts was occupied during the 1916 Rising, but little damage was caused. However, in 1922 forces opposed to the Anglo-Irish Treaty took control of the building, and these were later shelled from across the river, thus beginning the Civil War. A three-day battle ended in a huge explosion and fire which destroyed the dome and the nearby Public Records Office with its irreplaceable documents and maps.

These days, the building is a constant hive of activity as solicitors and barristers meet with their clients in its corridors. The public can attend most courts, but since even the defendants have difficulty finding out what's going on, don't expect instant entertainment or enlightenment.

The beauty of the Four Courts is best appreciated by crossing the Liffey at the next bridge. This trip can be combined with a refreshment stop at Dublin's oldest pub, the Brazen Head, which lies metres away on Bridge Street.

Turn right after the Four Courts, up Church Street. On the left is **St Michan's Church** (telephone 01–8724154. Tours of the church and vault 10 a.m.–12.45 p.m. Monday–Saturday, and late March–October also 2–4.45 p.m. Monday–Friday). The site dates from the eleventh century, though the present church is a nineteenth-century reconstruction of a seventeenth-century building. Handel is said to have played the organ here, but St Michan's real claim to fame is in its vaults, where a number of preserved corpses, probably dating from the seventeenth century, are laid out. The mummified bodies have been preserved from decomposition by the water-absorbent limestone walls in which the vaults were cut.

If whiskey is to your taste, then take a detour to the **Irish Whiskey Corner** (for details see page 56). To get there, turn left down May Lane, left again and the centre lies on the left. Jameson's whiskey distillery was built here in 1791 and today the site is the headquarters of Irish Distillers. One of the old bonded warehouses has been turned into a whiskey museum that re-creates the atmosphere of the old distillery using memorabilia and an audio-visual presentation. Best of all is the tasting session when you're invited to try the different blends of Irish whiskey and compare them to their scotch and bourbon rivals.

Turn left on leaving the museum and take the first right, which brings you to **Smithfield**, scene of an early-morning horse fair on the first Sunday of each month. The former markets area is much ruined today, its buildings dilapidated and its large cobbled expanse home to abandoned and burned-out vehicles. There is still some trading activity around Smithfield, but the main Dublin Corporation Fruit and Vegetable Market, a Victorian building of some charm and atmosphere, lies on the other side of Church Street, on St Michan's Street.

Turn right and walk up to the top of Smithfield. Take a right onto North King Street, which leads back to Church Street, then turn left and climb up Constitution Hill until the gates of the **King's Inns** are reached on the right. This was the last of Gandon's great public buildings and was designed as a study centre and boarding-house for barristers. Although the foundation-stone was laid in 1795, it wasn't until 1817 that the work was finished by one of Gandon's pupils. The two elaborate caryatids in the façade are dedicated, for no apparent reason, to Ceres and Bacchus.

Walk up the driveway to the building (look out on the left for a charming park bench near the entrance that is being slowly enveloped in tree bark). Since the building is not open to the public, pass under the central arch and out through the gateway to **Henrietta Street**, one of the hidden gems of Dublin. This street was for most of the eighteenth century the most fashionable address in the city, but today it stands as an oasis of Georgian Dublin in a desert of dereliction and inferior modern development. Once described as 'the grandest cul-de-sac in Europe', the street was home to numerous peers, bishops, judges and politicians in its heyday around the 1750s. Some of the houses, such as the library of King's Inns or a convent, are well maintained, but most were stripped of their finery and converted at the start of this century into grimy tenements. Number 9, owned by the Daughters of Charity, is generally considered the best, and can be viewed on summer afternoons on request. Blessington House (No. 10), which was originally the home of Luke Gardiner, also boasts a fine interior. All the houses are worth examining for the traditional hallmarks of Georgian architecture — the doorcases, railings, balconies and plasterwork.

At the end of Henrietta Street turn left and then right onto Lower Dominick Street, another once-elegant street ravaged by decay and little improved by urban renewal (although some well-preserved Georgian houses survive in the upper end of the street). Turn left onto Parnell Street and right at the Parnell monument to reach O'Connell Street once more.

## TOUR 4: WEST OF DUBLIN

Modern Dublin is expanding rapidly, and many of the former villages in the west of the county have been subsumed into the city. The spread of the suburbs has reached the neighbouring county of Kildare, and even further out quiet country villages have become dormitory towns for the workers of the big city.

Yet even long-time western suburbs like Inchicore and Chapelizod retain a village-like atmosphere, notwithstanding the problems caused by through traffic. On the plains of Kildare, trisected by two canals, the horse is still king and the bogs that dominate the landscape of central Ireland begin.

### Kilmainham

Just beyond the Guinness Brewery, about 1.5 miles/2.5 km west of Dublin, is the inner suburb of Kilmainham, which contains an interesting variety of public buildings and monuments spanning 300 years of Irish history.

The starting-point of the tour is **Kilmainham Gaol** (for details see page 56). Now converted to a museum, this forbidding building has been unwelcome home to the cream of Irish political revolutionaries over the past 200 years, many of whom were executed here.

It was built in 1792, in the aftermath of the French Revolution, when the authorities feared that radical ideas might take root in Ireland. Their fears proved well grounded, and successive generations of Irish rebels were locked up in its dark recesses over the following 130 years. The leaders of the 1916 Rising were taken here and executed in gruesome circumstances. The last prisoner to be held in the gaol, Éamon de Valera, who went on to become Taoiseach and President of Ireland, was released in 1924.

The prison, with its dark passages, heavy iron doors, execution yard and hanging room, remains a gloomy fortress. An excellent guided tour and audio-visual presentation takes the visitor through Irish history from a nationalist point of view.

A short walk from Kilmainham Gaol is the **Royal Hospital**, which has recently been restored at a cost of £21 million and is now the Irish Museum of Modern Art (IMMA). The hospital was built as a retirement home for old soldiers between 1680 and 1684, along the lines of Les Invalides in Paris. It was the first such building of its kind in the British Empire and stood for years as a lone and impressive outpost at the western edge of the city. That such a handsomely proportioned building should be constructed for the welfare of retired soldiers says something about the generosity of the age in which it was conceived.

It continued to serve its original purpose up to the present century, when it was closed in 1928. After decades of the building acting as temporary home for the police headquarters, the national folklore collection and a statue of Queen Victoria that once stood in front of Leinster House, it was decided to establish Ireland's national gallery for modern art there. The alterations made during renovations were heavily criticised by some observers, but the result has undisputedly provided a fine exhibition space for painting, photography and sculpture.

The problem for a new gallery such as IMMA (for details see page 58) is that building up a collection of modern art requires time and, more importantly, money. As a consequence, the permanent collection of the gallery is short on famous names and — it has been said — quality. However, there are usually a number of interesting visiting exhibitions on show. The Royal Hospital is also the location for frequent classical music concerts and children's events and there is a café onsite.

Down the lane from the Royal Hospital is Dr Steevens' Hospital, the city's oldest public hospital, built by Thomas Burgh in 1721. No longer used as a hospital, it has been beautifully restored by the Eastern Health Board to serve as offices. Opposite is the squat form of Heuston railway station, built in 1845 and formerly known as Kingsbridge. Cross the river here and veer left towards the gate of Phoenix Park. If the weary walker is in need of rest, Ryan's pub on Parkgate Street, with its distinguished mahogany furnishing, is recommended.

## Phoenix Park

The Phoenix Park (open daily 6.30 a.m.–11 p.m.) is Dubliners' favourite place of play. Covering 1,752 acres/710 hectares, it is the largest enclosed park in Europe. Within its circumference of 7 miles/11 km lie gardens, a zoo, playing-fields for football, cricket, polo and other sports, ponds, a bandstand and the homes of the Irish President and US ambassador.

If the visitor is coming direct from the city centre, the park can be reached by taking the 10 bus from O'Connell Street, or the 25/26 from Middle Abbey Street. The park can be toured by car or on foot, but probably the best way to see everything is to rent a bicycle in town for an afternoon. All the principal features are well signposted. (Note: do not camp in the park. Not only is it forbidden, but it can be dangerous.)

The park is not named after the mythical bird, as you might expect; 'phoenix' is a corruption of the Gaelic 'fionn uisce', meaning 'clear water'. The area originally belonged to the medieval priory at Kilmainham, but after these lands were seized during the Reformation a vice-regal country lodge was erected in the early seventeenth century. Later, a royal deerpark was created and a surrounding wall built. Today, deer still roam the park, which was laid out properly and opened to the public by Lord Chesterfield in the 1740s.

Enter the park by its main gate on the south-eastern corner, at Parkgate Street. The main avenue extends straight ahead for 3 miles/5 km through a green and wooded landscape. To the left is the Wellington monument, a 205-foot (62 m) obelisk — the largest in Europe — erected in 1861 to celebrate the victory of the Dublin-born general at the Battle of Waterloo in 1815. The plaques around the side of the monument were cast with cannons captured at Waterloo. Wellington, it has to be said, hated his country of birth. Asked once if he were Irish, he is said to have replied: 'Just because you were born in a stable doesn't mean you're a horse!'

First on the right is the floral colour of the People's Garden and, further on, **Dublin Zoo** (for details see page 63). The Zoological Gardens, as they are properly called, are the second oldest in Europe and have almost a thousand animals, many of them rare. Dublin Zoo has a fine record for breeding lions and one of its inmates later achieved fame in Hollywood as the MGM film lion. There is a Children's Corner and a restaurant.

Beyond the zoo is **Áras an Uachtaráin**, the official residence of the President of Ireland, Mrs Mary Robinson. It was built in 1751 and greatly enlarged in the next century to serve as the British viceroy's home. Although not open to the public, the current President's 'open door' policy has ensured that thousands of people have visited the residence.

The Phoenix Park has been the scene of a number of celebrated murders, the most famous of which was committed on 6 May 1882, when the Chief Secretary and Under Secretary to Ireland were stabbed to death near the house. Four members of a rebel group known as 'the Invincibles' were hanged in Kilmainham Gaol for the killing.

**Ashtown Castle**, at the north end of the park, is the oldest building in the area (the tower dates back to the fifteenth century) and served for many years as the Apostolic Nunciature. It has recently been renovated and is now used as a visitor centre for the area. (For details see page 54.)

On the other side of the main road is the US ambassador's residence, which was formerly the Chief Secretary's Lodge. The Fifteen Acres (actually 200 acres/81 hectares) behind the house is the main sports area, where thousands of Dubliners play football, hurling and cricket every week. Overlooking the area is the papal cross erected to commemorate the visit of Pope John Paul II in 1979, when over one million people gathered for mass in the Phoenix Park.

## TOUR 5: KILDARE

Kildare, its rich, flat pastures drained by the Liffey and the Barrow and traversed by the Royal and the Grand canals, is the capital of Ireland's horse world. While the east of the county is gradually being swallowed up by the expanding city, the peatlands of the west belong firmly to the country. The county is dotted with the grand homes of the Protestant Ascendancy, several of which are well worth visiting on a day-trip from Dublin.

**Castletown House** (telephone 01–6288252. Open April–October 10 a.m.–5 p.m. Monday–Friday, 11 a.m.–6 p.m. Saturday, 2–6 p.m. Sunday. November–March 2–5 p.m. Saturday/Sunday. Bus 67 to Celbridge from Middle Abbey Street), at the northern edge of the village of Celbridge, is the largest private house in Ireland and an architectural masterpiece of remarkable beauty. It was built for William Conolly, the speaker of the Irish House of Commons, work beginning in 1722.

Conolly, a wealthy man who had houses aplenty, wanted a palace appropriate to his leading position in society. He commissioned Alessandro Galilei, who designed the face of St John Lateran in Rome, to draw up the plans for a Palladian-style mansion. By the time the Irish architect Sir Edward Lovett Pearce finished off the building with curved colonnades on each side of the gracefully proportioned central block, Conolly was dead. However, later owners continued his work and commissioned the Italian Lafranchini brothers to do the plasterwork, as well as adding the great staircase and numerous sculptures.

Castletown House was sold to developers in 1965 and its contents auctioned off. Houses were built right up to the avenue and it seemed very likely that the house itself might be pulled down. However, conservationists led by the Irish Georgian Society rescued the house from such an undeserved fate and have restored it lovingly over the past twenty years.

**Carton House** (telephone 01–6286250) is a sister palace to Castletown, and has suffered similar uncertainties in this century. Situated at the eastern end of Maynooth, Carton was built using local materials by Richard Cassels (or Castle) in 1739 for the Earl of Kildare. The house was designed in the classical style and its original estate covered 1,000 acres/405 hectares. The baroque plasterwork inside was again done by the Lafranchini brothers.

Today, Carton stands idle but may soon be developed as a hotel and golf course. The grounds and Shell House (the interior is decorated entirely with sea-shells) are open to the public. The house can be seen by appointment.

Maynooth itself is a pleasant university town. **Saint Patrick's College** has been the principal centre for the training of Catholic priests in Ireland since 1795, but the lay university has been expanded greatly in recent years. The college buildings are pretty austere and are a mixture of classical and Gothic revival styles. The library has a large collection of Irish manuscripts and books, and there is a museum (telephone 01–6285222) containing a collection of ecclesiastical works of art and early electrical equipment. To the right of the college gates are the ruins of a medieval keep associated with the FitzGeralds, the Earls of Kildare.

Cassidy's Roost, a pub not far from the college on the town's main street, is worth a visit. A modern re-creation of classical (and many other) styles, the design appears to have been inspired by someone's Mediterranean holiday. The combination of balconies, balustrades, caryatids and urns amounts to kitsch *par excellence*, but the student drinking clientele seems happy enough.

The **Curragh**, on the main road south-west through Newbridge, is the headquarters of the Irish horse-racing industry. Horses appear to thrive on the grassy limestone plains here, and the whole area is unfenced to allow the animals to gallop. The Irish Derby is the biggest race run at the racecourse here; buses leave Busáras in Dublin on racedays.

The **National Stud** (telephone 045–21251. Open April–October 10 a.m.–5 p.m. Monday–Friday, 10 a.m.–6 p.m. Saturday/bank holidays, 2–6 p.m. Sunday) is the State-run bloodstock farm. Originally established at the turn of the century by an eccentric Anglo-Irish colonel who practised astrology on his horses, the stud was turned over to the Irish Government in 1943. The museum here traces the evolution of the horse and there is also an exhibit devoted to Arkle, Ireland's best-loved steeplechaser.

Attached to the stud are the Japanese Gardens (telephone 045–21251. Open daily Easter–October). These were laid out in 1906 by Eito, a Japanese gardener brought to Ireland by the same Colonel Hill-Walker who founded the stud next door. The gardens lead the visitor through the seven ages of man from birth to death and eternity.

## TOUR 6: THE CITY BY THE SEA — A TOUR ON THE DART

*'riverrun, past Eve and Adam's, from swerve of shore to bend of bay, brings us by a commodius vicus of recirculation back to Howth Castle and Environs'*

James Joyce, in the opening lines of *Finnegans Wake*, fittingly recorded the all-pervasive role of water in the life of Dublin. From Howth in the north to Killiney in the south, no part of Dublin Bay is much more than

105

# DUBLIN AND ENVIRONS

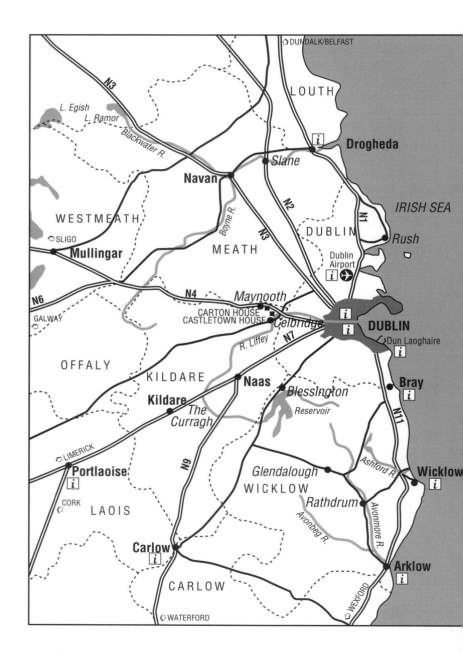

half an hour from the city centre. The fishing ports, dormitory towns and suburbs along the coast are all dominated by the majestic semicircular sweep of the bay and the weather it brings in off the sea. Each of the towns and villages has more in common with one another than with inland places, which is why this itinerary ties together the coastal strips on each side of the Liffey.

Most, though not all, of the destinations in this tour can be reached by the DART, Dublin's efficient and clean system of suburban trains which snakes up and down the coastline. Alternatives are given where there is no DART access. City-centre DART stations are at Connolly Station on the north side, and Tara Street and Pearse Station on the south side. The number of attractions listed is too long to be visited in a day, so the difficult choice of which sights to stop off at, and which to see from the train, is left to you.

## Southwards

Take the DART south from a city-centre station. The first beach the train passes is **Sandymount Strand** (DART stop: Sandymount), a vast expanse of sand 3 miles/5 km in length, dominated by the twin towers of the electricity-generating station at Poolbeg.

The strand figures extensively in *Ulysses* and today a pair of sculptures marks the spot where Leopold Bloom watched Gertie MacDowell lean back and reveal her drawers. This fictional encounter had resonances in real life; Joyce and Nora Barnacle walked out here while on their first date on the evening of 16 June 1904. The anniversary of this date, the day on which the events of *Ulysses* unfold, is now celebrated as Bloomsday in Dublin and throughout the literary world.

Sandymount is too polluted to be considered as a bathing-spot, but it is a pleasant place to stroll. Look out for the first of a series of low, cylindrical fortifications, known as Martello towers, which dot the eastern coastline. These squat granite buildings were erected in the early nineteenth century as an early-warning system in the event of an invasion from Napoleon's France (the expected attack never came). There are fifteen such towers between Dublin and Bray, all with walls 8 feet/2.5 m thick.

A longish and bracing walk can be enjoyed by heading in the direction of the towers at Poolbeg, ignoring the foul smell emanating from the water-treatment plant nearby. This leads to the magnificent South Wall, a breakwater which extends 1 mile/1.5 km into Dublin Bay. The walk combines fresh sea air with wonderful views of Howth to the north and Dún Laoghaire to the south.

**Booterstown Marsh** (DART stop: Booterstown. Buses 6, 6A, 7A, 8, 45 also follow the coast road) is a tiny bird sanctuary sandwiched between the road and the railway line. It is, nonetheless, one of the largest wildlife preserves in the Dublin area and there are information boards by the road with pictures of the migratory birds which are found there. It may even be possible to see herons, curlews, kingfishers and other birds from the train.

Although a much-sought-after residential district, **Blackrock** has lost a lot of its character in the past few decades as traffic volumes through the town have increased and at least one aristocratic mansion has been demolished to make way for a shopping centre. However, there are still elegant terraces of Victorian houses at Idrone Terrace and Maretimo Gardens and the People's Park above the town is well landscaped.

The next DART stop, Seapoint, is a beach popular with Dubliners, mainly because it lies so close to the city centre. Although the water quality has improved greatly in recent years, it still possesses a somewhat grimy feel and is best left to the birds.

**Dún Laoghaire** (pronounced Dunleary) is the largest coastal settlement in County Dublin apart from the capital itself. As the most Anglicised part of the country since the last century, it has its own distinct feel, more genteel than the rest of the county. The liberal sea airs of Dún Laoghaire have allowed both conservatives and radicals to flourish within its boundaries, and the town is justly proud of its separate identity and traditions.

Dún Laoghaire grew from a small eighteenth-century fishing village into the fastest-growing commercial and residential region in the Victorian era. The port was renamed Kingstown in 1821 after a visit from King George. The key to its success was the construction of the harbour between 1817 and 1842, which facilitated rapid communications with Britain. This achievement was capped by the building of the Dublin to Kingstown railway, the first in Ireland, in 1834, which provided the impetus for rapid expansion along the coast, as merchants and professional people moved out of the city centre and built mansions and fine Victorian terraces in the town. Kingstown became Ireland's first proper suburb.

Two views
of Dún
Laoghaire

Today, Dún Laoghaire (it was rechristened in 1921) is home to four yachting clubs and the car ferry terminus for boats going to Holyhead, across the Irish Sea in Wales. The long, curling fingers of the two piers in the harbour are much loved by locals for bracing weekend strolls; the East Pier, nearer Dublin, is quieter and favoured by fishermen, while the West Pier attracts families. In summer, small boats ply the waters off Dún Laoghaire, providing short tours along the coastline.

Remnants of the town's Victorian heyday are still to be seen in the seaside grand hotels and the bandstand on the promenade. Inland, there is a wide range of shops on the narrow main street and the lanes leading off it. There is also the National Maritime Museum (for details see page 56), an endearing collection of maritime exhibits from all ages.

Walk south 0.5 miles/1 km along the coast towards Sandycove (or take the DART to the station of the same name, which still leaves a walk to get to the sea). The **Martello tower** that is the location for the opening scene in *Ulysses* is visible across the bay; so too, just in front of the tower, is an interesting modern house built to a nautical design by the architect Michael Scott as his home.

The writer and surgeon Oliver St John Gogarty leased the tower while still a student in 1904 and invited the young James Joyce to come and live with him. Joyce was uneasy and mistrustful in the presence of his bombastic colleague and fled in fear of his life after an incident one night when a third occupant discharged a pistol in the direction of an imaginary enemy worryingly close to Joyce's bed. The tower was opened as a museum in 1962 and today houses a rich collection of Joyceana, including first editions of the writer's books, original manuscripts, some of his clothes and his guitar, as well as Joyce's death-mask. The museum also provides a fascinating insight into what life must have been like in these squat fortresses. For details of the James Joyce Museum see page 56.

Just down from the tower is the splendid bathing-place known as the Forty Foot, which also features in the opening pages of *Ulysses*. The sign still says 'Gentlemen only' but the battle for equal access for women has long since been won. Joyce's 'snot-green' waters can be choppy at times and there's no beach here, but there really isn't anywhere so near the city to match the Forty Foot for swimming and diving. The name, incidentally, comes not from the depth of the water, but from the 40th Foot Regiment, which manned the gun-battery placement above in the last century.

**Dalkey**, three DART stops beyond Dún Laoghaire, is a delightful and genteel seaside village with a self-contained air about it. The medieval village was walled, and known as the Town of Seven Castles; two of these remain, the sixteenth-century Archbold's Tower and the modern-day Town Hall. On or near the main street are numerous fine restaurants, a few pleasant pubs and some good bookshops.

A short distance from the village, down Coliemore Road, is Coliemore Harbour, from where it is possible to take the short boat-trip over to Dalkey Island. Today, the island is home only to sheep, another Martello tower and the ruins of a Benedictine church, but it all makes for an enjoyable afternoon excursion. George Bernard Shaw spent his boyhood years in a cottage above the village, on Dalkey Hill, but this is not open to the public. In compensation, however, there are splendid views of Dublin Bay and the coastline.

The view from the top of **Killiney Hill**, or even from the coastal Vico Road, is better again. The broad sweep of Killiney Bay was heavily touted in the last century as the rival in beauty of the Bay of Naples (the road-names in the area — Sorrento, Vico, etc. — reflect the developers' thinking), and these days it's certainly less polluted. It is a steep climb to the summit, from where the Howth peninsula and the city can be seen to the north, and the Bray Head and Sugarloaf Mountain stand out to the south. The obelisk at the summit was built in 1742 as a famine relief project after a prolonged and harsh winter when the Liffey froze. As an alternative to climbing, the visitor can opt for the pleasures of Killiney Strand, most likely the finest (stony) and longest beach south of Dublin.

The DART train line stops at **Bray**, which lies just inside Co. Wicklow. Like so many satellite seaside resorts which have lost out to foreign tourism, the town has probably seen its best days. The centre bustles healthily enough, but the long esplanade is something of a honky-tonk freeway, with its gaming halls, gambling machines and other noisy amusements. At the northern end of the esplanade, No. 1 Martello Terrace is one of the many former family homes of James Joyce; the film director Neil Jordan also lived on this pretty terrace.

The seafront at **Bray** is dominated by the looming hunk of Bray Head, south of the town. This promontory can be climbed in less than an hour; an alternative is to take the coastal path which leads to Greystones, a pretty fishing village further south. Take the 84 bus from Greystones to return to the city centre.

## Northwards

North of Dublin, the DART follows an inland route, through grey and sometimes grim suburbs, so the train is less useful as a means of touring the coastline. It does, however, deliver the visitor to Howth, the last stop and a must for a day-trip on a sunny day.

The northern coastal suburb of Clontarf was where King Brian Boru defeated Danish forces in a fierce battle on Good Friday 1014. The Irish chieftain and his two sons were killed that day, but the power of the Danes was finally broken. Nearby Dollymount Strand is one of the most traditional bathing-places in Dublin, and is invariably packed with families on hot summer days. Bus 30 from Lower Abbey Street provides access to both destinations.

The North Bull Wall was originally built in the last century to prevent silting in Dublin port. However, a more significant by-product of its construction has been the creation of the North Bull Island through the build-up of sand against the wall. The island today is still growing, and is home to a wide variety of plants and animals to be found in the sand dunes and salt marshes. Most importantly, tens of thousands of geese, ducks and other birds roost there in the winter months. The North Bull also boasts two golf clubs, Royal Dublin and St Anne's.

St Anne's Park, in Raheny, is a large park with wonderful plant beds and rose gardens that burst into colour in the summer. The main avenue is one of the longest, straightest stretches of road in a city that is largely bereft of boulevards and regal splendour.

**Howth** is both a fishing village and a popular suburban resort. It offers the visitor fine sea and hill walks, several interesting sights and a number of excellent seafood restaurants. Of these, the King Sitric is probably the best known, though it's also the most expensive. For more modest outlay, the pizzeria on the West Pier serves unpretentious food and cheap Italian wine.

The name Howth comes from the Danish word 'hoved', meaning 'head'. The train stops in the fishing village, just across the isthmus on the north coast of the peninsula. Above the village rises the 560-foot (170 m) Howth Head, from the summit of which can be seen the Wicklow Mountains to the south, and occasionally on very clear days the Mountains of Mourne to the north and the mountains of Wales across the Irish Sea. Also visible are the small offshore islands of Ireland's Eye and Lambay Island to the north. The novelist H.G. Wells called the view from the Head 'one of the most beautiful in the world'. A cliff path spirals its way around the nose of the promontory and takes in all these sights.

Howth Harbour was built at the start of the last century to accommodate ferryboats destined for Britain, but it was quickly superseded by Dún Laoghaire. Today, it's one of the five biggest fishing ports in Ireland, and also has a large yacht club. Howth Abbey, the ruins of which overlook the harbour, is said to have been founded by the Viking King Sitric; the existing ruins, however, date from the Norman period.

Across Abbey Street from the ruins of the fifteenth-century Collegiate building, which is attached to the Abbey but has an appalling modern shopfront, is a path leading to the Martello tower in Howth. This was the site of the first, wooden, Norman keep and offers good views of Howth Harbour and the offshore islands.

From Easter until October there is an erratic ferry service to Ireland's Eye. It is normally operational in good weather, especially at weekends. On the days that it is running, it leaves every half-hour — be sure to catch the last boat back to the mainland at 6 p.m. Bring food and drink as the island is barren and uninhabited, except for rats and seabirds.

The island has a ruined Celtic church from the pre-Viking period and yet another Martello tower. Along with its twin on the mainland opposite, it was used to guard the harbour entrance during the Napoleonic Wars.

To the west of the harbour is Howth Castle, home of the St Lawrence family since 1177. The present building dates from 1564, but has been rebuilt or modernised in each of the succeeding centuries. The house is closed to the public, but the gardens can be visited. The demesne is famous for its 2,000 varieties of rhododendrons and its azaleas, which are in full bloom between April and June. There are also forest and hill walks accessible from the grounds, which contain a public golf course.

In the stables beside the castle is the Howth Transport Museum (for details see page 55). Aside from old double-decker buses and a horse-drawn fire engine, the museum houses the Hill of Howth tram, which ran from 1901 to 1959 and is fondly remembered as a memento of a bygone age before the ill-advised decision to pull up the city's tramtracks.

The 1.5 mile/2.5 km cliff walk begins from the East Pier, leading to the white Baily Lighthouse, which was built in 1814. The lighthouse itself can be visited, but only by prior permission from the Commissioners for Irish Lights (telephone 01–6682511). The walk can be continued to Red Rock in Sutton, but you would need to set aside about four hours for this trek. There are no shops or other facilities on this route but plenty of good picnic sites.

See pages 108–9 in the Dublin Ecotour for more information on the flora, fauna and geology of Howth.

## TOUR 7: SOUTH SUBURBS

All Dubliners are lucky to have the sea in close proximity; southsiders are doubly blessed with the Dublin Mountains never more than half an hour away. These hills provide the southern border of the city, which spills down further along the flat coastal strip to Dún Laoghaire and Bray.

The south side of the city includes most of the wealthiest suburbs, though there are pockets of deprivation too. It is also the most Anglicised part of Ireland; a village like Dalkey would not look out of place in England. The area covered here is that south of the Grand Canal, that peaceful length of water which defines the city boundary and was so beloved of the poet Patrick Kavanagh. A canal-bank seat and statue near Baggot Street Bridge honours this complex, difficult man, and another bench opposite is inscribed with one of his poems (which was just what he wanted: 'O commemorate me with no hero-courageous/Tomb — just a canal-bank seat for the passer-by').

The road out of the city from here to Ballsbridge passes the distinctive cylindrical form of the US Embassy, which was built in 1964. Further on, after the bridge over the Dodder, are the headquarters of the **Royal Dublin Society** (telephone 01–6680645. Library open 10 a.m.–5 p.m. Tuesday–Friday, until 7 p.m. Wednesday/Thursday, 11 a.m.–5 p.m. Saturday), where the Dublin Horse Show is held in August. This body was formed in 1731 to promote Irish agriculture, industry, arts and sciences, and it retains an old-world, even dusty, atmosphere to this day.

The first Spring and Horse Shows were held in 1881. The Society, which had been based in Leinster House, moved to Ballsbridge in 1923 when that building became the Irish parliament. The Simmonscourt Pavilion at the RDS is the venue for trade exhibitions and large rock concerts. While the Horse Show and its highlight, the Aga Khan Nations trophy, continues to thrive, the Spring Show was abandoned in 1992, a victim of declining interest in agricultural matters.

Further on, turn right down Shrewsbury Road and follow the signpost right to reach the **Chester Beatty Library and Gallery of Oriental Art** (for details see page 58), one of the world's finest collections of oriental manuscripts and art. Sir Alfred Chester Beatty was an American mining engineer and millionaire who travelled extensively in the Middle and Far East and developed a passion for oriental objects and manuscripts. He bequeathed his collection to the Irish nation, of which he was made an honorary citizen in 1957.

The Gallery contains items from China, Japan, Persia, India and the Middle East, including the 1,259 manuscripts of Omar Khayyám. There is also a collection of Chinese snuff boxes and clay tablets from Babylon dating back to 2700 BC. And although the museum's treasures are mainly oriental, there is a remarkable collection of graphic works by Albrecht Dürer, purchased by Beatty at the turn of the century.

The road directly south from Christ Church Cathedral leads through Harold's Cross and Terenure before coming to **Rathfarnham**, 5 miles/8 km from the city centre. On the left, Rathfarnham Castle (bus 16 from

O'Connell Street), a fine building begun in the Elizabethan period, is currently being restored after long years of use by the Jesuits. The castle was built for Archbishop Loftus in the sixteenth century, and bought by William Conolly (who owned Castletown House) in 1723. The interior plasterwork is lavish, and the ceiling paintings have been attributed to Angelica Kauffmann.

If driving, turn right at the Yellow House pub and fork left at the Tuning Fork pub until **St Enda's Park** (bus 47A from Hawkins Street) is reached on the left. Located in the middle of a charming park with playing-fields and woodland walks, the Pearse Museum (for details see page 57) commemorates the educational and revolutionary activities of Patrick Pearse, the poet and teacher who led the 1916 Rising and was executed after it. The house itself was in the early years of the century the site of a progressive boys' school founded by Patrick Pearse and his brother Willy.

Leaving the park, turn on to Grange Road and walk or drive up the hill for about 1 mile/1.5 km until **Marlay Park** is reached. This is a far larger park with extensive woodland and nature walks; it is also the starting-point for the Wicklow Way, the long-distance trail that traverses the mountains of Wicklow. The estate originally belonged to the Huguenot banker David La Touche but was left to the State to be used as a park. The stables and courtyard have been converted into a craft centre, which is well worth visiting.

### Hill walks in the Dublin Mountains

The Dublin Mountains are miraculously near to the city. The vast suburban housing estates have spread almost to the base of the mountains, but the uplands themselves are relatively untouched by development. Although not much more than 1,000 feet/300 m in altitude, the mountain terrain is often rough and waterlogged and the weather can be very severe. For those without a car, though, the main problem is access; few of the city bus routes really penetrate the mountains, and those that do are infrequent.

Virtually any walk or drive south will reward the visitor with fresh air, tranquillity and extensive views of the city, but the following short tours are suggested for a summer afternoon or evening.

### Hellfire Club (Distance 4 miles/6.5 km)

Correctly called Montpelier Hill, this climb 4 miles/6.5 km south-west of Rathfarnham offers wonderful views of Dublin City and Bay. From Rathfarnham, turn right at the Yellow House pub and stay on the main road until two sets of traffic lights are passed (keep your eyes peeled for two oddly decorated private houses on the left). Turn right over the River Owendoher and then left, and follow the climb for several miles until a car park in the forest to the right is reached. (Buses 16, 16A or 47 come nearest to the start of the walk.)

This is the base of Montpelier Hill, from which the summit is easily attained (climb directly upwards from the car park or take the gentler but longer route which follows the forest trail winding around the back of the hill). The bleak shell of the Hellfire Club, which dominates the top of the hill, was probably built as a sporting lodge by William Conolly, who died in 1729. Later, it became the meeting-place for the rakes of the Hellfire Club, who drank and gambled their time away there. There are many stories associated with them, the most famous being that the devil appeared at one of their card-games.

The drive on to Killakee rewards the visitor with further pretty views of Dublin. Loop back via the Pine Forest to return to the city.

### Glenasmole (Distance 5 miles/8 km)

Follow the same route as above to Rathfarnham, turning right at the Yellow House pub. Turn right at the first traffic lights onto Ballyroan Road and left at the next traffic-light crossroads. Travel straight on for about 4 miles/6.5 km, past the roundabout and Bridget Burke's pub, until the road makes two sharp turns to cross the River Dodder. The reservoir at Glenasmole lies on the left. This area was dammed in 1888 to create an additional water supply for Dublin, and the walk around the two lakes here (there is little climbing involved) makes for a very pleasant afternoon. The granite spillways, canals and dams built a century ago have all aged beautifully and merge with the scenery. Kippure, the mountain at the top of the valley, is easily recognisable because of its TV mast.

Walk up the tarmacadamed road to the reservoirs, and proceed in an anti-clockwise direction around the two areas of water. The first part of the return is very boggy.

### Three Rock Mountain (Distance 3 miles/5 km)

Same route as above. After the Yellow House pub, turn left at the second traffic lights and continue straight on past the Grange golf club. Continue to Lamb Doyles pub on the Blackglen Road and take the road to the right, Woodside Road, facing it. Stop 1 mile/1.5 km further on at the Blue Light pub.

The 44B bus also travels this road but is very infrequent. The 44 bus is more frequent and stops near Lamb Doyles.

Walking back towards Dublin, take the first side road left. Turn right onto a steep path before the quarry. Further up, turn first left to gain the forest edge and follow the side of the forest to the summit of Three Rock (1,479 feet/450 m), which is home to a motley collection of unsightly radio masts along with the three granite boulders which give the mountain its name. On a good day, there are fine views of Dublin and the Wicklow Mountains from this point. The descent is achieved by dropping south to the forest line and taking a gravelled path down the back of the mountain until the road is reached.

A more strenuous variation is to continue from Three Rock via the Fairy Castle to Two Rock Mountain before returning via the back of the mountain.

## Other routes

There are many other gentler routes suitable for short walks and which do not require special clothing or equipment. These include:
— The River Dodder from Ringsend to Rathfarnham (6 miles/10 km)
— Dalkey and Killiney Hills (3 miles/5 km)
— Bray to Greystones coastal path (with diversion to top of Bray Head) (5 miles/8 km)
— The Grand Canal from Grand Canal Street to Harold's Cross (2 miles/3 km)
— The Royal Canal from Newcomen Bridge (near Connolly Station) to Clonsilla and beyond (at least 7 miles/11 km)
— Sandymount to the South Wall and Poolbeg Lighthouse (5 miles/8 km).

## TOUR 8: NORTH SUBURBS

The north side of the city, too, is hemmed in by a canal. The Royal Canal, neglected but still pretty, arcs around the northern border of Dublin, neatly dividing city from suburb. This side of Dublin is flatter and poorer, but is nonetheless steeped in history and tradition.

**Glasnevin** is a pleasant inner suburb with a lot to offer the visitor. To reach it, drive from the city centre by Dorset Street and turn left after the bridge over the canal. Follow the canal for about 0.5 miles/1 km and turn right onto Prospect Road, then left onto Finglas Road. Alternatively, take bus 40/40A from Parnell Street.

Glasnevin Cemetery, on the right-hand side of Finglas Road, is the best-known burial-ground in Ireland, and a fascinating place to while away a few hours. It contains the graves of many Irish leaders, including Éamon de Valera, Charles Stewart Parnell, Daniel O'Connell (commemorated with a round tower) and Michael Collins. The poet Gerard Manley Hopkins is also buried here. The nearby Gravediggers pub is recommended for liquid refreshment.

From the eastern side of the cemetery, enter the **National Botanic Gardens**, founded by the Royal Dublin Society in 1795. These feature a remarkable 20,000 varieties of plant, a rose garden and a vegetable garden. The Curvilinear Range of glasshouses, a magnificent cast-iron and glass construction originally built between 1843 and 1869, was restored in 1991. The Palm House was erected in 1884 and contains orchids, palms and tropical ferns. Open daily free of charge.

The **Casino** in the suburb of Marino (telephone 01–8331618. Open 9.30 a.m.–6.30 p.m. daily mid-June to September) is one of Dublin's best-hidden beauties. To reach it by car, follow the Malahide Road from the north city centre for 2.5 miles/4 km. You can also take bus 20A, 20B, 27, 27A, 27B, 32A, 42 or 42B from the city centre.

The Casino, which has nothing to do with gambling, was built as a summerhouse for Lord Charlemont, whose main residence on Parnell Square is now the Municipal Gallery of Modern Art. His idea was to retire to the clean air of Marino and to enjoy the sea view, but this idyll was ruined shortly after the building was completed in 1771 when a neighbour in Fairview put up a terrace which blocked off any glimpse of the sea from this site.

William Chambers drew up the plans for the Casino without ever leaving England, but these were brilliantly executed by the Irish workmen and the Roman builder and sculptor Simon Vierpyl. The building, a palace in miniature, cost £20,000, a fortune in those days, to erect. Everything about it is not as it first seems; it looks small enough, yet there are sixteen rooms within, on three floors. The building plays gentle tricks with the observer; the vertical columns are actually hollow and serve as downpipes, and the garlanded urns on the roof hide the chimneys.

The main mansion on Lord Charlemont's estate was demolished in 1921 but the Casino survived, almost by an oversight. It passed into State hands in 1930 but was allowed to fall into disrepair. Today, the site is surrounded by housing estates and the traffic nearby creates a constant din. However, the Casino itself has been restored to something approaching its former glory in a renovation programme that began in 1974.

**Malahide Castle** (for details see page 56), one of Dublin's oldest estates, lies just south-west of the pretty seaside village of Malahide. To get there, travel north from Dublin on the R107 for 9 miles/14.5 km, take a train from Connolly Station or take bus 42 from Beresford Place.

The Castle was occupied virtually continuously by the Anglo-Irish Talbot family from 1185 until 1976, when it was bought by the State. Many of the paintings were purchased by the National Gallery and returned on loan. The Castle itself is an amalgam of many different periods and styles; the three-storey tower house is the oldest part and dates from the twelfth century. The medieval Great Hall is the only one of its type to be preserved in its original form. The interior is well decorated with portraits and has fine furniture from the seventeenth, eighteenth and nineteenth centuries. The Castle is surrounded by extensive gardens and parkland with thousands of species of plants. The Fry Model Railway in the park contains a rare collection of handmade models of Irish trains, built by a railway enthusiast, Cyril Fry, in the 1920s and 1930s.

For astronomy enthusiasts, **Dunsink Observatory** (telephone 01–8387911) is well worth a visit. One of the oldest observatories in the world, it was founded in 1783 by Trinity College and taken over by the Irish Government in 1946. The 12-inch (30.5 cm) optical refractor telescope was built in 1863 and is still in use today. Admission is free, but tickets for open days on the first and third Saturday of each month from September to March must be obtained by post. Write enclosing a stamped addressed envelope to the Secretary, Dunsink Observatory, Dunsink, Co. Dublin.

**Newbridge House** (for details see page 57) at Donabate, a seaside resort 12 miles/19 km north of Dublin, is the ancestral home of the Cobbe family. More intimate in scale than many of the Big Houses, this is an otherwise typical eighteenth-century Georgian house set in 350 acres/142 hectares of parkland. The house contains many examples of period furniture and plasterwork and the museum features a collection of coaches, including the Lord Mayor's.

# ECOTOUR

An ecotour of the Dublin area can be undertaken by public transport (the DART and buses), by car or, for the more energetic, by bicycle. We start on the north side of the city, on the coast, and travel south, with one or two forays inland to the city proper. The Bull Island is explored in depth as it is unique, a habitat of international importance for a large number of birds and an excellent example of how sand-dune systems are formed, and of the plants that colonise them.

The location of Dublin, on a river by the coast, is similar to that of many other cities. Access to the sea is essential for trade and the river has acted as a waste-disposal system through the centuries. Though environmental legislation now controls pollution, much of the city's raw sewage is

still dumped at sea just outside Dublin Bay. European Community legislation will prohibit the dumping of sewage sludge at sea after 1998 and require local authorities to deal with it in other ways. This should bring about changes in the nutrition of Dublin Bay, where raw sewage enters the waters at Howth Head, and waste from the secondary treatment of sewage at Ringsend. Will the reduction in nutrients affect the large populations of waders and other birds that feed on the mud-flats around the bay? It will certainly make bathing a lot less worrying: in spite of

St Columba's Church and Round Tower in Swords, Co. Dublin

Corporation assurances, one always feels nervous stepping into the sea knowing what is being dumped in there at the same time.

**Link** North County Dublin, Rush, Rogerstown Estuary

We begin the tour proper at Howth Head but those with an interest in ornithology could profitably take in areas of the coast further to the north. C.D. Hutchinson's *Watching Birds in Ireland* (1986) lists important sites and for the north of the county includes Rush and its surrounds, which hold large numbers of tree sparrows and finches in the winter. The area can be reached by turning right off the N1 about 4 miles/6.5 km north of Swords at Blake's Cross and heading out along the coast road.

**Stop** Rogerstown Estuary

Two habitats separated by the railway viaduct, this site has an abundance of eel-grass, tassel weed, alga, glasswort and invertebrates which makes it an excellent feeding ground for wintering wildfowl and waders. Brent geese and pintail feed here in the winter, as do teal, widgeon, shelduck, godwits and ringed plover. Hutchinson recommends starting at the Dublin County Council tip-head, where rare gulls may be spotted along with snow buntings and Lapland buntings. Little stints, curlew, sandpipers and ruffs may also be found in the estuary in autumn.

**Link** Swords, Malahide, Portmarnock and Howth

Further south along the N1 is Swords, where we turn right to the coastal town of Malahide. The estuary here holds a similar range of water-fowl and waders but in fewer numbers. South from Malahide is Portmarnock; the area of sand dunes around the golf course is the remnants of a once-rich dune system that had a well-developed flora. Keep an eye out for waders and water-fowl along the bay as far as Sutton, where we go out to Howth Head above Howth Harbour. Take the road directly above the east pier that runs along the coast to a car park and cul-de-sac. Ireland's Eye lies just north of Howth below us.

**Stop and walk**

Leaving the car here, we will walk around Howth Head by the cliff path. In a scene that rivals Wicklow for a feeling of wilderness, the slopes around us are covered in autumn gorse, ling and bell heather. Heather or ling has tiny leaves that are pressed tightly against the stem and pink flowers borne in clusters at the ends of its branches. Bell heather has longer leaves that stand out from the stem; its flowers are bell-shaped and a dark pink to purple colour. Along the cliffs we find breeding colonies of guillemot, razorbill, and kittiwake in the spring and early summer. The area is also known for the regular occurrence of aberrant monster forms of the red ant.

The name Howth is derived from the Old Norse word 'Hoved', which simply meant a headland. John Dalton gave an account of the north Dublin area in his *History of Drogheda with its environs and a memoir* *of the Dublin and Drogheda railwa*y (1863). He speaks fondly of Howth, where

> [the] descent to the new lighthouse abounds with enchanting landscapes . . . such splendid sights, it may be expected, will be, ere long, diademed with villas, the shores offering, in several places, the greatest facility for bathing . . . while in others they are indented with creeks . . . in which seals and porpoises may often be seen rolling their unwieldy bodies.

Robert Lloyd Praeger in 1937 worries about the spread of housing:

> As I first knew Howth, half a century ago, it was a delightful old-world place. Now houses and bungalows, most of them inartistic eyesores quite out of keeping with their setting, encroach more and more on the open spaces; along the southern shore with its superb view across Dublin Bay, the greed of land-owners confines the visitor to a narrow muddy track between high barbed-wire fences.

Praeger finishes his lament by appealing for the preservation of what remained of the open spaces of Howth Head for the people of Dublin. This was achieved when An Taisce purchased the open areas of heathland on the Head, which they now manage.

The rock of Howth Head is similar to that of Bray Head across the bay, a worn-down knob of siltstones and quartzite, the much-altered sands and muds of a sea that existed some 600 million years ago in the Cambrian era. At the Sutton end, carboniferous limestones, the calcareous deposits of a more recent tropical sea — 300 million years ago — brush up against the quartzite.

The gorse on the Head is a favourite spot for the stonechat. This bird is about the size of a robin and has a distinctive chattering call akin to the sound of pebbles being banged together in the hand. The male is a darker brown than the female and has white markings on the throat; both have red breasts and white wing-bars. They perch on the gorse bushes, calling and making brief flights before returning to their branch.

It is possible to walk around Howth Head, along the coast and down to Sutton; from where we parked it would take about 2.5 hours. The terrain is not difficult apart from a point on the southern side of the Head where the narrow path gives way to some rocks. A trail and footholds have been worn at this point, and the agile will be able for the challenge. A more restrained walk might be to the Summit, an area that overlooks Baily Lighthouse and the cliffs. We can then return to the car by the same coastal track, the whole walk taking about 1 hour.

In the sea below, all along the coast from Skerries to the Bull Island, there are frequent sightings of both the common and the grey seal. The grey seal breeds in the area on Lambay Island.

**Link** Howth, St Anne's Park, Bull Island

From Howth we head south along the coast road. The next stop of interest along the way is the Bull Island. As we reach the causeway that joins the mainland and the island we are also close to St Anne's Park, a good sanctuary for wildlife in the city. Badgers and foxes as well as squirrels are found within the extensive parkland.

Bull Island is to the left across the causeway. Cars can be driven out onto the beach at this point. The access of cars to the beach is gradually being restricted to protect the dune systems, which have come under increasing pressure from trampling in recent years. Restricting access reduces the damage as people seldom wander far from their cars. An interpretative centre is open throughout the year on the island at the end of the causeway.

**Stop and walk** (6 miles/9.5 km)

Another way on to the island is via the wooden bridge further south along the coast at Clontarf. This is easier for bus-users; the causeway is a little remote from bus stops. The views from the bridge give a good idea of the island's structure. It is possible to walk the length of Bull Island and back in 2–3 hours.

## DUBLIN BAY AND BULL ISLAND: A POTTED HISTORY

The development of Bull Island is closely linked with the development of Dublin Bay. Over the centuries the Liffey was burdened with silt and clay from the soils it passed through, and also with sewage and waste from the streets of an ever-growing city. The Dodder, Tolka and numerous other streams around Dublin Bay carried their own loads of sediment into the sea.

By the latter half of the seventeenth century, ships were forced to unload their cargoes for the city at Ringsend or the Pigeon House, from where goods were either carted into the city or transported on smaller boats to the quays. Merchants' demands for improved access were eventually heeded at the end of the century, when the Liffey was dredged and work on the South Wall began. In 1711 a channel was made as far as the outlet of the Dodder above Ringsend and the embankment on the south side was continued for a further 3 miles/5 km. By 1730 the embankment, The Piles, was completed and in 1761 the construction of a stone pier was initiated. In 1796 the South Wall was finished. Today we see it jutting out across the bay from below the two tall chimney stacks at the Pigeon House.

While all this building was going on, 100,000 tons of gravel was dredged from the channel each year. This material was sold as ballast, or used as infill on the South Wall and embankment and at the site of the Custom House, built between 1781 and 1791. Throughout the nineteenth century an estimated 32 million tons of material was dredged from the bay.

The fine organic material that made up much of the sewage and street waste deposited in the Liffey was swept out across Dublin Bay, and on meeting the currents at Howth Head swept back towards Sutton. Water lost its momentum on the turning tide and the organic debris settled out on the sands of the North Bull. The city's ooze was thus deposited on the higher parts of the North Bull Sands and in turn acted as a trap for the accumulation of more sand and the development of Bull Island.

In a survey of the bay in 1800 Captain William Bligh (of *Mutiny on the Bounty* fame) had marked in the Bull as a small, dry, sand island. By 1803 reports stated, 'a considerable stripe of [the North Bull] remains dry at high water and has a growth of marine plants'. A map prepared in 1819 by Francis Giles, an English engineer, shows the Sand Island as some 2 miles/3 km long. A timber bridge was built out to it that autumn, leaving a channel free for movement of waters around the island.

In 1825 the North Bull Wall was completed. This focused water leaving the port area of Dublin into a narrow channel between the North and South Walls, causing it to scour sediments from the basin there. Sediment has continued to build up on the northern, Sutton, side of the island so that the Bull Island is now about 3 miles/5 km long and 1 mile/1.5 km wide in some places.

The North Wall was built from carboniferous limestone rocks quarried locally in Clontarf. These rocks are about 330 million years old and contain the evidence that at that time Clontarf, and much of Ireland, was submerged in a shallow tropical sea. Ferns and colonial sea animals (corals) are preserved in the rock as fossils and can be inspected on the walk out along the Wall.

## THE NATURAL HISTORY

The main habitats on the island are the beach, the dune system, the alder marsh, the salt marsh and the mud-beds. Each of these has attractions for plants or animals as sites suitable for growth or feeding grounds.

### The beach

The beach is at its most interesting following a storm. The turbulence of the sea sweeps in sand-dwelling cockles and gastropods. Cast up on the hard sand, they are unable to burrow and are fed upon by the waders that congregate on the shoreline. Mussels are common in the bay, again often found on the beach after storms. Tubes of the sand mason are carried in on a regular basis, and in recent years the beach has been inundated with the remains of algal mats that grow through the summer in the bay and are then churned up by the sea and cast ashore, where they rot on the sand.

Clinkers from coal-burning ships are still washed up, large quantities being found in the dunes after a particularly high tide.

## The dune system

The development of sand dunes is a continuous process and the ridges of rising and falling dunes that run from the south to the north along the island can each be dated from historical accounts and maps. Much of the older section of the dune system has now been altered beyond recognition by the Royal Dublin and St Anne's Golf Clubs. On the seaward side of the island the dune formation process continues and is best observed at the most northerly tip of the Bull.

In the spring and autumn, high tides deposit a line of organic material, seaweed, shells and algal mats on the beach at the high-water mark. This debris is soon covered in sand and the nutrition from the decomposing organic matter is used by sea couchgrass, which rapidly establishes itself and begins the dune formation process. Winds from the sea carry sand up from the exposed beach; the wind speed drops and with it the sand. The accumulation continues but the couchgrass is unable to grow above the rising mounds.

At this point marram grass, which grows out of reach of the salt water, begins to colonise these mini-dunes. Marram dunes can attain a height of 164 feet/50 metres in some locations, though on the Bull Island they are generally below 33 feet/10 metres. The grass is ideally suited to these conditions: it traps more and more sand and carries on growing by sending out rhizomes that allow it to keep its green leaves above the surface. Nitrogen for its continued growth is derived from the grains of sand the grass traps and perhaps from nostoc, a free-living blue-green alga and a nitrogen-fixing dune inhabitant which forms small green gelatinous spheres in wet weather.

Towards the beach are the incipient or fore-dunes, which are newly stabilised by colonising grass. Circular dunes surround Green Island at the northern end of the Bull. This area was isolated in 1869 but by 1902 had been incorporated into Bull Island. At the tip, growth continues with the formation of what is termed a recurve, a semicircular sweep of sand deposited by the sea as it rounds the Bull and slows down on meeting water coming out from Sutton.

## Nutrition within the dunes

Nitrogen fixation, the trapping of nitrogen from the atmosphere by bacteria that live in the root nodules of legumes, is most active in the slacks between the dunes and nearest the water table. Rainfall on the dunes maintains a lens-like fresh-water table below the island. In this area we see legumes such as vetch, clover and bird's-foot trefoil growing in abundance.

Mycorrhizal systems of grasses and orchids assimilate nitrogen from the organic matter. Mycorrhiza are fungi that grow in through the roots of the plants; they increase the surface area of the roots available to absorb nutrients from the surrounding soils, and may obtain sugars or other carbohydrates from the plants.

Yellow rattle is a hemiparasitic plant which overcomes the problem of nutrient shortages by taking its nitrogen from other plants around it.

Thallose lichens in the thirty- to forty-year-old dunes are blue-green algal symbionts, a mixture of fungus and algae that live hand in hand. The fungal part of the lichen provides a shelter and structure while the algal portion traps sunlight and converts the energy to sugars which the fungus can use for its growth.

As dunes increase in age more organic matter accumulates in them. The youngest dunes on the island are now forming behind the lines of boulders which prevent cars moving onto them; these are mainly sand. As we move back from the beach, dunes increase in age and in their organic matter content. It is now difficult to dig one's hand into the sand; a barrier of roots and old plant material binds it, and the process of soil formation is under way in the older dunes. The oldest dunes, almost 200 years in existence, have been claimed by the golf courses.

Between the Royal Dublin golf course and the seashore, a line of old shelters stands hidden from the sea by sand dunes which formed after their construction. Growth of the dunes is an ongoing process that can still be witnessed today.

### The alder marsh

The alder marsh is the lowest point on the island. It is surrounded by two ridges, on the landward side corresponding to the 1906 shoreline and on the seaward side to the 1936 shoreline. About 12 inches/30 cm of peat material overlies the sand within the alder marsh area. This material has accumulated as a result of the high-water table in the winter months and the proximity of the fresh-water table to the surface throughout the summer. In the wet conditions organic matter cannot decompose fully and so has gathered with the passing years. Alders can grow in soils low in nitrogen because their roots contain lumps or nodules with bacteria that trap nitrogen from the air. Alder nodules continue to fix nitrogen into the autumn months.

### The salt marsh

The salt marsh lies between the dunes and the lagoon on the landward side of the island. At the dunes' boundary, the limit of penetration of the highest spring tide, there is a sharp vegetation change. From the grasses and flowering plants of the dunes, the vegetation becomes a mat of *Festuca rubra* and sedges.

On the lagoon side of the salt marsh a ridge of 16 inches/40 cm coincides with the natural high-water mark. Within the marsh, drainage creeks cut through the crust to the underlying sand and give it the look of an area permeated by hundreds of river channels. Elsewhere in the salt marsh are pans, shallow, steep-sided, subcircular depressions, floored with bare mud.

Dense stands of *Salicornia* stems encourage the accumulation of sediment in the mud-flats on the margins of the salt marsh.

## BIRDS OF BULL ISLAND

The most spectacular event on the Bull Island is the arrival of the overwintering flocks of waders and wildfowl, who come to feed on the abundant nutrient reserves that have built up over the summer months. Protection from hunting (a no-shooting sanctuary was first declared at the Bull in 1931) and from harsh climatic conditions are also factors that determine where birds roost and feed. The winter months are without doubt the most important times for birds on and around the island.

The Brent geese arrive in Ireland from Arctic Canada and Greenland in October. The flocks of Brent consist of family groups that feed together in areas where eel-grass grows, both in Dublin Bay and at other estuaries around Ireland. On the Bull they are seen feeding north of the causeway from Sutton to Kilbarrack.

Shelduck breed all around the Irish coastline but in July adults leave the ducklings in crèches in the care of a few adult birds and head to Heligoland, off the north German coast, to moult. They are found in their greatest numbers at the Bull in the month of October, when they are feeding on a tiny snail called *Hydrobia ulvae* along the island coast between Raheny and Kilbarrack north of the causeway.

Widgeon congregate about 658 feet/200 m north of the causeway in the winter months, having spent the summer in Iceland, Scandinavia or Russia.

Teal are found in flocks of up to 1,000 in the salt marsh on the island's landward side. Though teal breed in Ireland in the summer, many more arrive from Scandinavia and the Baltic from August until December, in which month peak numbers are recorded at sites throughout the country.

The pintail is a very rare breeding bird in Ireland. In the winter, numbers are in the region of 300 to 400 at the Bull, where they are found feeding between Raheny and the causeway. When the tide is in, they move to the salt marsh in Dollymount. Most of these birds are thought to be from Russia, though a few do come from France and Italy.

The shoveler is another rare breeder in Ireland. Numbers at the Bull start to increase in August and reach their highest point in November. They feed mainly in areas north of the causeway.

Waders are the most numerous group of birds at Bull Island. They stand patiently along the shoreline feeding as the sea retreats and allows access to the sands and shells cast ashore. Their main roost is between the wooden bridge and the causeway along the salt marsh. 24,000 waders were counted in the 1970s; 20,000 is sufficient to register the site as a mud-flat of international worth.

Waders which feature in abundance at Bull Island include oystercatcher, turnstone, curlew, lapwing, knot, dunlin, bar-tailed godwit, redshank and greenshank. The wooden bridge at low tide offers a good opportunity to get close to these birds and find out what they are like in the field.

Among the other birds seen on Bull Island are long-eared owls that come in from St Anne's Park; short-eared owls have also been seen. Kestrels feed daily on the island, along with sparrow-hawks and pere-grines. The peregrines cross the bay from the city, where a pair roost and have bred young. Food for all these raptors comes in the form of mice and the many meadow pipits and skylarks that nest among the dunes.

The most important site on the Bull Island is the breeding grounds of the little terns. These small gull-like birds with forked tails and thin pointed bills are sometimes referred to as sea swallows. The nest is a shallow scrape on the shingle or sand of a beach. As there are fewer than 300 pairs of this bird nesting in the country, protection of the sites is vital. The colony at the northern end of Bull Island is Ireland's largest. Each May the terns travel from west Africa to nest here. Because they nest on the ground the area is fenced off from walkers; people are asked not to walk across the sand in case eggs are broken.

## MAMMALS OF THE ISLAND

The most famous in natural history terms is the Bull Island Mouse. For all its notoriety it is now known never to have existed. In the latter part of the last century, when Darwin's Theory of Evolution was the hot news, it was thought that a population of mice had evolved on the Bull that were different to those on the mainland. Mice trapped on the island, by Mr Lyster Johnson, seemed to have a lighter-coloured coat than their mainland counterparts. This, it was argued, was due to pressure from predators: only the paler varieties could survive and breed on the island as they had the advantage of camouflage on the light sands. In 1929 the Bull Island Mouse became a separate species, *Mus jamesonii*.

In the 1960s, just prior to the building of the causeway, Azzo von Rezzori and Fergus O'Gorman trapped more mice on the island to determine if the theory held true. On examining the newly trapped specimens and the skins of those initially trapped, von Rezzori and O'Gorman came to the conclusion that the Bull Island Mouse was a mythical creature. The pale fur was, they considered, in all probability due to a small population of light-coloured mice interbreeding in the early years of the island's history.

Hares are also plentiful on the island. Pressure on the hare population comes from illegal hunting with dogs and the presence of two golf clubs on the island. Foxes have been seen, though it is thought that they cross from St Anne's Park rather than live permanently on the island. Bats have been attracted to roost in special boxes attached to poles in the vicinity of the information centre. The bats originally roosted in the trees of St Anne's Park — and no doubt still do — and fed over the island on the insects that abound.

**Link** Bull Island, Clontarf, the Tolka

From Bull Island we cross through the city of Dublin, coming in via Clontarf. A pub in the village is known as The Sheds, a name that refers to a time long past when wooden buildings there were used for curing fish. In the nineteenth century there was still a profitable oyster-bank in the sea off Clontarf. We pass through Fairview and over the Tolka River. John Dalton, writing in 1836, described the Tolka as a picturesque trout stream, but at this point it is one of the most badly polluted rivers in Dublin. The presence of swans from time to time may be an encouraging sign but on several occasions they have had to be rescued after severe contamination of the waters by oil.

## DIVERSION — ALONG THE TOLKA TO BOTANIC GARDENS — TOWN THROUGH PHOENIX PARK

We can follow the Tolka back along its course to the suburbs, passing a number of city parks created over the years on its banks. At Fairview Park we veer right along Fairview Strand and right again down Richmond Road to Lower Drumcondra Road. Here we turn left and then right onto Botanic Avenue, at the end of which are the Gardens that give the road its name. Established in 1790, the Botanic Gardens have continued to develop since then; a pleasant few hours can be spent going through the collections of plants both indoors and out.

Prospect or Glasnevin Cemetery surrounds the Botanic Gardens on two sides and further west along the Finglas Road is the Tolka Valley Park, which reaches out into the countryside at Dunsany.

The return journey to the city takes us along River Road to Ashtown Road, where we turn right to the Phoenix Park. The Park is large enough to lose oneself in for an entire day. All the features of a city park that attract wildlife are found here in the 707 hectares/1,752 acres of grassland and wooded areas.

Any open stretch of grassland is a feeding ground for birds such as gulls, oystercatchers, rooks, magpies, blackbirds, thrushes and starlings. Food found includes earthworms, leather-jackets (the larvae of 'Daddy Long Legs'), slugs, snails, butterfly and moth caterpillars. In one acre (a half-hectare) of grassland alone there may be 809 kg of earthworms (four-fifths of a ton).

Grassland sites such as football pitches afford plenty of food for birds and also allow them to feed in relative safety. In large flocks the amount of time each bird has to spend looking around for predators is reduced and so feeding becomes more efficient. Flocks of oystercatchers, interspersed with a few gulls, are a common sight on playing-pitches, particularly in the winter months. With their smart black-and-white plumage and long orange beaks, oystercatchers are distinctive birds. They come to the parks to feed on leather-jackets, larvae and worms when conditions by the sea are not favourable. Oystercatchers on the coast are territorial about their feeding areas and a young bird may be forced inland to such poorer sites.

Earthworms and insects are major components of the badger and fox diet, so open grassland is important for both populations. In more remote situations the abundance of earthworms in soils will determine the density of badger population in any particular area. In a suburban situation waste food discarded by humans may make up 50 per cent of a badger's diet and mask the importance of this other source.

Rabbits will be found feeding on the grass and perennial weeds (daisies and dandelions) at dusk and dawn. The woodland and shrubs that border playing-fields act as cover and refuge from predators. In the 1940s and 1950s the rabbit population was very high and the rabbit was having a profound effect on the ecology of many plant species, so efficient was it at grazing. The introduction of myxomatosis, a viral infection, devastated the population in a very short time. The results were dramatic. Areas that had been cropped for years were suddenly producing swards of grasses and herbs. The populations of predators rose for a short while and then fell.

Standard trees are a feature of all city parks. These stand alone in the parkland and will develop the large crowns typical of trees that grow in the open, in contrast with the same species in the woods, where, drawn up by the light, the trees grow tall and produce few side-branches.

In some city parks, remnants of woodland isolated by grassland may still be found. In these patches of trees and shrubs — in effect small clumps of woodland edge — birds can forage and shelter and small mammals can take refuge. In the older parks they often survive from days when a private estate flourished in the area, and are a mixture of beech, ash, sycamore and a range of exotics that would have been planted to enhance the landscape features.

Any wood can be divided into four vertical layers, each typified by particular plant species or plants of a certain size.

**Field layer**

At ground level, the field layer is in the shade of the vegetation above for much of the year. To overcome this problem, plants may grow and flower early in the year, taking advantage of the light available on the short winter and early spring days. The cover of trees and leaf litter on the soil surface means temperatures do not fall as much as they might in a more open situation, so faster growth is possible in woodlands. Snowdrops, wood-sorrel, lesser celandine and wild garlic are some of the species encountered on the forest floor. Ivy takes on a creeping growth form and can cover much of the floor.

Enclosing the woods prevents trampling by the park-users, which would mean that much of the field layer was lost and regeneration of seedlings was impaired

On the woodland floor is a layer of leaf litter, an important source of nutrients for the plants and animals of the wood. The large roots running up into trees like buttresses are there for support only; within the litter layer fine tree-roots extend in all directions absorbing moisture and nutrients from the decaying litter.

## Shrub layer

Shrubs in the wood often include snow-berry and bramble, whose bushy growth allows them to exploit patches of sunlight on the forest floor; the creeping growth form of bramble means it can reach into areas of light in the canopy. Honeysuckle is also found at this layer, climbing through the shrubs.

## Under storey

Holly is the main under-storey species. Because it is evergreen it can take advantage of the absence of leaves on the trees above it in the winter months to continue its photosynthetic activities. There are also many young deciduous trees in this layer of vegetation. Beech and oak trees when juvenile retain their lower leaves until late in the year; this allows them to create more food reserves while the trees above are bare.

## Canopy

High above us is the woodland canopy. The mature oak, beech and other trees shade the remaining layers in the spring, summer and autumn. Leaves from the canopy fall to the forest floor and give rise to the litter layer above the soil surface. The canopy accommodates a myriad of leaf-eating and predatory insects (as are all other layers of the wood). The squirrel is at home here feeding on oak, beech and pine seed and lying up in dreys during poor weather. The main predator of the squirrel in suburbia is the domestic cat. The Botanic Gardens has long had a population of red squirrels but in recent years the number of stray cats in the area has taken its toll on the population.

In the Phoenix Park a population of grey squirrels, introduced to Ireland from America in 1911, has become established. The grey squirrel prefers broadleaves to conifers and is at home on the ground feeding on the fallen seed of beech and oak. The red is more suited to life in conifer woodlands; it feeds on the seed from the cones and is more agile in the canopy than on the ground.

The largest mammals within the Phoenix Park, apart from those at the zoo, are the fallow deer. Up to the 1980s cattle were grazed in the park but this practice was stopped with the detection of tuberculosis in the herd of deer. Fallow deer are not a native species; they were introduced into Ireland by the Normans as a ready source of venison and for the hunt. Herds were kept by Normans throughout Ireland and wild populations of fallow deer can now be found in most Midland counties, particularly in and around forests. The palmate antlers of the male are distinctive, setting it apart at once from the native red and from introduced sika species, both of which have the pointed tines we associate with deer.

It is possible to observe the rut in progress in the park. Go up there in late September or early October to hear the stags in song. One stag tends to be favoured above all others by the hinds and so gets to father most of the calves in the park that year. The result is a preponderance of deer with little variation in coat colour until the current favourite falls from grace or, more likely, is killed by a passing car. What is it that proves to be such a potent attractant to the hinds? The most probable factor seems to be the cry or song of the stag.

**Link** Phoenix Park, city centre

We leave the Phoenix Park by the main entrance at Parkgate Street and head east along the Liffey to the centre of Dublin city. A city centre offers little prospect of wildlife but Dublin's main thoroughfare, O'Connell Street, is the site of a roost for pied wagtails.

**Stop** O'Connell Street and O'Connell Bridge

During autumn and winter several hundred pied wagtails may congregate in the plane trees that line the central island of O'Connell Street. They come in from the suburbs, where temperatures may be 3–5° Celsius cooler at night. The city centre is a heat island: heat from the day's sun is trapped in the concrete and road surfaces and released slowly at night. For birds with a reduced food supply in the winter months, the energy saved by staying warm at night could mean the difference between life and death.

Another bird of inner-city Dublin is the peregrine, a predatory bird whose diet consists entirely of other birds. The list of species that make up the diet of the peregrine runs to 117 birds in Britain and Ireland. At the top of that list come the feral doves and pigeons. With Dublin's burgeoning population of pigeons it is small wonder that a pair of peregrines set up shop on a gasometer in Dublin docks. From this site pigeons feeding on spilt grain from trucks entering and leaving the port were easy prey. The speed at which a peregrine can strike has been estimated at 120 miles/192 km per hour; a blow to the neck in mid-air leaves the pigeon senseless.

The gasometer (which was dismantled in 1993) had other attractions for the peregrines. Height and cliff-like sides made the structure an almost perfect mimic of the sheer rock-faces the peregrine frequents in the wild.

In addition to extracting rich pickings around the docks, the peregrines venture across the bay to Bull Island, where a little more variety is added to the diet. Meadow pipits and skylarks, common among the dunes, are also fancied.

The appearance of peregrines in the city tells us the population of this bird is at a healthy level in the country. In the 1960s the population had fallen to around 60 pairs, due to poisoning by pesticides such as DDT, then in widespread use on grain crops. Pigeons ate the grain and peregrines ate pesticide-packed pigeons. With controls on the use of DDT and dieldrin the population has gradually risen, and today there are in excess of 300 pairs in the country. Now one of the major threats is egg collectors plundering the nests. Last year one of the Dublin birds was poisoned by bait left out to kill pigeons.

Expansion of the population is limited by the number of nest sites available — ledges on high rock exposures are the favoured spots — and a move into cities may indicate the saturation of sites outside. The loss of the gasometer site to a new development project is to be offset by attempts to coax peregrines to nest at the tall Pigeon House chimney stacks. The address might seem a little unfortunate if the peregrines do move in.

The swift is as accurate a harbinger of summer as we are likely to get on this island; high in the mid-May skies above Dublin its screams tell us the summer is just around the corner. Gilbert White, of Selborne, writing of the swift in the 1770s, noted that it spent considerable time in the air, was observed mating on the wing, and fed on insects at high altitude (*A Natural History of Selborne*, 1967 facsimile). He was, however, sceptical about the idea that it migrated. He found that swifts produced only one clutch of three young per year and that the parents were rather negligent at times, leaving young unfed for days at a stretch. More recent texts on the swift offer little that is new. The young can remain without food for up to three days, going into a kind of stupor as they wait for parents to return with insects. And, of course, we now know that the swift migrates to Africa each year.

Prior to the advent of towns the swift nested in embankments, on cliffs and in tree-holes. Now it finds a perfect site in the eaves of houses from the city centre out to the suburbs. Returning to the nest is a noisy affair. The approach is marked by high-pitched screams and a number of fly-bys before the swift alights on the wall and scurries into the nest.

Plants that colonise city sites have to adapt to the harsh conditions: a lack of soil and moisture, searing heat in the middle of the day and polluting fumes of traffic are just some of the dangers. Among the most successful is buddleia. The flowers are a distinctive purple in long spear-like clusters at the end of a slender branch which almost droops under their weight. The leaves are a dull green, lighter underneath than on top. The plant is an exotic; it originated in the Orient and was introduced into Ireland in the 1890s. In the garden it is a well-mannered plant and can be kept firmly under control. In the city and town it is a plant of altogether wilder habits; it can be seen sprouting from gutters, from crevices in walls and along window-ledges where some debris has gathered.

The merit of buddleia from a wildlife perspective is its attraction for butterflies; it is often referred to as the butterfly bush. The draw for the butterfly is the flowers of the plant and the nectar therein.

Many other plants are found along the gutters and broken drainpipes where water is in greater supply. *The Flora of Inner City Dublin* by Peter Wyse Jackson and Micheline Skeffington (1984) details the location and biology of many of the plants found in the city.

**Link** City centre, quays, canal dock

We keep going east along the quays and cross the Liffey when past the Custom House. Walking east along the river, we turn on to Lombard Street East and then right along Pearse Street. We are now heading to the Grand Canal Docks. This is the end-point of the Grand Canal, which has connected the Shannon and the Midlands with Dublin for almost 200 years.

**Stop** Grand Canal Quay

On Grand Canal Quay just before Victoria Bridge there is a museum or interpretative centre on the canals. This is worth a visit to put into context the role of canals in both history and natural history.

**Link** Grand Canal Quay, the Dodder, Ringsend, Irishtown and Sandymount

We cross the canal and then the Dodder River. Swans will often be seen along the Dodder and around the canal basin. Another common sight is cormorants at rest on pillars or any other projections, wings extended as they dry their flight feathers.

The Dodder flows from the northern slopes of Kippure Mountain in Wicklow through Glenasmole, Tallaght, Firhouse, Templeogue, Rathfarnham, Milltown, Donnybrook and Ringsend. From the suburbs of Milltown to Templeogue a linear park has been established along the river. A most informative account of the river is given by Christopher Moriarty in *Down the Dodder* (1991).

We pass through Ringsend and out onto the coast road at Irishtown and Sandymount.

**Walk** Irishtown Wildlife Park, South Wall, Poolbeg Lighthouse

We can park the car here or take the bike with us through the park. The Irishtown Wildlife Park, a quiet place to walk, runs along the coast in the direction of the Pigeon House. It is built on a massive infill site that has been planted with a wide variety of plants, some native, others exotics more at home in a well-manicured garden. Swallows, skylarks and meadow pipits are here in the summer months. Herons feed along the shoreline where a small stream enters the sea. In the winter months Brent geese will be seen feeding on the eel-grass along the shore and on the grass sites around the power station at the Pigeon House.

It is possible to walk from Irishtown right out to the end of the South Wall — it is a long walk, admittedly, but the view from the South Wall of Dublin Bay is unsurpassed. Keep to the coast all the way. The strong smell on leaving the Wildlife Park behind the Pigeon House is the Ringsend sewage-treatment plant. At the moment these are just settling tanks. The solids are pumped onto a ship and dumped at sea off Howth Head. The liquid fraction is released to sea at the start of the South Wall, a point where gulls congregate when the tide is out and flow from the plant is at a maximum.

Poolbeg Lighthouse at the end of the pier is a good place for observing birds such as the common scoter, great crested grebes and divers at sea. On the way out along the wall look for groups of turnstones feeding on insects that are found among the seaweed and under debris and stones. Purple sandpipers feed in the same areas but are a mottled brown colour in contrast to the reddish-brown and white of the turnstone.

**Link** Sandymount, Merrion Gates, Booterstown

Follow the coast road along the Sandymount seafront past the level crossing at Merrion Gates and on to Booterstown Marsh.

**Stop** Booterstown Marsh

Booterstown Marsh is leased by An Taisce, which manages the area as a bird sanctuary. Though small, 10 acres/4 hectares, the site is frequented by mallard, moorhen, shelduck, heron, sedge-warbler and reed-bunting in the summer months. In winter, lapwing, snipe, curlew, teal, widgeon, oystercatcher and dunlin are seen at the marsh. It is possible to observe the birds from the roadside or in the DART station on the other side of the marsh.

The water in the marsh varies between fresh and salt water. Along the road at the Dublin end the influence is mainly a freshwater one. Reed-beds of sea club-rush, glaucous lake-rush and jointed rush provide shelter and food for ducks and moorhens. At the eastern end of the marsh the influence is predominantly from saltwater and the plants of the salt marsh are found here. Sea aster, sea milkwort, salt-marsh grass and arrow-grass occur. With a muddy surface that is rich in organic matter and invertebrates, snails, worms and larvae, there is plenty of food for the birds.

**Link** Booterstown, Blackrock, Dún Laoghaire

Keep south along the coast past Blackrock Park on to Dún Laoghaire Harbour. Here we can go out the West Pier to get a good view of some seabirds of the area. From the West Pier observations have been made on migrants passing north and south on the Irish coast. This information is used to determine the importance of routes which these birds follow during migration passages. There is no use protecting areas such as Bull Island and the Slobs in Wexford if other sites along the flight path of birds are ignored. The loss of resting and feeding grounds may, in the long term, damage bird populations irreversibly.

**Link** Dún Laoghaire, Killiney Hill

From Dún Laoghaire we head south once more. Killiney Hill is at a high point on the coast above Killiney Bay.

**Stop** Killiney Hill

Killiney Hill is a public park and there is car parking available. From the hilltop the view south includes the conical peaks of the Great Sugar Loaf and to its east Little Sugar Loaf and then Bray Head with its more rounded outline. Both Sugar Loaf mountains escaped the abrasive effects of glaciers that passed over the summit of Bray Head and rubbed it smooth. Killiney Head was glaciated at the same time, as is demonstrated by the large granite rocks at the summit, smoothed and rounded, each in the same direction. The ends of the rocks were plucked off by the passing glacier to leave them with an abruptly truncated outline. In geological circles they are referred to as roches moutonnées due to their perceived similarity to a moutonnée, a type of sheepskin wig in fashion in the nineteenth century.

**Link** Killiney Hill, Killiney beach

We move south again to Killiney beach. There is a car park at the DART station, and access to the beach is via a tunnel under the railway from here. The beach is a narrow and very stony affair. The water deepens suddenly just metres from the shore and there can be a strong undertow. The DART runs regularly from Killiney station and we may either head back into town or go further south to Bray and Co. Wicklow.

# WICKLOW

Glenmacnass, in the heart of Co. Wicklow

Wicklow, the county directly south of Dublin, is an area of contrasting terrains but consistent beauty. Deriving its English name from the Viking words 'Wyking alo' or 'Viking meadow', it can be divided into three geographical areas: the fertile coastal strip whose floral beauty and great demesnes have earned the county the title of 'Garden of Ireland'; the bleak but beautiful uplands in the centre which make up the country's largest continuous mountainous region; and the more gently sloping farmlands of west Wicklow, which look down on the plains of central Ireland. Much of its coast comprises rocky cliffs and excellent sandy beaches.

As the historic stronghold of Gaelic clans and fugitive bands, Wicklow resisted British domination for centuries, and was one of the last areas to be constituted formally as a county. Wicklow Town was a Norse harbour, but inland the countryside remained in native hands. MacMurroughs,

# COUNTY WICKLOW

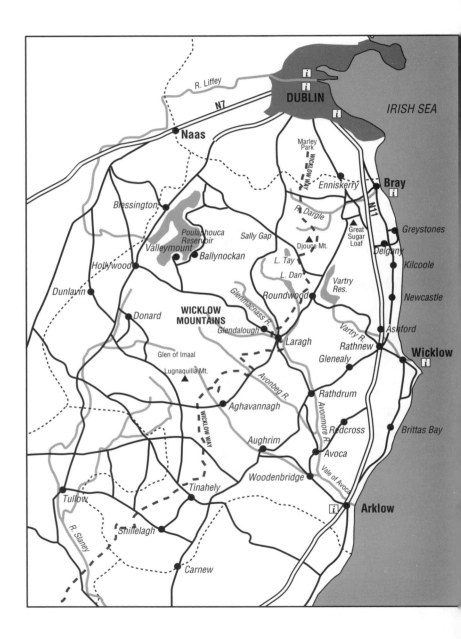

O'Byrnes, O'Tooles and others constantly raided the lower lands of the Pale until 1601. Wicklow men were involved in the failed Wexford uprising of 1798. It was only with the construction of the Military Road after 1798 that the region was made to submit to the British. This road, which bisects the mountains and runs from Rathfarnham in County Dublin to Aughavannagh in the far south of County Wicklow, is still the only north–south route through the upland areas today and runs at a height of over 1,000 feet/304 m for more than 20 miles/32 km. When it was built, the road was fortified with military barracks at various stops along the route, such as Glencree and Aughavannagh.

Apart from the north of the county, most of Wicklow is sparsely populated; indeed, one of Dublin's most endearing charms is that it has such a rural area on its doorstep. The Ice Age left the area with a chain of rounded granite peaks, cut by deep river valleys and home to numerous corrie lakes. The highest summit is Lugnaquilla, at 3,039 feet/924 m. The environment in the mountains is sufficiently severe to deter most human settlement, though in consequence this has the disadvantage for the visitor that transport services are poor, and a car (or, for the fit, a bicycle) provides the only practical way of seeing everything. Alternatively, try out one of the coach tours offered by Bus Éireann (see 'Travel' in the Dublin section, pages 17–18).

# ESSENTIAL INFORMATION

## BANKS: PRINCIPAL OFFICES

### Allied Irish Banks:
**Arklow**, telephone 0402–32529, open 10 a.m.–4 p.m. weekdays (5 p.m. Monday)
**Blessington**, telephone 045–65151, 10 a.m.–1 p.m. Tuesday and Thursday
**Wicklow**, telephone 0404–67311, open 10 a.m.–4 p.m. weekdays (5 p.m. Monday).
Closed lunch 12.30–1.30 p.m.

### Bank of Ireland:
**Arklow**, telephone 0402–32004, open 10 a.m.–4 p.m. weekdays (5 p.m. Monday)
**Rathdrum**, telephone 0404–46162, open 10 a.m.–3 p.m. weekdays (4 p.m. Monday).
Closed lunch 12.30–1.30 p.m.
**Tinahely**, telephone 0402–38121, open 10 a.m.–3 p.m. weekdays (4 p.m. Monday).
Closed lunch 12.30–1.30 p.m.
**Wicklow**, telephone 0404–67376, open 10 a.m.–4 p.m. weekdays (5 p.m. Monday)

There are also branches of the main clearing banks in Bray and Greystones.

## BICYCLE HIRE AND REPAIR

County Wicklow offers thrilling but energetic touring for fit cyclists. See 'Bicycle Tours', page 151.

Bicycles can be hired or repaired at:

E.R. Harris, 87c Greenpark Road, Bray, telephone 01–2863357

Wicklow Hire Service, Abbey Street, telephone 0404–68149 (hire only)

J. Caulfield, King's Hill, Arklow, telephone 0402–32284

J. Owens, 2 Church Buildings, Arklow, telephone 0402–32638

T. McGrath, Main Street, Rathdrum, telephone 0402–46172

J. Kenny, Laragh, telephone 0404–45326.

The following shops also do repairs:

Ashford Bicycle Centre, Esso Station, Ashford, telephone 0404–40605

P. Kelly, 13 Main Street, Arklow, telephone 0402–39989.

## BUREAUX DE CHANGE

All commercial banks cash traveller's cheques and exchange currency. Traveller's cheques and major credit cards are accepted by most hotels, large shops, travel and transport companies.

## CAR REPAIRS

**Arklow**
Kavanagh & O'Reilly Motors, Wexford Road, telephone 0402–32200
Kavanagh's, Ferrybank, telephone 0402–32224
Mayfair Garage, Main Street Upper, telephone 0402–32578
Sheehan's Motor Services, Knockenrahan, telephone 0402–32391

**Aughrim**
G.S. Autos, Cronebe, telephone 0402–36323

**Blessington**
Ryall Motors, Main Street, telephone 045–65749

**Brittas Bay**
Timmons Motors, Barndarrig, Kilbride, telephone 0404–48104

**Dunlavin**
H.J. Coleborn, Main Street, telephone 045–51200

**Glenealy**
Glenealy Garage, 0404–44663

**Rathdrum**
Michael Stedman, Ballygannon, telephone 0404–46322
Webster Garage, Ballinacarrig, telephone 0404–46358

**Redcross**
Aidan Furlong, Kilpatrick, telephone 0404–47274

**Tinahely**
Rothwell's Garage, telephone 0402–38113
Tinahely Motors, Churchland, telephone 0402–38101

**Wicklow**
Blainroe Garage, telephone 0404–67428
William Cuffe, Castleview 0404–67292
Porter Brothers, South Quay, telephone 0404–67142
Sinnott Autos, Bollarney, telephone 0404–67212

# CHURCHES

Catholic mass is available throughout the county both on Saturday evenings and on Sunday mornings.
Church of Ireland service in Greystones is at 10.30 a.m.
Methodist service in Bray is at 10.30 a.m. on Sundays.
Presbyterian service in Bray is at 11.30 a.m. on Sundays.

# CRÈCHE AND BABYSITTING SERVICES

Euro-placements, 59 Waterloo Road, Dublin, telephone 01–6603926

# EMERGENCIES AND MEDICAL MATTERS

In cases of emergency, ring 999 from any telephone, and say which service you require — fire brigade, police or ambulance. The call is free.

**Hospitals:**
St Colman's, Rathdrum, telephone 0404–46109
County Hospital, Wicklow, telephone 0404–67108
District Hospital, Wicklow, telephone 0404–69236.

# GARDAÍ (POLICE)

If an emergency arises ring 999 and ask for the Gardaí/Police. This call is free.
Otherwise, contact the local Gardaí at:
**Arklow:** telephone 0402–32304
**Ashford:** telephone 0404–32986
**Aughrim:** telephone 0402–36142
**Avoca:** telephone 0402–35102
**Blessington:** telephone 045–65202
**Donard:** telephone 045–54612
**Dunlavin:** telephone 045–51211
**Hollywood:** telephone 045–64172
**Rathdrum:** telephone 0404–46206
**Tinahely:** telephone 0402–38102
**Wicklow:** telephone 0404–67107

# LAUNDERETTES

**Arklow**
Fleming's, Fairgreen, telephone 0402–31757

**Bray**
Crescent Cleaners, Bray Shopping Centre, telephone 01–2863189

# PHARMACIES

**Arklow**
R.D. Arnold, 40 Main Street, telephone 0402–32456
Duffy's Medical Hall, 46 Main Street, telephone 0402–32457
O'Meara's, 30 Main Street, telephone 0402–32045

**Ashford**
Paudie Doyle, telephone 0404–40439

**Aughrim**
O'Byrne's, telephone 0402–36148

**Ballymore Eustace**
J. Blake, The Pharmacy, telephone 044–64247

**Blessington**
Blessington Pharmacy, Main Street, telephone 045–65197

**Dunlavin**
O.J. Roche, telephone 045–51319

**Rathdrum**
John & Michael Tierney, Main Street, telephone 0404–46157

**Tinahely**
Gilsenan Pharmacy, telephone 0402–38168

**Wicklow**
Gleeson Pharmacy, Abbey Street, telephone 0404–67451
John Holly Pharmacy, 1 Main Street, telephone 0404–67855
Leonard Mulvey, Butler's Medical Hall, Abbey Street, telephone 0404–67355
Shine's Pharmacy, Main Street, telephone 0404–67444

## POST OFFICES

Post offices are generally open 9 a.m.–5.30 p.m. Monday–Friday and can be found in most towns and villages.
Details of telephone services are in the Dublin section (page 17).

## TAXIS

**Arklow**
Shaun Carey, telephone 0402–39894

**Blessington**
Blessington Cab Hire, telephone 01–582730

**Bray**
Bray Taxi Service, 5 Main Street, telephone 01–2829826

**Wicklow**
Sadie Dolan, telephone 0404–67420

## TOURIST INFORMATION OFFICES

The Wicklow Town Office is at Rialto House, Fitzwilliam Square. Opening hours are 9.30 a.m.–5.30 p.m. Monday–Friday in winter and 9 a.m.–6 p.m. Monday–Saturday in summer. Telephone 0404–69117/69118. The office at Bray, telephone 01–2867128, also opens all year round.
During the summer months, temporary tourist offices are open in:
Arklow, telephone 0402–32484. Open July/August.
Blessington, telephone 045–65850. Open May–October.
Laragh, telephone 0404–45482.
Rathdrum, telephone 0404–46768.
Further tourist information points are being established at Carnew and Baltinglass.

## TRAVEL

### Buses

Provincial bus services for Wicklow leave Dublin from Busáras, the central bus station, at Store Street. Express routes follow either the N11 towards Wexford or the N81 to Blessington.

A number of local bus routes from Dublin also extend as far as Wicklow; for example, the 65 bus goes to Blessington, with infrequent variations to Ballymore, Donard and Ballyknockan. The 84 bus passes through Bray, Greystones, Delgany and Newcastle, while the 45 bus travels as far as Bray and the 44 goes to Enniskerry.

The privately owned St Kevin's Bus Service, telephone 01–2818119, leaves Dublin (from the College of Surgeons on St Stephen's Green West) at 11.30 a.m. daily for the ancient monastic settlement of Glendalough. The bus stops at Bray Town Hall at 12.10 p.m. and returns from Glendalough at 4.15 p.m. This is the only bus service that enters the mountains.

## Trains

Train services run the length of the Wicklow coastline, leaving Dublin from Connolly Station (Amiens Street) and Pearse Station (Westland Row) and stopping at Bray, Greystones, Wicklow, Rathdrum and Arklow.

## Horse-drawn caravans

Perhaps not a serious option for the traveller in a rush, but Clissmann Caravans, Carrigmore Farm, Wicklow, telephone 0404–48188, is worth considering for the ultimate in slow-paced, relaxing holidays.

## WEATHER FORECAST

The weather forecast for Leinster (including County Wicklow) can be obtained by ringing 01–8425555.

# FESTIVALS AND SPECIAL EVENTS

## March

Arklow Music Festival

## June

County Wicklow Gardens Festival. A celebration of the public and private gardens of Wicklow. Includes flower shows, garden parties and woodland walks.

The Synge Summer School in Rathdrum provides a forum for discussing the life and work of one of Ireland's best-known playwrights, John M. Synge. The school also debates aspects of modern Irish theatre.

International Cartoon Festival, Rathdrum. Cartoonists from around the world, street entertainment and exhibitions.

## July

Bray Seaside and Arts Festival
Wicklow Regatta Festival

## August

The Parnell International Summer School in Rathdrum attracts historians, politicians and other people interested in the legacy of Charles Stewart Parnell, the nineteenth-century statesman once called 'the uncrowned King of Ireland'.

## September

The County Wicklow Lamb Fair, Blessington, features sheep-shearing, dog trials, country markets and seminars.

# WHERE TO STAY

This list includes hotels, guesthouses and hostels approved by Bord Fáilte (Irish Tourist Board). B&B accommodation is too plentiful to list in full; for information enquire directly at houses displaying the sign for approved accommodation (a green shamrock) or ask at the local tourist information office.

Bord Fáilte grades hotels and guesthouses separately, depending on facilities. Hotels range from five-star luxury to modest, usually family-run, one-star establishments. Guesthouses are classified separately, from four stars to one star. As prices vary according to season and inflation, a rough indication is given based on the cost of overnight single accommodation (double accommodation may cost up to 50 per cent less for two people sharing). The categories are as follows:

| | |
|---|---|
| Economy: | £15 to £25 |
| Budget: | £25 to £35 |
| Moderate: | £35 to £45 |
| High: | £45 to £60 |
| Very high: | £60 and more |

When asking the price, check whether a service charge is added. The price quoted usually includes an Irish breakfast, except in some of the larger hotels.

## HOTELS AND GUESTHOUSES

### Arklow
Arklow Bay Hotel, telephone 0402–32309. Grade **. Modern hotel with 38 bedrooms. Rating: budget.
Bridge Hotel, telephone 0402–31666/31655. Grade *. Rating: economy.
Marine Hotel, telephone 0402–32355/32436. Grade *. Rating: economy.

### Ashford
Bel Air Hotel, Cronroe, telephone 0404–40109. Grade *. Family-run hotel with surrounding gardens, 1 mile/1.5 km from village. Riding school. Closed at Christmas. Rating: budget.
Cullenmore Hotel, telephone 0404–40187/40108. Grade **. Modern building on main road 2.5 miles/4 km north of village. Accommodation for disabled guests. Rating: economy/budget.

### Aughrim
Lawless's Hotel, telephone 0402–36146. Grade **. Free trout fishing available to guests in Avoca River. Rating: budget.

### Baltinglass
Germaine's Guesthouse, telephone 0508–81005. Grade *. Rating: economy.

## Blessington

Downshire House Hotel, telephone 045–65199. Grade **. On main street of town. Tennis. Closed at Christmas/New Year. Rating: budget.

## Bray

Cois Farraige Hotel, Strand Road, telephone 01–2862293. Grade *. Rating: economy.
Crofton Bray Head Guesthouse, Strand Road, telephone 01–2867182. Grade **. Rating: economy.
New International Hotel, Seafront, telephone 01–2867950. Open May–September. Rating: economy.
Royal Hotel, Main Street, telephone 01–2862935. Grade ***. Largest hotel in Bray, which can be reached in little over thirty minutes by train from Dublin. Rating: high.
Ulysses Guesthouse, Centre Esplanade, telephone 01–2863860. Grade *. Rating: economy.

## Delgany

Delgany Inn Hotel, telephone 01–2875701. Grade **. Rating: budget.

## Donard

Chrysalis Centre, Donoughmore, telephone 045–54713. Something completely different — a holistic retreat centre located in a restored eighteenth-century house. Three single rooms and three dormitories. Vegetarian cooking and a library of alternative books. Regular personal growth (yoga, spirituality, etc.) courses and workshops. Rating: economy.

## Dunlavin

Rathsallagh House, telephone 045–53112. Grade ****. A family-run guesthouse set in 500 acres/202.5 hectares of parkland. The farmhouse was converted from Queen Anne stables when the original house burned down. Indoor swimming pool. Tennis. Closed at Christmas. Rating: very high.

## Enniskerry

Enniscree Lodge Inn Hotel, telephone 01–2863542. Grade **. Open February–December. Small hotel with 10 bedrooms in charming location in Glencree Valley. Rating: high.
Powerscourt Arms Hotel, telephone 01–2863507. Grade *. Rating: budget.

## Glendalough

Glendalough Hotel, telephone 0404–45135. Grade ***. An old-fashioned hotel in one of the most beautiful glens in the county. Rating: budget/moderate.

## Glen of the Downs

Glenview Hotel, telephone 01–2873399. Grade ***. Rating: moderate.

## Greystones

La Touche Hotel, Trafalgar Road, telephone 01–2874401. Grade **. Rating: moderate.

## Rathdrum

Avonbrae Guesthouse, telephone 0404–46198. Grade **. Open April–November. Rating: economy.

## Rathnew

Hunter's Hotel, telephone 0404–40106. Grade ***. The first hotel on this site on the banks of the River Vartry was opened in 1830, and an old-world atmosphere still lingers. Rating: moderate.

Tinakilly House Hotel, telephone 0404–69274. Grade ****. Victorian mansion with impressive views of the Wicklow landscape. Tennis. 2.5 miles/4 km from village. Rating: very high

## Tinahely

Murphy's Hotel, telephone 0402–38144. Grade *. Rating: budget.

## Wicklow Town

Blainroe Golf Hotel, telephone 0404–67500. Grade **. 3 miles/5 km from town. Golf course and leisure facilities. Private beach. Rating: moderate.

Grand Hotel, telephone 0404–67337. Grade ***. A refurbished Victorian building on the main Dublin road. Rating: moderate.

Old Rectory Country House, telephone 0404–67048. Grade ****. Former nineteenth-century rectory located on a hillside just off the main road from Dublin 0.5 miles/1 km before Wicklow. Offers country-house cooking with an accent on seafood and organic vegetables. Closed October–Easter. Rating: high.

## Woodenbridge

Valley Hotel, telephone 0402–35200. Grade *. Rating: budget.

Woodenbridge Inn Hotel, telephone 0402–35146. Grade **. A 12-bedroomed hotel in the Vale of Avoca with golf and fishing nearby. Rating: budget.

# HOSTELS

An Óige (the Irish Youth Hostel Association) runs a network of youth hostels ideally situated for walkers and cyclists visiting the main scenic areas of Wicklow. Membership of An Óige or of a national youth hostelling association is required. Contact An Óige head office in Dublin (61 Mountjoy Street, telephone 01–8304555) for more information.

Aughavannagh House, Aughrim, telephone 0402–36102
Ballinclea Youth Hostel, Donard, telephone 045–54657
Baltyboys Youth Hostel, Blessington, telephone 045–67266
Glencree Youth Hostel, Enniskerry, telephone 01–2867290
Glendalough Youth Hostel, telephone 0404–45143
Knockree Youth Hostel, Enniskerry, telephone 01–2867196
Tiglin Youth Hostel, Ashford, telephone 0404–40259

## Other hostels

YWCA, Coolnagreina Holiday and Youth Centre, Trafalgar Road, Greystones, telephone 01–2874221

# CAMPING AND CARAVAN SITES

Johnson's Caravan and Camping Park, Redcross, telephone 0404–48133. Open from mid-March to mid-September. From Dublin, take N11 to Wexford. Turn right at Rathnew, then left under railway bridge. Travel 7 miles/11 km to Doyle's pub, from where the site is signposted.

River Valley Caravan and Camping Park, Redcross, telephone 0404–41647. Open from mid-March to mid-September. Directions as above.

Roundwood Caravan and Camping Park, telephone 01–2818163. Open from early April to mid-September. Park is situated near Roundwood village, on left if approaching from Dublin. Bike hire. Daily bus service to Dublin.

## SELF-CATERING

A wide range of holiday accommodation is available for rent on a weekly and long-term basis through Bord Fáilte, telephone 044–48761. Advance booking is essential in peak season.

# WHERE TO EAT

All restaurants are required by law to display their menu and prices outside the premises. The list below is not in any sense a 'good food' guide, though some indication is usually given as to what can be expected from a restaurant. The ratings used refer to the approximate price of a meal for one person, wine not included. These are as follows:

```
Economy:    under £5
Budget:     under £10
Moderate:   under £15
High:       over £15
Very high:  over £25
```

### Arklow
Stone Oven, telephone 0402–39418. Bakery and coffee shop. Specialises in confectionery and German bread. Rating: budget.

### Bray
Tree of Idleness, Seafront, Bray, telephone 01–2863498. Award-winning Greek-Cypriot restaurant. Open 7.30–11 p.m. Monday–Saturday, 7.30–10 p.m. Sunday. Rating: high.

### Dunlavin
Rathsallagh House, telephone 045–53112. Country-house cooking using local vegetables, beef and lamb. Hotel. Closed at Christmas. Open 8–9 p.m. Monday–Saturday, 2.30 p.m. only Sunday. Rating: very high.

### Enniskerry
Enniscree Lodge Hotel, Glencree Valley, telephone 01–2863542. Terrace restaurant with superb mountain views. Open 7.30–9.30 p.m. Tuesday–Sunday, also 12.30–2 p.m. Sunday. Rating: high.

### Glendalough
Glendalough Hotel, telephone 0404–45135. Hearty helpings of meat and fish. Rating: high.

### Greystones
The Hungry Monk, Main Street, telephone 01–2875759. Family-run restaurant with fish specialities. Open 7–11 p.m. Tuesday–Saturday, 12.30–3 p.m. Sunday. Rating: high.

### Rathnew
Tinakilly House Hotel, telephone 0404–69274. French/Irish cuisine. Duck, lamb and quail specialities. Famous brown bread. 2.5 miles/4 km from village. Open 12.30–2 p.m., 7–9 p.m. daily. Rating: very high.

Two views of Glendalough

## Wicklow Town

Old Rectory Country House, telephone 0404–67048. A former nineteenth-century rectory located on a hillside just off the main road from Dublin 0.5 miles/1 km before Wicklow. Offers country-house cooking with an accent on seafood and organic vegetables. Closed October–Easter. Open 8 p.m. only Sunday to Thursday, 7.30–9 p.m. Friday/Saturday. Rating: high.

Things to Eat, 6 Main Street, telephone 0404–68720. Home-made soups, breads, cakes and pastries. Open 8 p.m. only Sunday–Thursday, 7.30–9 p.m. Friday/Saturday. Rating: economy to budget.

## Woodenbridge

Woodenbridge Inn Hotel, telephone 0402–35146. Full restaurant and bar food. Rating: budget to moderate.

# SHOPPING

Many talented craftworkers have made their home in County Wicklow and many of their studios are open to visitors. These include:

*Arklow Pottery*, South Quay, Arklow, telephone 0402–32401. The country's largest pottery factory. Factory tours available from mid-June to the end of August (except last week July/first fortnight of August). Pottery shop open all year.

*Avoca Gift Centre*, Avoca, telephone 0402–35241. Hand-knit mohair, Aran sweaters and cotton garments.

*Avoca Handweavers* in Kilmacanogue, telephone 01–2867466, and Avoca, telephone 0402–35105. The oldest handweaving mill in Ireland is still in use at Avoca producing intricately woven tweeds. Restaurants at both sites. Open 9.30 a.m.–5.30 p.m. (until 6 p.m. May–November).

*Ballinastoe Studio Pottery*, Roundwood, telephone 01–2818151. 3 miles/5 km from Roundwood on the Enniskerry road.

*Bergin Clark Studio*, Ballinaclash, Rathdrum, telephone 0404–46385. Batik and silk prints.

*Boswell's*, The Mall, Main Street, Wicklow Town. This firm's gourmet natural sausages contain no preservatives and have to be consumed within twenty-four hours, so they're not suitable to bring back home. Do try them, however, as they taste delicious. Over twenty varieties made from pork, lamb and beef, including Beef and Guinness, Wicklow Lamb and Mint, and Spanish Chorizo.

*Elderbush Pottery*, Three Wells, Aughrim, telephone 0402–36468. Handmade pottery and ceramics with hand-brushed glazes.

*Glendalough Craft Centre*, telephone 0404–45156

*Mount Usher Craft Courtyard*, Ashford, telephone 0404–840205. A collection of potters and other craftworkers located at the entrance to the Mount Usher Gardens.

*Patrick Howard Pottery*, Church Hill, Wicklow, telephone 0404–67229

*Powerscourt Gardens Craft Shop*

*Tweedle Craft*, The Forge, Redcross, telephone 0404–41615. Upholstery, wrought-iron work.

*Wild Irish Crafts*, near Shillelagh, telephone 0503–56228. Natural pressed flowers. Visitors welcome.

Other craft outlets worth a visit are *Glendarragh Pottery* and *Wicklow Willow Crafts*, both in Roundwood, and *Holly Farm Pottery* in Rathdrum.

# DAYTIME ACTIVITIES AND SPORT

## ADVENTURE SPORTS

The Tiglin Adventure Centre, at the Devil's Glen near Ashford (3.5 miles/6 km), specialises in weekend and weekly courses in orienteering, caving, hang-gliding, hiking, mountaineering, rock-climbing, canoeing, snorkelling and surfing. For further details and booking, telephone 0404–40169.

Blessington Lakes Leisure Pursuits Centre, Burgage, Blessington, telephone 045–65092. Canoeing, hill-walking, sailing, pony-trekking, fishing, tennis, orienteering.

## ANGLING

Many of the rivers and lakes in County Wicklow abound in small brown trout, the principal stretches being the Rivers Aughrim, Avonmore, Avonbeg, Dargle, Liffey (below Golden Falls Lake), Slaney (below Blessington), Vartry Reservoir at Roundwood and the lakes at Poulaphouca. The latter lakes are also very good for coarse fishing. Sea trout can be had in the lower reaches of the Dargle, the Potters River (night fishing) and the Ennereilly River.

Along the coast, shore fishing is also popular at Greystones, Kilcoole, Arklow and Wicklow. The main fish are whiting and codling in winter, and bass and flat fish in summer.

## AQUA SPORTS

Many locations along the Wicklow coast including Bray, Brittas, Greystones, Wicklow and Arklow are suitable for sailing, windsurfing and boating.

## CYCLING

Bicycle hire, see page 138.

Guided cycle tours through Wicklow are organised each summer, telephone 0404–69117. Routes for individual cycle tours are detailed on pages 151–3.

## GAELIC GAMES

Wicklow's Gaelic football and hurling teams play regularly at the county grounds in Aughrim.

## GOLF

### 18-hole courses

Arklow Golf Club, telephone 0402–32492
Blainroe Golf Club, telephone 0404–68168/68246
Charlesland Golf and Country Club, telephone 01–2876764
Delgany Golf Club, telephone 01–2874536
The European Club, Brittas Bay, telephone 01–2804077
Greystones Golf Club, telephone 01–2874136

### 9-hole courses

Baltinglass Golf Club, telephone 0508–81350
Bray Golf Club, telephone 01–2862092
Coolattin Golf Club, telephone 055–29125
Kilcoole Golf Club, telephone 01–2872066
Tulfarris Golf Club, telephone 045–64574
Wicklow Golf Club, telephone 0404–67379
Woodenbridge Golf Club, telephone 0402–35202

## Par 3 courses
Bray Head, telephone 01–2865077
Rathdrum, Fun Park, telephone 0404–46149
Djouce Mountain Golf Club, off main Bray–Roundwood road, telephone 01–2818243

# HILL-WALKING

## The Wicklow Way

The first long-distance path in Ireland, opened for public use in 1981, the Wicklow Way follows a roughly north–south line, over the eastern flanks of the Dublin and Wicklow Mountains. The Way extends from Marlay Park in south County Dublin to Clonegal, County Carlow, traversing 82 miles/131 km of the largest unbroken area of high ground in Ireland. The whole region is very sparsely populated.

The route follows sheep tracks, forest firebreaks and old bog roads. Stout footwear and warm, waterproof clothing are essential. Strong walkers might expect to cover up to 20 miles/32 km in a day, but many may prefer to walk the entire Way in a week or more. Walkers are asked not to damage fences, crops or property belonging to farmers along the Way. Dogs should not be taken on the walk as it runs mainly through sheep country.

There is much wildlife to be seen along the route. Red deer and sika deer graze on many mountain slopes; hares, foxes, grouse and occasionally badgers appear, and squirrels frequent the forests. Watch out too for ravens, as well as herons and otters near rivers.

## How to get there

Take the 47 or 47B bus from Hawkins Street in Dublin to get to the starting-point of the Way in Marlay Park. Alternatively, take the buses that travel to Glencullen (No. 44B, quite infrequent), Enniskerry (Nos. 85/44) or Roundwood/Laragh (St Kevin's Bus Service) to join the Way at a later stage.

For information about hostels and guesthouses along the Way, see 'Where to Stay', page 142. The Ordnance Survey has published a special map covering the route. There's also a book, entitled *The Complete Wicklow Way Walks*, by J.B. Malone, whose idea it all was.

Comprehensive information on other walking routes in Wicklow is contained in several small, locally published books, most notably *Hill Walker's Wicklow* and *Hill Stroller's Wicklow* by David Herman. The first book lists a number of routes for climbing Lugnaquilla, Wicklow's highest peak.

Local tourist offices can also supply details of other walking possibilities. Wicklow Tourism publishes a series of six trail-sheets featuring walks at Annamoe, Laragh, Great Sugar Loaf, Baltinglass, Hollywood and Avoca. Each sheet features a circular walking route of about three hours' duration.

# HORSE-RIDING

County Wicklow offers wonderful opportunities for equestrian sports, and there are plenty of riding schools in the region:
Bel-Air Riding School, Ashford, telephone 0404–40109
Broom Lodge Stables, Nun's Cross, Ashford, telephone 0404–40404
Brennanstown Riding School, Hollybrook, Bray, telephone 01–2863778
Broomfield Riding School, Tinahely, telephone 0402–38117
Castle Howard Equestrian Centre, Avoca, telephone 0402–35164
Clarabeg, Roundwood, telephone 0404–46461
Clara Vale Riding Stables, Rathdrum, telephone 0404–45327
Cooladoyle Riding School, Newtownmountkennedy, telephone 01–2819906

Devil's Glen Holiday and Equestrian Village, Ashford, telephone 0404–40637
Forest Way Riding Holiday, Roundwood, telephone 01–2818429
Laragh Trekking Centre, Glendalough, telephone 0404–45282
Wicklow Trail Ride, Calliaghstown, telephone 01–4589236.

## PITCH AND PUTT

Arklow, telephone 0402–39016
Aughrim, telephone 0402–36267
Blessington, near ESB station, Poulaphouca

## SWIMMING
### Beaches

At least one-third of Wicklow's 30 miles/48 km of coastline consists of sandy beaches. Wicklow Town has a sand-shingle beach extending several miles north of the town. To the south are Silver Strand, Maghermore, and Jack's Hole, as well as Brittas Bay beach, which is 3 miles/5 km long. The beach at Bray and at Naylor's Cove, as well as the sandy beaches on each side of Arklow, are also safe for swimming. Only Brittas Bay (South and North) currently qualifies for the Blue Flag awarded by the European Community to beaches with high standards of water quality and beach management.

### Swimming pools

Avonbrae Guesthouse, Rathdrum, telephone 0404–46198
Old Court Park Sports & Fitness Centre, off Boghall Road, Bray, telephone 01–2829120
Presentation College, Bray, telephone 01–2867517
Corna Bay Leisure Club, telephone 0404–47228

Swimming in lakes and rivers is not recommended; both are prey to hidden currents that can cause problems through their force or the extreme coldness of the water. Swimming in reservoirs is prohibited.

## TENNIS

There are a number of tennis clubs in Wicklow which are open to visitors for a small charge:
Arklow Sports and Leisure Centre (indoor/outdoor, and squash), telephone 0402–39016. Opening hours 12.30–11 p.m.
Bray Lawn Tennis Club, Vevay Road
Avonbrae Guesthouse, Rathdrum, telephone 0404–46198. Grass court; summer only.
McGrath's, Rathdrum, telephone 0404–46327. Hard court; open all year.
Gelletlie's Jewellers, Main Street, Wicklow. Contact for four hard courts; open all year.
Greystones Lawn Tennis Club, telephone 01–2876505
Rivervalley, Redcross, telephone 0404–41647.

# CHILDREN'S ACTIVITIES

An Bóithrín Cam, Valleymount, Blessington, telephone 045–67332 is a traditional Wicklow hill farm which is open to the public. Meet the animals — cattle, pet lambs, pigs, goats, etc. — walk the farm or have a picnic on the grounds.
Annamoe Leisure Park (between Roundwood and Laragh) offers trout fishing, canoeing, a children's play area, picnic and barbeque facilities. Telephone 0404–45145. Open 10.30 a.m.–6.30 p.m. weekends in May/September, daily in June–August.

*Blue Gates Farm*, Ashford, telephone 0404–40573, is open to the public.
*Clara Lara Fun Park* (between Rathdrum and Laragh) has an adventure playground, junior play area, fishing, crazy golf, picnic and barbeque facilities. Telephone 0404–46161. Open Easter to October, 10.30 a.m.–6.30 p.m.
*National Aquarium*, Bray, telephone 01–2864688. Situated on the seafront in Bray, the aquarium holds more than 10,000 fish from all over the world. Open April–September 10 a.m.–9 p.m., October–March 10 a.m.–6 p.m.
*Par 3 Golf Course*, Rathdrum, features a boating lake, river fishing, children's play areas, picnic facilities as well as golf. Telephone 0404–46149.
An attraction of interest to adults and children alike, *Peatland World* in Rathdangan, Co. Kildare, telephone 045–60133 is an attempt to interpret the wildlife, flora and fauna of the boglands that dominate the landscapes of central Ireland. It also looks at man's exploitation of the bogs for fuel and fertiliser, among other things.
*Turlough Hill* is an underground power station close to Glendalough. Water, pumped up to a reservoir overnight, is released to generate hydroelectricity as needed during the day. The view from the reservoir in clear weather is spectacular. Open April to October by appointment only (telephone 0404–45113). No charge.

# BICYCLE TOURS

County Wicklow, with its quiet roads and wonderful scenery, is ideal terrain for the energetic cyclist. Those less accustomed to long hours in the saddle are advised to stick to the flatter coastal strip, but the mountains offer the most exciting routes, as well as the most peaceful roads. The routes described in 'Wicklow Tours' can just as easily be cycled as part of a multi-day tour as driven. Although guesthouses are few and far between in the mountains, there is a good network of quite spartan youth hostels and it isn't hard to find suitable areas for camping. Travel equipped with repair kits and wet-weather gear, as shops and shelter are not always at hand.

There follows a selection of day tours starting in Dublin, and a number of all-Wicklow itinerary suggestions. Consult the ensuing sections for information on the towns and sites visited; see also the bicycle tours suggested for the Dublin area.

**Sugar Loaf** (34 mile/54 km round trip from city centre)
The big Sugar Loaf is by no means Wicklow's highest mountain, but it is certainly the county's most distinctive peak. It looks like a volcano, but the quartzite rock of which it is composed was formed 500 million years ago and has remained undisturbed since.

Head south from Dublin's city centre towards Dundrum. Continue south on the Sandyford Road, climbing gradually towards the Scalp, where the steep valley sides are strewn with giant boulders seemingly ready to fall down onto the road. The road drops into the secluded village of Enniskerry, with its central square and the Powerscourt Estate and Waterfall nearby. Continue straight on, passing the Catholic church, which dates from 1843 and was the first Gothic-revival-style church in the country. The Protestant church is further on on the left.

Cross the Dargle River at Tinnehinch and push upwards, ignoring the first signpost for Kilmacanogue and turning right, away from this destination, at the second signpost. Near the top of the climb, turn left to where the path leading to the summit of the Sugar Loaf begins. This point offers fine views of the surrounding mountains to the west and south, but the view is even better from the summit, which is relatively easy to climb.

Return to Dublin by descending eastward on a narrow and twisting route to the main Dublin–Wexford road. This road suffers from heavy traffic but provides the quickest return to the capital.

**Glencree** (Round trip 29 miles/46 km)

This route follows the Glencree Valley, one of the most beautiful in County Wicklow, to the small hamlet of the same name. Glencree is home to a reconciliation centre and war cemetery but no pub, a youth hostel but no hotel.

Head south from Dublin to Rathfarnham. Turn right here past the Yellow House pub and continue straight on to Ballyboden. After two sets of traffic lights, turn right over the Owendoher River and then left. From here there is an unceasing heavy climb into the mountains for 8 miles/13 km, but it's well worth the effort.

The route passes the car park leading to the Hellfire Club (see pages 114–15) on the right and emerges at Killakee, where the splendour of Dublin Bay unfolds. Continue climbing over the Featherbed Mountains into County Wicklow. The road is less steep here, and surrounded by peat bogs. Far below, the reservoir at Glenasmole can be seen and the peak of Kippure with its TV mast lies at the head of the valley. Eventually, the road drops into the valley formed by the River Glencree. Continue until you come to an abandoned cottage on the right. Behind this is the charming Lough Bray, tucked below the Eagle's Crag east of Kippure.

Double back and take the second turn right to Glencree. Be sure to visit the tranquil German War Graves Cemetery before travelling down the valley towards Enniskerry. After Curtlestown, turn left towards Glencullen up and down an extremely steep valley. Return to the city via Stepaside and Sandyford.

The following itineraries are suggested for longer trips on the bicycle:

— Bray — Enniskerry — Glencree — Sally Gap — Lough Tay — Roundwood — spur to Lough Dan — Newtownmountkennedy — Glen of the Downs — Bray. 40 miles/64 km. A tough climb into the heart of the mountains, but well worth it on a fine day.

— Blessington — Russborough House — Poulaphouca — Dunlavin — Baltinglass — Kiltegan — Rathdangan — Glen of Imaal — Donard — Castleruddery — Blessington. 60 miles/96 km. A lengthy tour of west Wicklow, including the isolated Glen of Imaal, nestling under Lugnaquilla, the highest mountain in the county.

— Blessington — Sally Gap (lake road) — Glenmacnass — Laragh — spur to Glendalough — Wicklow Gap — Valleymount — Ballyknockan — Blessington. 50 miles/80 km. The mountains again, approached from the west of the county.

# WICKLOW TOURS

### TOUR 1: EAST WICKLOW

The coastal towns of Bray and Greystones are dealt with in 'Dublin Tours' and are easily accessible by train or Dublin Bus. This route therefore enters Wicklow inland at Enniskerry. A car is necessary to cover the complete route, but individual stops can be reached using public transport and connections are indicated where appropriate.

To get to Enniskerry, which is 12 miles/19 km south of Dublin, take the No. 44 bus from Hawkins Street.

**Enniskerry** is a pretty village, built around a central square and surrounded by wooded hills. However, the main reason for coming to the village, and a very good one it is too, is to visit the nearby Powerscourt Estate and Gardens (telephone 01–2867676. Open daily 9 a.m.–5.30 p.m., March to October). Powerscourt House was one of the great Georgian houses of Ireland until it was burned down accidentally in 1974. Today only a shell of the building designed around 1730 by Richard Cassels, the architect of Russborough House (see below), remains. However, the gardens at Powerscourt, which were first laid out between 1745 and 1767 and redesigned between 1843 and 1875, survive intact.

Powerscourt House was built using granite quarried locally and commanded beautiful views of the Dargle Valley and the mountains behind. Ironically, it had just undergone costly refurbishment and was about to be opened to the public when disaster struck in 1974. The owners threw a party before the official opening and lit a fire in the Morning Room, which had not been used for a long time. The chimney caught fire but the blaze was extinguished — or so it was thought. That night, the house burned down.

Since then, several plans to rebuild the mansion have been put forward, but so far nothing has come of these and the house remains a ruin to this day.

The gardens were inspired by Italian models, and feature sweeping terraces, classical sculptures and a circular pond. With the mountain backdrop the overall effect is dramatic, if a little kitschy. But the vast grounds have much more to offer, and are ideal for a brisk walk or a picnic. There is an arboretum with a Sitka spruce thought to be Ireland's tallest tree, a Japanese garden and a pets' cemetery. At the far end of the estate — there is a path but most people will want to drive the 3 miles/

5 km to get there — is the Powerscourt waterfall (open daily 10.30 a.m.–7 p.m.). Nestling under Djouce Mountain, this cascading 400-foot (122 m) waterfall is the largest in the British Isles.

Gardening enthusiasts might wish to indulge their passions a little more by making a detour to the nearby Dargle Glen Gardens, 2 miles/3 km south of Bray. The ornate gardens and canals of Kilruddery House (telephone 01–2863405. Open daily 1–5 p.m. in May, June and September), immediately off the Bray–Greystones road just south of Bray, date back to the seventeenth century and are also worth a visit.

Our main tour, however, proceeds southwards from Enniskerry to **Roundwood**, which at an altitude of 900 feet/274 m is said to be the highest village in Ireland. Turn right in the village (there's also a turning before the village) in the direction of Sally Gap. This narrow road rises steeply into the heart of the Wicklow Mountains, offering breathtaking views of its peaks and passing two beautiful lakes, Lough Tay and the more distant Lough Dan, far below on the left. The area around the lakes forms part of a large estate owned by the Guinness brewing family. The area is private property and not open to cars, but you are allowed to walk down to the lakes. The stretch between Lough Tay and Lough Dan is one of the nicest easy walks (the valley floor is flat) in the whole of Wicklow.

The road continues through bare uplands, devoid of any cultivation or settlement apart from a few meagre tree plantations. It peaks at the barren crossroads at Sally Gap — Sally is derived from the Irish for willow — where we turn left towards Glendalough. This route is the Military Road, built by the British after the rebellion of 1798 to fight off attacks on Dublin from Irish marauders taking refuge in the hills. The road bisects the Wicklow Mountains, starting at Rathfarnham in County Dublin and ending at a military barracks at Aughavannagh in the deep south of County Wicklow.

The road continues through the upland bogs until it drops onto the floor of the valley formed by the Glenmacnass River — stop at the top, before the descent begins, to admire the lovely waterfall of the same name, on the right. Take due care on the rocks.

At the end of the valley is Laragh, the nearest village to the ancient monastic site of Glendalough, which is 2 miles/3 km to the west.

Apart from its historical heritage, **Glendalough** ('glen of the two lakes') is one of the most beautiful valleys in Ireland. It can also be one of the most crowded, especially at weekends and at peak season. Those without a car can reach it using the St Kevin's Bus Service (see 'Travel', pages 140–41) which offers a daily round trip that makes for a pleasant excursion.

Glendalough has a youth hostel and a hotel, so it's a good place for an overnight stop. There is also plenty of B&B accommodation on the road to Laragh.

It was St Kevin, reputedly of a noble family, who first came to the secluded valley in the sixth century to live the life of a hermit. However, his peace was short-lived as acolytes came to visit from near and far, and a monastic settlement was founded by the lakes in 545. In spite of repeated attacks from the Vikings in the ninth and tenth centuries, the settlement continued to grow until English forces overran it in 1398. Substantial ruins remain about both lakes and all are freely accessible to visitors. There is also a modern visitors' centre, which has an audio-visual presentation explaining the history of Glendalough and provides guided tours on request. Open 10 a.m.–5 p.m. daily, longer in summer (closed Mondays from November to mid-March), telephone 0404–45325.

The most distinctive building here is the perfectly preserved round tower, probably built in the eleventh or twelfth century, which stands 100 feet/30.5 m high. Entry to the first storey of the tower, which rises 25 feet/7.5 m off the ground, was by means of a ladder; this could be pulled in rapidly in the event of a Viking attack. The largest building is the roofless cathedral, which dates from the ninth century at the latest. Nearby is St Kevin's Cross, 11 feet/3.5 m high and the best-preserved cross on the site.

St Kevin's Church is an early example of an oratory, and has two storeys and a high-pitched stone roof. While the ruins by the Lower Lake are the largest and most important on the site, those by the Upper Lake are generally the oldest. Both Teampall na Sceilig (Church of the Oratory) on the southern shore of the Upper Lake, and Reefert Church, at the south-east corner, date from St Kevin's time. On the far side of the lake, inaccessible except by boat, is St Kevin's Bed, a tiny cave in the rock-face about 30 feet (9 m) above the water level. This is where the saint is said to have hidden away as a hermit.

The whole area is covered by nature trails and pathways, and is well signposted. For more serious walkers, it's a good base for longer walks into the heart of the mountains, and rock-climbers are attracted to the rock-faces up the valley from the Upper Lake.

From Glendalough return to Laragh and drive south in the direction of **Rathdrum**, 13 miles/21 km away. About 1 mile/1.5 km south of the town is the entrance to Avondale Forest Park, which spreads over 500 acres/202.5 hectares and covers the old demesne of Avondale House (telephone 0404–46111. Open daily 10 a.m. to 1 p.m., 2–6 p.m. May–September, 12 noon–6 p.m. at weekends October–April).

Avondale is famous as the birthplace and home of Charles Stewart Parnell, the Protestant landlord who espoused the cause of Irish nationalism and became the most revered Irish politician of the nineteenth century until his downfall as a result of an adulterous affair. Parnell's love for Kitty O'Shea, wife of a parliamentary colleague, scandalised Victorian society and split the Irish nationalist movement in two. After Parnell died in

Brighton in 1891, at the age of only forty-five, the scars ran so deep in Irish society that they took a generation to heal.

The house at Avondale was built in 1779 and acquired by Parnell's great-grandfather at the end of the eighteenth century. In recent years, it has been thoroughly restored and today contains a museum devoted to Parnell, his life and his fight for home rule for Ireland. The surrounding estate is heavily planted with trees, and in 1904 was the first forest to be taken over by the State. There is an enjoyable 3.5 mile/6 km walk which takes in much of the estate and skirts the Avondale River.

A few miles further south is the small village of **Avoca**, set in densely wooded hills near where the Avonmore and Avonbeg Rivers join. This spot, supposedly, is the inspiration for Thomas Moore's famous song 'The Meeting of the Waters':

> There is not in the wide world a valley so sweet
> As that vale in whose bosom the bright waters meet . . .

Moore, who penned many celebrated songs in the early nineteenth century, is commemorated with a statue at the junction of Dublin's Westmoreland and College Streets (his figure stands by a public toilet, prompting scurrilous comments by Joyce and others about another 'Meeting of the Waters'). When Moore was asked afterwards exactly where he was describing in the song, he couldn't remember, so this legend may be nothing more than good old-fashioned Irish blarney.

Avoca Handweavers (telephone 0402–35105), the oldest handweaving mill in Ireland, is well worth a visit. The way south leads to the pretty village of Woodenbridge, where the Avonmore and Avoca Rivers meet (was this the real Meeting of the Waters?). This was the area where the gold for many of the great artefacts displayed in the National Museum was mined, and there was a latter-day gold rush here in 1795 after a large nugget was found locally.

**Arklow**, 5 miles/8 km to the east on the coast, is a largish industrial and fishing centre that has little to offer the visitor except a small Maritime Museum near the railway station and wonderful expanses of sandy beach. These extend for miles north and south of the town. Further to the north, Brittas Bay is the best-known beach in the county.

The far south of County Wicklow is marked by more gentle scenery than in the mountains to the north; the attractive village of Shillelagh with its stone cottages and Coolattin Wood, 2 miles/3 km to the east, are worth a detour. Coolattin is one of the last native woods in the country and supplied the timber used in the roof of St Patrick's Cathedral in Dublin. Sadly, its survival is threatened by the desire of business interests to fell many of the trees.

The main tour, however, continues north from Arklow along the coastline towards **Wicklow Town**. On the way, there are many excellent bathing-spots, most notably Brittas Bay and, further north, Silver Strand. Wicklow Town itself is unremarkable, though the area around the port is pleasant. South of the harbour is the ruin of the Black Castle, which was built by an Anglo-Norman lord who arrived with the English invasion of Ireland in 1169. The town's Protestant church is an eighteenth-century building, but it stands on a more ancient site, and the Romanesque door in the porch dates from the twelfth century. There are fragments of a thirteenth-century Franciscan friary on the main street. Nearby is a Heritage Centre which provides information on the county's history as well as genealogical services.

From Wicklow Town, drive 4 miles/6.5 km north-west towards **Ashford**. Just before the village are the Mount Usher Gardens (telephone 0404–40205), which cover 20 acres/7 hectares on each side of the River Vartry. Over 5,000 different species of trees, shrubs and plants are collected here in an exotic blaze of eucalyptus, azalea, rhododendrons and much more. The site was formerly a mill, but was converted to gardens by the Walpole family from 1868. There are also a number of craft shops, a restaurant and a bookshop, grouped together at the entrance.

A few miles up the road towards Annamoe, the Devil's Glen is a wooded chasm where the River Vartry tumbles and cascades downwards amid the thick forests. The area is well signposted and the trails reveal the plunging river in all its beauty.

Return via Ashford to the main Dublin–Wexford road, from which the capital can be reached in less than an hour.

## TOUR 2: WEST WICKLOW

Leave Dublin on the N81 by the south-western suburb of **Tallaght**. A quiet village until twenty-five years ago, Tallaght was the place to which many former residents of Dublin's inner city were relocated, and it is now one of Ireland's largest towns. However, for years its lines of solid, grey houses were unbroken by the most basic of facilities such as shops, churches or schools. Of late, there has been some catching up, and today the main road to Blessington passes the country's biggest shopping and cinema complex (known as The Square, though its large glass roof is shaped like a pyramid) on the right.

**Blessington**, 20 miles/32 km from Dublin, is a market town laid out on one long, broad street by Michael Boyle, an Archbishop of Dublin in the seventeenth century. The Protestant church, with its four-pointed tower, was begun about 1682. Much of Blessington was destroyed in the rebellion of 1798, but rebuilding started early in the nineteenth century. Today, the town thrives as a tourist centre and day-trip destination for Dubliners, who throng its pubs and hotels at the weekends. The No. 65 bus from Crampton Quay, by the Ha'penny Bridge, travels to the town.

About 2 miles/3 km south of the town is **Russborough House** (telephone 045–65239. Open 10.30 a.m.–5.30 p.m. Sundays/public holidays from Easter to the end of October, except June–August when the house is open daily), a fine Palladian mansion built in grey Wicklow granite between 1740 and 1750 by the architect Richard Cassels (or Castle). Unlike so many other Irish great homes, Russborough and its surrounding estate have survived the years intact, so the house and its location can be viewed as they were originally conceived.

At 700 feet (210 m), the frontage is the longest in Ireland and consists of a central block and two semicircular arcades extending to embrace the wings. The approach is from one side, so the length and richness of the façade unfolds itself gradually. As one writer put it, 'no other Irish house is strung out so extravagantly as Russborough'.

Inside, the lofty rooms are lavishly decorated with the baroque plasterwork of the Lafranchini brothers which is found in so many of the great Irish houses of the mid-eighteenth century. The house is furnished with a fine collection of period furniture, statuary and porcelain.

However, Russborough's chief joy is its art collection, which includes works by Goya, Velázquez, Gainsborough, Vermeer and Rubens. While the first paintings were bought in Rome by the original owner of Russborough, the bulk came with the current proprietor, Sir Alfred Beit, a South African-born millionaire who bought the house in 1952. The best paintings were taken for ransom by the IRA in 1974, but were quickly recovered. In 1987 Sir Alfred donated seventeen of them to the National Gallery, but before these were transferred, a number of paintings were stolen again and have remained missing. Every so often one turns up (in one case, as far away as Turkey), as criminals trying to sell them on the black market are exposed. The hope is that all will eventually be recovered.

The house stands in 200 acres/81 hectares of wooded estate, with an artificial lake and views of the Poulaphouca Reservoir and the Wicklow Mountains beyond.

Two west Wicklow scenes: magnificent Russborough House (*left*) and a peaceful corner of Blessington lakes (*above*)

Return to Blessington, and branch right after the village in the direction of Manor Kilbride. (An alternative route is to continue south to Hollywood, and then turn left to reach Glendalough over the Wicklow Gap. Glendalough is covered in the East Wicklow tour.)

The great Poulaphouca Reservoir, which provides most of Dublin's water, lies on the right. Originally, Poulaphouca was a succession of cascades down which the River Liffey rushed from the mountains, but today with the flooding of the area for the reservoir and hydroelectric scheme, it's a much more peaceful place. The drive around the perimeter of the lake is pleasant; on returning from Russborough, take the first right turn from the main road before Blessington and travel anti-clockwise around the lake, keeping it on the left at all times. This route passes through the small villages of Valleymount, Lackan and Ballyknockan before rejoining the main tour on the Blessington–Manor Kilbride road.

Follow the signs for Manor Kilbride and turn right, onto the R759 towards Sally Gap. The surrounding bog is big and wild, and only a few sheep survive up here. The road passes the Coronation Plantation to the right, which was started to celebrate the coronation of King William IV in 1830 but quickly became a failure.

Turn left at Sally Gap crossroads, towards Glencree and Dublin. Look out for people cutting turf; it's possible to lease a plot of bog for this purpose. The turf is cut out of the bog in big slabs and chopped into manageable lengths. It is then left in piles to dry out (somewhat) before being taken down to the city. During World War II, or the Emergency as it was known in Ireland, imported fuel was scarce and large areas of the Wicklow Mountains were mined for turf. The tradition survives today as a cottage industry practised by the hardy few.

The narrow road from Sally Gap at one stage crosses a bridge only metres from the source of the great River Liffey, at this point only a trickle from the bog. Kippure Mountain with its TV antenna atop looms to the left and behind it lies Upper Lough Bray. Just before Glencree, beside an abandoned cottage on the left (the first sign of human settlement for miles) is Lower Lough Bray, which is very near the road but not visible from it. This is a splendid little lake which nestles under a cliff known as the Eagle's Crag. The walk through the gorse to the upper lough and on up to the clifftop reveals lovely views of the lakes and the beautiful Glencree river valley stretching towards the sea.

John Millington Synge (1871–1909), one of the founders of the Abbey Theatre and the author of *The Playboy of the Western World* and *Riders to the Sea*, spent many summers from boyhood on walking, cycling and fishing both here and throughout Wicklow. Synge drew inspiration from the county and its people for his lyrical essays, a number of his poems and four of his seven plays.

The second turn on the right leads down to the hamlet of Glencree, where the former military barracks now serves as a centre for reconciliation. The village also contains a tastefully laid-out German War Graves Cemetery, a poignant reminder of the horrors of the two world wars this century, and of Ireland's good fortune not to have participated in either of them (hundreds of thousands of Irish fought with the British Army in both wars, but there was no conscription here during the First World War and the newly independent Irish Free State remained neutral during the Second World War).

The final section of the Military Road before Dublin is as beautiful as any that has gone before. The road climbs from Glencree and rises high above the Glenasmole Valley (the Thrush's Glen) and its small reservoir, below on the left. At Killakee, a stunning panorama of Dublin Bay and the city unfolds. The return to the city centre is via Rathfarnham and Terenure.

# ECOTOUR

The ecotour of Wicklow covers an extensive area and may best be undertaken by car. Public transport, train or bus, will take us part of the way, through the coastal regions of the county or from Dublin south to Glendalough. The rest of the region has to be traversed by car, bicycle or on foot.

The ideal way to explore Wicklow is on foot, and the best route to take is the Wicklow Way. This brings the hiker from Marlay Park in south County Dublin across the hills that rise above Dublin city and from there into Wicklow. One passes through a number of conifer woodlands that are managed by Coillte, the semi-state forestry company. On other sections one is alone on vast stretches of blanket bog or crossing quiet mountain streams or rivers. The route can be covered in seven or eight days' walking and is well worth the effort if you have time and energy to spare. Bring wet-weather clothing, invest in a good map and a guidebook and make sure people know what your itinerary is. Do not be lulled into a false sense of security: people have been lost for days on the Wicklow and Dublin Mountains in spite of the number of hikers and climbers that use these hills.

## BRAY

Our journey through Wicklow starts at the town of Bray south from Dublin along the N11. Drive into the town and take the first left turn to the DART station and the esplanade on the coast. Not far down the promenade is the National Aquarium, which boasts the most extensive collection of marine organisms in the world and is worth a visit if time permits.

**Stop and walk** Bray Head to Greystones 3 miles/5 km

We park at the foot of Bray Head and make our way along the coast to the old cable-car line, about 10 minutes away. After this the walk levels out around the headland and slopes gently into Greystones, the rocks rising above and falling away below. As is to be expected on a coastal cliff walk like this, seabirds abound. There are colonies of nesting gulls, and it is an excellent site at which to observe guillemots: these auks are black, with the exception of their white wings, and nest in scattered groups along the cliffs. The other bird of note is the Manx shearwater, an elusive creature that nests in burrows in the soils above the cliffs. It comes and goes mainly at night and so is impossible to see by day; the noise of it returning to its burrow may be the only way to 'observe' this bird. But if you are going out at night to listen, remember this is a cliff walk.

Cormorants and shags both nest on ledges along the rocks below the cliff walk.

The rock of Bray Head is quartzite interlayered with bands of shale and dates back over 600 million years to the Cambrian era. In the shale the fossil remains of a simple seaweed, *Oldhamia radiata*, are found. The quartzite is composed of old sandstones altered by heat or pressure into the present structure. Resistant to the weathering forces of wind and rain, it now stands out above the softer rocks that once overlay it. During the most recent glaciation of the Wicklow region, Bray Head was covered by a glacier and its top smoothed off; otherwise it would have a conical outline much like that of the Little and Great Sugar Loafs.

The plants seen include bracken, ling and bell heather in heathland areas. Along the cliffs are sea pink, sea campion and white stonecrop, and the less common sea mallow and sea samphire.

At a leisurely pace this walk can be done in 2–2.5 hours. Spectacular views across the Irish Sea and of the cliff below accompany us along the route round the head.

After 1 hour the cliff gives way to woodland and grass pastures. On the seaward side the rocks are replaced by glacial drift and the line of the land is seen to be straight as far as Greystones. The sea is slowly but steadily wearing away at the soft drift material. The path reaches sea level at Greystones and one can walk along the beach of mainly shingle. Turnstones, purple sandpiper and ringed plover are among the birds to look out for here.

Between Greystones and Wicklow Town the coastline is, for the most part, trouble-free. Indeed a relatively undemanding walk is possible from Greystones south to Wicklow, with the sea on the east and the railway track and land to the west.

**Link** Greystones to Kilcoole 2.5 miles/4 km

A better strategy may be to continue by road from Greystones to Kilcoole, where a left turn takes us down to the coast. Parking at the old railway station, we head out onto the beach at this point. Along the landward side a series of wetlands provides refuge for wildfowl in the winter. This area is an important wintering site for the swans of Dublin city too. Many of the flocks congregate to feed in the reeds and rushes; in the summer the unpaired swans may remain here.

Also in the summer little terns nest along this section of coast. Any developments that increase traffic here are a threat to the habitat of these birds. The Irish Wildlife Federation has a scheme to protect these ground nesters during their most vulnerable periods at the nest.

Below Newcastle and on the way to Wicklow reed-warblers are heard, if not seen, from the beds of reeds and rushes abundant in the area.

**Link** Wicklow Town to Rathdrum 9.5 miles/15 km

From Wicklow Town we take the T7 north to Rathnew and then south-west through Glenealy to Rathdrum. The valley through which we drive is wooded with a selection of conifer and deciduous species. This gives us a picture of what Ireland would be like if forests took up between 20 and 35 per cent of the countryside, as they do in Europe. Wicklow is Ireland's most heavily wooded county, with about 23 per cent of the land devoted to forestry.

Rathdrum village is set in on the hillside overlooking the Avonmore River.

**Link** Rathdrum to Avondale 1 mile/1.5 km
**Stop and walk**

Just south of the village is Avondale Forest Park, former home of Charles Stewart Parnell and now used as a facility for forest management courses and as an amenity park by Coillte.

One of the key features of this park is the large selection of conifers and broadleaves that were planted there. The State Forestry service planted as wide a range of trees as possible in order to determine what species were best suited to Irish conditions. The two trees that today dominate Irish forestry, Lodgepole pine and Sitka spruce, do not feature as good specimens because soil and climatic conditions militate against them at this site, but there are splendid examples of Western hemlock, redwoods, Douglas fir, Spanish chestnuts and Serbian spruces to be seen. Near the house a stand of eucalyptus towers above the surrounding trees. Close by is a collection of maples from around the world.

A wide, grassed avenue runs from the house downhill towards the Avonmore River. Along this avenue blocks of different tree species were planted; at the edge of each block is a sample that shows what an open situation and plenty of light can do for a tree.

The river is wide and curves gently through the valley, giving us a broad view and a chance to glimpse a kingfisher in flight.

**Link** Rathdrum to Laragh via Clara Valley 7.5 miles/12 km

We leave Rathdrum by the T61, which follows the valley through which the Avonmore River flows from Laragh. Much of the route along this road is forested with Scots pine, larch, Douglas fir, Norway spruce and Western red hemlock.

About 4.5 miles/7 km from Laragh the woodlands change from conifers to oak with a mixture of ash, rowan, beech and sycamore. Many of these trees are over a hundred years old and merit a brief stop for a walk through them. There is little evidence of regeneration, a result of sheep, deer and rabbits constantly grazing on the woodland floor and preventing the growth of saplings. In some areas the woods have been fenced off, which has the effect of immediately allowing growth of young trees, and a more mixed group is seen. Where trees fail to generate, the woods become even-aged and might as well be managed for timber, so little variety is there.

On the forest floor the vegetation is mainly deer-grass, a broadleaved grass with hair-lined margins. Deer-grass is found growing with bilberry in these woods; their presence indicates the acid nature of the soil and the moist conditions which prevail.

These woodlands are man-made, planted at a time when oak would have been used in charcoal and fence-post production and managed for such products through the practice of pollarding. Pollarded trees were cut back to the base of the trunk and new stems sprouted from the stump remaining. At first there would have been many of these stems; with time some were thinned out, the first cut yielding light stakes and the later harvests heavier stakes suitable for fencing. Some may also have been cut for charcoal production. A few were left to thicken and eventually just one stem may have been left on the stump to mature for 100 years or more. It is still possible to pick out trees where two or even three stems are growing from one stump, a sign of the management that has taken place. Indeed, as already noted, unless woods such as these are managed, animals like deer and rabbits will effectively kill the trees off in a few decades by preventing their regeneration.

The woods of Ireland had all but vanished by the end of the seventeenth century. A growing population hungry for fuel, bands of travelling saw-millers, and charcoal manufacturing for the smelting of ores were the main reasons for the depletion — that and a failure to replant trees. By the eighteenth century most of the landscape had a denuded appearance about it. Where people could no longer find wood or turf for fuel, gorse or furze was burned.

The result of all this felling has been the total annihilation of native woodlands. Today the oakwoods that do remain are at best semi-natural, the consequence of replanting on sites considered too poor for the production of tillage crops. Estimates of the area of these semi-natural oakwoods are about 210,000 acres/85,000 hectares.

### Stop and walk

If there is time we can walk through the oakwoods down into Glendalough and the interpretative centre there. Turning left onto the Military Road that leads to Drumgoff bridge and Glenmalure Valley, we enter the oakwoods on the right about 658 feet/200 m up the hill. This is part of the Wicklow Way and is signposted as such. Even though the direction of the route is southerly it takes us back towards Laragh and the Glendalough Valley.

### DIVERSION INTO GLENMALURE 4.5 MILES/7 KM

We follow the Military Road across the hill to the site of the ruins of Drumgoff barracks. On the northern side of the road is Cullentragh Mountain while on the south is Kirikee, and as we enter Glenmalure Carriglinneen Mountain rises steeply above the road. Once at the crossroads we are in Glenmalure Valley. Standing on the bridge, over the Avonbeg River and near the ruins of Drumgoff barracks, we get a view of the shape of this countryside. The valley is broad and flat-bottomed, which hints at the factors in its shaping. No river gorged out this valley, otherwise the walls would slope in to give a V-shape. Instead what we see is the work of a glacier that moved along this valley well over 10,000 years ago, between the peaks of Mullacor and Lugnaquilla, Leinster's highest mountain. As the ice melted, the glacier retreated and the valley floor was left with a mix of coarse-textured gravels of granite origin. At the western end of the valley the Avonbeg rises on Table Mountain and its narrow twisting route into Glenmalure gives some indication of what the valley looked like prior to the appearance of the glacier. Several rivers flow in from the surrounding mountains, crossing valleys which were abruptly truncated by the same glacier, now termed hanging valleys.

Lugnaquilla is a mountain of interest to geologists and climbers alike. The peak is at 3,039 feet/924 m, which just qualifies it as a Munro, a mountain over 3,000 feet/912 m high. All the peaks of Britain and Ireland above this arbitrary cut-off point were identified and now are a challenge to a particular breed of mountaineer. The Munro-baggers climb with only one objective, the summit and a tick against that peak on their log of Munros. The more climbed in one day the better.

As a geological phenomenon the peak of Lugnaquilla marks the heart of the Wicklow granites. Above the granite here is a layer of schist, rock that covered the region and into which molten granite poured from deep below the earth's crust some 300 million years ago.

The climb to the summit is a relatively easy one from the car park at the western end of the valley. A number of guides to routes up are available. Bring a good map and, if you can use one, a compass. Mists descend rapidly on this mountain and leave the walker cut off. Though the mountain is heavily used, many have been lost on the slopes.

We return to Laragh along the same road out of Glenmalure Valley.

On the road back the woodland floor is covered in hard fern, wood-sorrel and bluebells. Rhododendron, the scourge of Irish oakwoods, also occurs. This large and spectacular flowering shrub was introduced into Ireland as a garden plant and has taken well to the moist, damp and acid soils on which many of Ireland's oakwoods remain. The deep shade that it casts prevents the germination of other plants, and, to aggravate matters, deer do not feed on rhododendron and so its growth is unimpeded. In the national parks at Killarney and Glenveagh work-camps are organised each summer to combat this exotic, with groups of ten to fifteen people cutting, burning and spraying. As the plant produces a light seed in large quantities it can spread far and wide, so control of this weed will take years to achieve.

**Link** Laragh to Glendalough Valley 2.5 miles/4 km

On the road into Laragh we pass over the Avonmore River and into the village. Turning left at the village green, the road takes us into Glendalough Valley. On the southern side of the road is Derry Bawn while the hill on the northern side is called Brockagh. 'Broc' is the Irish for badger and the name here may refer to the dwelling-place of badgers.

The features of Glendalough Valley are attributable firstly to glaciers that scoured out the valley floor and left the two hollows now filled by the Upper and Lower Lakes, and, in the more recent past, to humans who cleared the woodlands from the area to produce charcoal for smelting of ores. Nineteenth-century prints of the valley show a devastated landscape. The tower and ruins of the churches stand alone in a barren and bleak vista. That the whole could be transformed so radically through the planting of trees shows the recuperative powers of nature. Along the valley walls of the Upper Lake scree tumbles into the transparent waters. The divide between the two lakes is gravel washed into the valley floor from the stream that enters the Avonbeg from the slopes of Mullacor.

**Stop and walk**

A car park at the Upper Lake gives access to the wooded sides of the valley. A number of guided walks are laid out along the rivers and up through the oakwoods. There is a small interpretative centre to the east along the valley which deals with the natural history of the area and is open in the summer months.

The clearness of most of Wicklow's streams and rivers is testimony to the chemistry of the waters and the underlying granite rocks. The brown coloration is due to humic acids extracted from the peats that the rivers all flow through. The clarity of the water is due to a lack of plankton, in turn a result of the acidity of the granite. With few nutrients in the water not many microscopic plants and animals live to cloud it. The natural acidity of these upland waters mean they are very vulnerable to additions of chemicals which further raise the level. When this happens aluminium in the surrounding soils may be released, affecting the eggs and gills of fish. An increase in acidity may also reduce insect numbers and thus the quantity of food available to fish in the waters. A suspect in the process of increasing river acidity in upland areas is conifer woodlands. The movement of rainfall through the canopy of these trees washes chemicals from the leaves into mountain streams and may cause acidity levels to go beyond a manageable level. Current planting policy in forests prevents the afforestation of upland areas on acid rocks in the vicinity of streams and rivers.

There are two ways out of Glendalough: the first is by Lough Nahangan and Blessington; the second is through Glenmacnass and over the Sally Gap. These routes are given as Links 1 and 2.

**Link 1** Glendalough, Lough Nahanagan, Blessington Reservoir, Blessington 19 miles/30 km

Leaving the valley by the R756 or L107 brings us our first real glimpse of the Wicklow uplands. The wooded valley slopes give way to open tracts of blanket bog as the road runs along the line of the Glendasan River.

On the left along the far banks the spoil from former lead-mines can be seen. The mining industry in Wicklow flourished for many years in an on-off fashion. One of the main attractions of the region was the gold to be found in the rivers. Some of Wicklow's rivers still yield gold to the patient prospector. Patience is the key word. Many hours of panning in freezing waters may grant only a few flecks of gold but gold there will be.

Along this road and to the left is Lough Nahangan. This lake sits in a corrie, a shallow depression scooped out of a mountainside in one of the several glaciations that occurred in the region. The term corrie comes from the Gaelic for a cauldron, an indication of the importance of the Irish landscape in the study of past glaciations and their impact. This lake provides evidence that there was 12,500 years ago a brief warming in the climate. Plants began to recolonise a slowly thawing Arctic landscape. Temperatures were as high as they are nowadays for a few hundred years and then suddenly there was a cold snap. The climate deteriorated and a small glacier formed again at the corrie where Lough Nahangan is now. The spell did not last long and about 10,000 years ago the Irish climate was much as it is today.

All the evidence for the theory lies in the muds that are found in ridges beneath the lake's waters. The muds contain the pollen of plants that grew between these cold spells; from an analysis of this, botanists can say what plants grew in the region and therefore what the climate was like. Lough Nahangan served as the first example of this warming and then abrupt but short-lived freezing, and gives its name to the Lough Nahangan interstadial.

Above the Lough is a power station and Turlough Hill Reservoir. The Electricity Supply Board pumps water from the Lower Lake at night when power consumption is low and allows the water from the upper reservoir to flow downhill through the turbines to generate the electricity. The flattened top of Turlough Hill stands out on the skyline from many of the higher peaks around Co. Wicklow and should be easily distinguished. A line of pylons marches east along the valley above the road carrying the power generated.

The road now passes through the Wicklow Gap. The mountain on the right or northern side of the road is Tonelagee or 'backside to the wind', a name that refers to the shape of the mountain and the exposed nature of the area. On the southern side of the road is The Fair Mountain.

The route takes us on to Blessington Reservoir. A former river valley, it was flooded in the 1930s and the dammed water used to generate electricity at the Poulaphouca station. 'Poulaphouca' means 'hole of the pooka or spirit', and may have been a fortunate choice of name for a place that was to supply power to Dublin. Today the importance of the reservoir is as a supplier of fresh drinking-water to the city. For this reason much of the area is fenced off and the sides of the reservoir afforested to prevent soil erosion into the lake and too rapid a siltation of the reservoir, though the problem of siltation is greatest for the generators of electricity. The woodlands planted around the lake are generally of Norway spruce, a tree introduced into Ireland but native to mainland Europe and the Scandinavian countries.

The reservoir is a nationally important site for wintering populations of greylag goose. Mallard, teal and widgeon also winter in the area in fairly substantial numbers.

All along the shoreline are narrow beaches. The sand is granite, either from rocks broken down by glaciers in the distant past or from rocks still weathering today. The material is rather coarse with few fine fragments. By following the lakeshore through Ballyknockan and Lacken we arrive at a bridge that crosses the lake to the town of Blessington. The N81 is then a direct route back to Dublin through the towns of Brittas and Tallaght.

**Link 2** Laragh, Glenmacnass, Sally Gap 8.5 miles/14 km

A better route across the Wicklow Mountains is along what is known as the Military Road. This route and a series of barracks were constructed by the British to keep the mountains free of rebels. Many had sought refuge in the inaccessible uplands of Wicklow, and the British knew this would be the only way of controlling them. The route takes us through the roughest and often the bleakest of Irish landscapes. It is also one of the most spectacular. The valley we follow is that of the Glenmacnass River.

On the way out of Laragh a lot of the surrounding country is shrouded by conifers. Many of the trees we see along this road will be a species called Sitka spruce, the mainstay of commercial forestry in Ireland. A native of the western seaboard of the United States and Canada, its range is limited to a narrow coastal band that on occasions extends inland along river valleys. It thrives in a region that is rain-soaked for much of the year. Transplanted to Ireland it finds a home from home and grows rapidly in even the most inhospitable places.

Some see these alien trees as a blight on the landscape. The woods are dark and empty places that acidify soil and rivers, damaging fish stocks. Many of the environmental problems facing foresters today are the result of past forestry policies. In the 1960s and 1970s the State was the main planter of trees in Ireland. The money available to the Forestry Service was limited and foresters had to compete on the open market for land which at that time was costly. Foresters found themselves planting trees high on the sides of mountains or out on vast expanses of blanket bogs. The cheapest land was all that could be planted, land of no value to farmers.

Now it is seen that many of these forests were planted in areas of great natural beauty. It may also be the case that many of the soils planted upon were the ones most vulnerable to the acidifying effects of conifers. Foresters are aware of this and today guidelines from the Forestry Department clearly stipulate that planting be kept clear of rivers. The afforestation of open tracts of bog in the west of Ireland is also discouraged.

In Wicklow the conifers are better suited to the landscape than in other areas. In the steep valleys they can be folded into the land and hidden from the eye to some extent. Another factor may be that forestry has had a long history in Wicklow. Trees other than Sitka spruce grow well in the area and, as noted, it is Ireland's most afforested county. In spite of all that, the presence of large tracts of conifers on an upland landscape of blanket bog is difficult to forgive.

As we pass through Glenmacnass the road gradually rises to a point where the end of the valley looms into sight. Here the Glenmacnass waterfall tumbles from the Wicklow uplands over a cliff and into the valley below. We at once recognise another valley scoured by a passing glacier ten millennia ago. The waterfall marks the junction of the Wicklow granite and the schists that surround it. On the valley floor, a series of moraines (piles of sand and rubble left behind by retreating glaciers) bears testimony to glaciations in the area.

## Stop and walk

Above the waterfall we are on the uplands proper of Wicklow. A number of lay-bys allow us to get out of the car and explore the area on foot. We are on the north-east flank of Tonelagee. High up on the side of the mountain is a corrie lake, Lough Ouler, which lies in one of the depressions left after the last remnants of the glacier melted. The lake waters are acid in chemistry while on the surrounding cliffs several of what are termed alpine plants occur, so called because of the altitude at which they grow. Adapted to the harsh conditions of the uplands, many Arctic plants in Ireland may have succumbed to warmer weather in the recent past. In such periods there were few retreats high enough for these plants and so the country's Arctic flora is a relatively poor one.

From Glenmacnass the Military Road winds between a number of Wicklow peaks. Because of the elevation of the road the mountains we pass seem fairly low-key. To the east as we drive north are Barnacullan, Mullaghcleevaun, Duff Hill, Gravale and Carrigvore. To the west are two river valleys. The first is that of the Inchavore River, which flows into Lough Dan. Beyond the summit of Knocknacloghoge is the Cloghoge Brook, which runs into Lough Tay. To the north of the brook is Luggala or Fancy Mountain.

The Military Road comes to a crossroads at the Sally Gap, and again we have a choice of routes. Straight ahead is Kippure and the Liffey Head bog, then the Dublin Mountains and the city. To the east is Lough Tay, Lough Dan and the rest of east Wicklow.

## A SHORT ACCOUNT OF LIFE ON THE UPLANDS

Much of the character of the Wicklow uplands stems from the vast tracts of blanket bog that make up the landscape, a lot of it now in the Wicklow National Park. This bog is the accumulation of vegetation that has been growing and only very slowly decomposing over the last 5,000 years. The main vegetation in the area is a mixture of heathers — ling and bell heather — with rushes and, at the heart of the bog's growth, the sphagnum mosses. Ling has tiny leaves pressed against the stem and pink flowers. Bell heather has longer leaves that stand out from the stem, and bell-shaped flowers of dark pink to purple. The mosses grow only in the wettest places on the bog, by and in the pools. Their cells are designed to absorb and hold as much water as possible; a special coating on the cell wall swaps hydrogen ions from the plant for nutrients in the rainfall. Since rain contains very little nutrition, a lot of it is required for a decent meal. All that rainfall comes from the excess of 50 inches/1,250 mm of rain which falls in the regions where blanket bog is formed.

The term blanket bog refers to the growth habit of this peatland type. These bogs spread out over the surface of the landscape and can grow on hillsides at slopes of up to 25°. The bogs of the west of Ireland are of a similar type, formed where rainfall again reaches levels of over 1,250 mm per annum. Do not therefore expect good weather when walking across these peatlands. Their very existence depends on a steady supply of rainfall, which not only provides nutrition but also prevents the normal decomposition process from taking place.

Plants and animals all decompose when they die, plants generally at a slower rate as they contain a lot of material hard to break down: in particular, compounds called lignins. Plants may also lack the quantities of nitrogen in the tissue that make animals such a bonanza for scavengers of all sorts, from foxes to carrion beetles and flies, and bacteria. In addition to this, if the plant lies in water after dying, the bacteria that do the decomposing take longer to work, as they need oxygen and oxygen in water is in short supply. As it accumulates, the plant material is buried deeper and deeper beneath the peat surface. Oxygen is becoming scarcer and eventually the decomposition process is almost at a standstill.

In Wicklow and many of the upland areas of Ireland, the intensification of sheep-farming has led to the destruction of this fragile habitat. 'Fragile' seems an odd description, as rain, frost, wind and snow make the uplands a harsh place, but these areas are very vulnerable to overgrazing and to trampling, as a walk across any of the bogs of Wicklow on a wet day will demonstrate. Along well-worn paths heather is replaced by grasses and bare peat. In wet weather the peat is cut up and reduced to a black oozy slime. In the summer this material dries out rapidly and can support no plants, so is vulnerable to erosion from trampling feet and the wind.

It is not just hikers that do this damage but the countless thousands of sheep that now dot the uplands of Ireland like a wondrous and all-pervasive montane dandruff. In some areas of the country, sheep have so ravaged the heather that craftsmen seeking mature heather plants for the construction of lobster-pots must search far and wide for what was once an abundant material. Sheep do, however, keep the heather short and in this way promote new growth. The spreading of fertilisers on the hills to encourage grasses is another obstacle to the maintenance of this delicate ecosystem.

In the past many estates that owned upland areas would burn the heather in strips, part of the management policy to foster the growth and health of the grouse populations in upland areas. The grouse is a bird with the stature of a stumpy but sturdy chicken, the wings seeming just a shade small for such a stocky body. Its coloration is a perfect match for the heather and it is generally seen only after it has been flushed from cover while one is walking across the upper slopes of heather-clad hills. When surprised, it rises with an explosive burst and makes off in low flight across

Glenmalure

the hillside. The energetic flapping of wings and deep and loud chuckling noise of the birds — there are usually three or four in a group — causes as much alarm in the walker as the walker has in the grouse.

Grouse depend on heather in many respects. The fresh growth is important as a food source; they eat little else. Grouse-droppings indicate the fibrous nature of the diet; these narrow, inch-long and rust-brown objects may be spotted in little clumps on stones or in clearings.

The heather also furnishes the grouse with cover from prey, important for adult and chicks alike. Peregrines are adept at hunting, as are kestrels on the uplands. To provide or increase the selection of heather types available for the grouse it was the duty of gamekeepers to burn the heather in strips along the hillsides (to burn all of it would result in new growth throughout, with no cover remaining). Today heather is still burned but mainly to provide new growth for sheep; substantial tracts are seen ablaze in upland areas each spring. This adds nutrients to the system, which would otherwise be depleted.

With nutrients in limited supply, only a few grouse can be supported over a large zone. Competition for mates and resources is therefore intense. One of the best ways of observing grouse in Wicklow is to get up early and head for the region around the Sally Gap. Try to arrive in the first few hours of the day, when you will hear the calls of the cocks from their territory. Each cock picks an area to hold and indicates this by the dawn calling. The hens choose a suitable mate and nest within that area. Any males that fail

171

to attract a hen are said to be supernumeraries, surplus to requirements. The territories they hold are in all probability marginal and would not support the young of a brood. A wasted effort is avoided.

A second bird of the uplands that is characteristic of the region is the raven. Ravens were in the past victims of both shepherd and game-keeper. In Ireland their numbers have steadily risen in the last century and they are now generally seen on most expeditions into the Wicklow hills. Isolation, wilderness and high mountain valleys characterise the domain of these splendid jet creatures of the skies. When you see one raven you will in most cases be rewarded with the sight of a second. Their flight is a majestic and carefree display against the backdrop of mountaintop or storm-filled sky. The call is a deep chortling gurgle. The two fly high, on occasions tumbling through the air. Their display appears to be an affirmation of their kinship and domination of the skies in the area through which we mere humans stumble below.

Food for the raven is mainly scavenged remains of animals on the hills. In the past a pair would have to range far and wide to find food. Studies have shown that in America ravens rely on members of the larger group to find carrion and then call on their colleagues. In Ireland the rise in the number of sheep on the hills, and thus in sheep carcasses, must be contributing to the prevalence of this bird.

One of the earliest migrating birds to return to Ireland in the spring is the wheatear. From mid-March onwards there will be few areas of the Wicklow uplands that will not have a pair of these robin-sized birds darting back and forth across the heather. The bird has a striking white patch on its rump. This is seen as a white flash when the bird is in flight and is the root of its name: 'wheatear' is Anglo-Saxon for 'white arse'. The wheatear ranges over the hillsides feeding on leather-jackets, cater-pillars, and other grubs it finds in the upland soils. It will be spotted perching on rocks and posts, its tail shooting up and down, and its call is a strident chirping sound.

The other small brown birds of the uplands are the native meadow pipit and the skylark. The meadow pipit is about the same size as the wheatear and flits around singing in flight that is undulating and low above the heather. It is by far the most abundant bird of the Irish uplands. In the winter months the meadow pipits may abandon the high ground for the more sheltered and milder lowlands, in particular damp grasslands and freshwater margins where insect larvae may still be found in the grasses and the soil. The flocks they form at this time of year reach up to 100 birds.

The skylark is a showier bird of the open spaces. In Wicklow any good spring or summer's day is marked by the song of the skylark high in the air above the walker. Its plumage is not remarkable; there is a crest of feathers on the head but otherwise it is the display and song of this bird that draws it to our attention. It will emerge abruptly from cover on the ground and rise to heights of 100 feet/30.5 m or more, from where its warbling song will be sustained for several minutes. Gradually it will then descend, all the time singing. On warm sunny days the heavens can be alive to the sound of this bird; it feels as if no other creature shares these open spaces, so all-pervading is the song. In the winter months the sky lark leaves the uplands to feed on the coast, where it finds food in the seeds of salt-marsh or sand-dune plants.

The mammal most characteristic of Irish upland areas is the mountain hare. The animal found here is an Irish subspecies, *Lepus timidicus hibernicus*. This differs from its counterpart in Scotland in having a coat that does not change to white in the winter months. It may gain small patches of white but retains a good amount of brown fur. The diet of the hare is comprehensive and incorporates many of the plants found growing on the hills; the vegetation is such that a wide-ranging diet is needed to get a full complement of nutrients. As there is limited scope for the animal, populations of mountain hare are low on Ireland's hills; the presence of sheep may also act as a depressant, as they take quite a proportion of the scarce resources.

Another mammal that may be encountered on the hill or forest walk is the pygmy shrew. Unfortunately the encounter will, in all probability, be with a dead animal. The rain-soaked corpses of these tiny creatures are a common sight along trails; by common I mean you are likely to see at least one on a long hike over high ground. Because of the shrew's size it needs a constant supply of food to keep warm and active. This in turn means it must spend a major part of the day hunting. If temperatures fall and it cannot feed, it rapidly burns up all its reserves and will perish. It is a popular item of prey for kestrels in the area. In hedgerows and long grass along banks and fences, the high-pitched squeals of shrews may be heard on still summer days. Finding the animals is difficult, however. The calls are almost ultrasonic so it is hard to pinpoint their source. The shrews will also be in heavy grass cover if possible, though they may be spotted in runs.

Deer are the largest mammals found in the Wicklow hills. There is an interesting story to the present mix of animals in these hills. In the last century the Powerscourt estate brought a small deer into Ireland from Japan. This animal was called the sika deer; its taxonomic name is *Cervus nippon*. The generic name *Cervus* hints at its close relation to the native Irish red deer or *Cervus elaphus*.

Sika deer are very small animals, no bigger than a Labrador dog, with slender legs and a more delicate build. The red deer is much larger. Standing 4 or 5 feet high at the shoulder (1.2–1.5 m), a fully grown red deer stag can be a formidable animal. The two seem like chalk and cheese but at Powerscourt they were cross-bred and viable offspring were produced. One of the defining characteristics of a species found in biology texts is the ability to reproduce and bear viable offspring, offspring that are fertile. It would seem that red and sika deer are one and the same species, though time and distance has produced a remarkable difference in their body-form.

To keep the deer in, the estate wall was constructed around what appears on our maps as the Deerpark above the Powerscourt waterfall. The wall still stands, up to 8 feet/2.5 m high in places, in others reduced to small piles of rubble. Once the hybrid animal had been produced it was possible for this species to cross with either red or sika deer. In time some of these animals made good their escape from Powerscourt and crossed with other deer in the Wicklow area. Today it is highly unlikely that any pure-bred red or sika deer remain here. What we have instead is herds of hybrid animals and a great range in body-size and coat-colour.

If you seek pure herds of either animal you must journey to Kerry, where herds of pure sika share the woodlands of Killarney with herds of pure red deer. No cross-breeding has occurred, perhaps because no attempt has been made to cross the animals, or because the breeding season of the animals is not synchronised and so males and females of each species offer no attraction to one another.

While walking in any of the conifer plantations from south County Dublin through to Wicklow you are likely to encounter one or two of these deer; if a group is seen it will almost certainly be a female, a hind, with young calves of that year. Such encounters usually occur as the deer pass from one block of trees to another across a forest road. On the open hill it may happen that you startle a deer that had been sheltering in a hollow from the wind and had not noticed your approach. After running for a few hundred yards the deer will probably turn to inspect the cause of the alarm and then gently canter away over the horizon, leaving the observer to wonder at its grace and agility on such an unforgiving terrain.

Stags are more elusive animals. In the summer months they move to the high ground and feed on grasses and heathers less nutritious than those found on the lower slopes, where the hinds are nursing the young born that spring. The stags are at these higher points to avoid the nuisance of flies. As their antlers grow they are nourished by a rich supply of blood found in the velvet that coats them. In the summer this velvet is shed and the smell of the rotting flesh is a great attraction for flies keen to avail of this feast. The flies can become a real worry to the deer, pestering them to such an extent that they feed but poorly and start to lose body condition. On the exposed high ground the flies are more likely to be blown away by the strong winds.

As the autumn approaches, the groups of stags start to split up and each stag becomes a competitor for the attentions of the hinds; this time of male display is termed the rut. The stag's antlers and mane, a thatch of fur beneath the neck and extending to the shoulders, are fully developed. The effect may be added to by the animal wallowing in mud and adding sphagnum mosses and mud to the antlers and mane to give a more bulky look. The shallow, muddy depressions are a common sight on open hillsides through the autumn. Also used by the females, they may in fact be just a site for grooming to get rid of fleas, lice and ticks or the irritation these little parasites cause. The stags avoid confrontation as much as possible through performances that consist of deep bellows and runs past one another.

In red deer the stag roars up to three times a minute twenty-four hours a day for three weeks in an effort to keep the harem together and deter other males from mating with his choice females. Whether this tactic is successful or not can really be judged only by close and constant observation of the hinds. Infidelity among females in the animal world is apparently more common than was previously thought. Among deer, Scottish observers found that as a rule hinds mated with one male. Frank Fraser Darling in *A Herd of Red Deer* (1937), describes stalking a group of red deer and observing one male with a large group of females; the stag spent most of his time chasing rivals away and by the end of several days had lost most of his harem and failed to mate.

The stag's interest and energy wanes after the three weeks, at which stage he has lost 20 per cent of his body weight and 80 per cent of his body fat (fat is essential for survival in the winter months) and it is imperative that he begin feeding again.

At the end of the rut the females return to their own groups and the males to theirs. The stags may be in very poor condition; many will have had little time to feed or may have been injured during the rut. The onset of winter will further debilitate them as food is now generally scarce and temperatures are falling. A harsh winter might kill them.

**Link** Sally Gap, Kippure, Lough Bray, Glencree, Dublin 10.5 miles/17 km

To the north, straight through the Sally Gap, is the Liffey Head bog. Above the bog Kippure ascends steeply to a height of 2,490 feet/757 m and is topped off by a transmission mast for the national television station, RTE.

The Liffey rises from one of the small streams that cross the road at the foot of Kippure and begins a long and tortuous journey into Dublin, which is only about 8 miles/13 km away from here. The Liffey instead goes off in the direction of Blessington and then Co. Kildare.

The bog around here is a fine example of high-level blanket bog. Annual rainfall in excess of 60 inches/1,500 mm means that waterlogged conditions prevail for much of the year, and so plant remains do not decay but accumulate. If you come across a turf bank along the road, what you are seeing is a section through time. It has taken almost 5,000 years for this peat to collect. The vegetation of the area is mainly bog cotton; grasses such as *Molinia* or purple moor-grass, heathers and sedges are also common. The main birds are meadow pipits, skylarks, wheatears, kestrels and the odd passing raven. The mammals are deer and shrews, with perhaps the occasional fox and mountain hare.

Past Kippure the road begins to descend to the Glencree Valley. It winds around and over the Upper and Lower Lough Bray. Both are corrie lakes, scooped out by glaciers and now filled with acid waters. We can stop along the road at the old quarry above Lower Lough Bray to walk onto the surrounding blanket bog. Glenmalure Valley is to the east of the road. Either of two roads to the right will lead through the valley and into the town of Enniskerry.

The road straight ahead leads into Co. Dublin above Glenasmole and the reservoirs that lie in the valley. On both sides of the road are the signs of turf-cutting operations. In recent years people have started to contract the cutting of turf to operators with what are best described as sausage-machines. The turf is extracted by a cutter that runs beneath the surface of the peat extruding a cylinder of peat looking for all the world like a giant roll of black pudding. This may have the initial effect of preserving the surface of the bog but a cursory inspection some weeks after harvesting reveals the destruction of the peat-surface vegetation. Without a cover of plant material the peat surface will dry out irreversibly in summer and erode or crack. The long-term consequences of the use of these machines is still under study in Ireland but the prognosis is not good. Along the sides of the upland areas here peat has been cut by hand for decades. Though the short-term effects of hand-cutting appear drastic, in the long term it seems to have a minimal impact on the character of the blanket bog.

This road continues to Killakee and a forest at the foot of Montpelier Hill and the ruins of the Hellfire Club. On the right-hand side of the road is a broadleaved woodland planted in the late 1930s. The trees are mainly beech and now form a closed canopy that blocks much of the light from the forest floor.

The road goes on downhill into the suburbs of Rathfarnham and Terenure.

**Link** Sally Gap, Lough Tay, Lough Dan, Djouce 3 miles/5 km

By turning east at the Sally Gap we travel along the R759 in the direction of Roundwood. On this road in early spring and early in the day can be heard the calls of red grouse announcing their territorial claims. Further along the road is a series of car parks and lay-bys.

## Stop

We draw in off the road at a point with a good view of the other side of the valley above Lough Tay. On the slopes running west from the cliff-face of Luggala, herds of deer may be seen if one is early enough. At first it is difficult to pick the rusty-red and brown coats out on the green and brown slopes. But a pair of binoculars and a slow steady sweep along the valley sides should be rewarding. After the first animal is spotted, others will begin to appear, as if by magic, from among the growth.

Lough Tay lies at the foot of Luggala on the south shore and at the sides of White Hill where we are on the northern shore. The space between these two valley walls was gouged out by a glacier, which scooped out the lake beneath and on melting left a pile of gravel (a moraine) that further dammed up the valley to deepen the lake. The woodlands on the southern flanks of the valley are in the main oak and birch, with a few conifers poking through the canopy here and there.

Lough Dan, seen to the south of the valley, lies in a depression that was also scoured out by a glacier. Both lakes are known to have stocks of Arctic char, in all probability trapped here since the passing of the last glaciation, when it was one of the few fish species abundant in the freezing waters.

**Walk** Djouce 2 miles/3 km Lough Dan 2 miles/4 km

There are two popular walks that can be done in this area. One brings us uphill to the peak of Djouce, while the second takes a downhill course to the shores of Lough Dan.

To climb to Djouce we park at Luggala woodlands and pass through a stand of conifers to the open heather slopes above. On the way uphill we pass large granite boulders strewn at random; these were once carried over the slopes by a glacier, the upper limit of the ice being the line currently reached by the trees. So 15,000 years ago a vast river of ice moved along the Cloghoge Valley to Lough Dan; then, at the height of these boulders, part of it shifted to our east and out onto the plateau of the Vartry.

One of the granite boulders has been taken as a memorial to the late J.B. Malone, author of *The Complete Wicklow Way Walks* (1993). Malone pioneered long-distance walking routes in Ireland and was the driving force behind the establishment of the Wicklow Way. His guide to the Way, regularly republished, is still the most authoritative on the intricacies of the route as well as aspects of the history and landscape of the area.

The climb to Djouce takes us up over White Hill and west along the line of the summit. The track is clearly marked, the effect of hundreds of pairs of feet tramping over the mountains week after week all through the year. This climb is among the most popular for people from Dublin as it can be done with relative ease in most weathers. Where people have been walking, the heathers and bog cotton are replaced with grasses. The grasses may be ripped out in wet weather and then deep gullies are cut into the peat. On any kind of slope the gullies soon cut down to the underlying rock and stone as rains carry away the peat.

On a summer's day the summit of White Hill seems alive with the white fluffy seed-heads of bog cotton. In late autumn the stems turn from green to red as the plant withdraws precious nutrients from the fading stem. Much the same process takes place in deciduous trees in the autumn prior to leaf-fall.

Amidst the bog cotton and heather is a plant giving an indication of the altitude at which we now stand. *Empetrum nigrum* or crowberry grows in a straggly fashion close to the ground and in among the other plants of the hill. The leaves are narrow, a dark but shiny green, and underneath are two distinctive white bands. The fruit appears in the early autumn and is a large, black and perfectly spherical berry. This plant was more extensive when the Irish landscape was tundra-like. With the warming of the climate it has had to retreat to hilltops. It is similar to the bilberry, which also grows here, but that produces a smaller and distinctly blue berry and its leaves are broad and light green in colour.

The view to the south from White Hill takes in many of Wicklow's peaks. Due south is Lugnaquilla, the highest. To the right is the flattened summit of Turlough Hill, and to its right stands Tonelagee, with Luggala in the foreground above Lough Tay. A short but steep climb brings us to the summit of Djouce, a place well worn by countless feet and the howling wind. At a height of 2,385 feet/725 m, it offers a splendid view of Wicklow and north County Dublin as well as the Wicklow coast from Bray south to Wicklow Head.

The Wicklow Way continues along the flank of Djouce, towards the woodlands above the Powerscourt estate, and encounters the Dargle River just before it enters the woodlands and joins the Powerscourt waterfall.

**Walk**

The alternative to a climb at the start of a walk is to go down to Lough Dan. This walk starts at the Pier Gates and follows the road almost to the shores of the Lough. It traverses the Cloghoge Valley, with the river cutting through the glacial till. A track brings you along the southern shore to the end, where a gravel beach has been thrown up in front of the Inchavore River on its entry to the lake. The result is that the waters overlying this white sand seem tropical while about 20 feet/6 m from the shore they remain glacial. From the high ground above the lake the cries of peregrines may sometimes be heard as they tumble and practise their hunting skills.

**Link** Roundwood 3.5 miles/6 km

If neither of these walks is to your liking, the R759 continues east to the Vartry Reservoir and in the direction of Roundwood. The first woodland we pass after the Pier Gates is Sleamaine Forest. The Wicklow Way goes through this to high ground above Lough Dan and then down into Oldbridge and to Laragh. The road we are on brings us to a T-junction at the R755. A left here leads to the Great Sugar Loaf and Bray, a right to Roundwood.

Circuit — Oldbridge (3 miles/5 km), Laragh (3.5 miles/6 km), Annamoe (2.5 miles/4 km) and Roundwood (2.5 miles/4 km)

A right turn after Sleamaine Forest takes us to Oldbridge after a drive of about 3 miles/5 km on a road that winds between well-developed hedgerows alive with birds.

As we approach Oldbridge, oakwoods close in over the road. On the east of the road is an even-aged stand of oaks that were in the past coppiced.

## Stop

We can pull up at the wood entrance and peer in for a while. The floor is covered in bilberry, which tells us that the soil is poor. There is in fact an accumulation of peat over an acid soil at this site. It is typical of the conditions under which most of Ireland's semi-natural woodlands now grow; the soils are far from optimal for oak but have little agricultural value either and perhaps for that reason alone the woods exist.

But why did peat form on this soil in the first place? The soils of the area are coarse-textured and would thus have been free-draining, which might have been the cause of later problems. As water moves through a soil it picks up minerals from the top parts and may deposit them lower down. Iron is one of the minerals that can be moved about a soil in this way. As iron is taken from the top layer, the soil develops an ashen yellow colour. The technical name for these soils in the literature derives from the Russian for ash, podzola. The iron is deposited in the lower levels or horizons of the soil as a band of deep red material. In some cases this band is so well developed that an impenetrable iron pan evolves. No water can now pass down the profile and the soil becomes waterlogged; this inhibits the decay of organic material and the peat forms.

The jay is a frequent visitor to these woods in the autumn. Its chest is a light red colour while the tail is black. A white patch is visible on the rump and the wings show blue and white patches. Somewhat akin to the magpie in manner, the jay is a very vibrant and noisy bird. In the autumn groups of three or four will be heard moving through the canopy, squawking and screeching like hoarse magpies or crows; the sound can be a little alarming at first. They seem to hop rather than fly from tree-top to tree-top. The jays are in the woods to collect acorns, a favourite food. Often buried for later consumption, some of the acorns are forgotten and may germinate the following year. Since they might be buried at some distance from the woods, this is one way oak could spread those heavy seeds across the landscape.

Though the oak produces thousands of seeds over the two or three centuries of its life, only one need survive to replace the tree. The acorns are also taken by squirrels and wood-mice, and many seeds survive predation and germinate. All sorts of obstacles face an oak seedling, however. At germination it may be consumed by insects or fungal pathogens. Later in life a rabbit, hare or deer could cut the sapling right back to the ground or open the stem to infection. In other areas of Wicklow we have seen the bare woodland floors which indicate that succession in the forest is being interrupted by the feeding and bark-stripping of the deer, rabbit and hare.

**Link** Oldbridge

The road continues to the bridge that crosses the Annamoe River: this is Oldbridge. There is a place to park a little further on the road.

**Stop**

Walking back to the bridge and looking downriver away from Lough Dan, you will in all likelihood see a dipper or two at work on the river. A bird of rough waters, the dipper likes its rivers to be rocky places, not too deep and with a good flow. This scenario puts it in the upper reaches of most rivers. The dipper may at first go unnoticed, but once seen it will never fail to catch your eye again. In size it is about half-way between a robin and a blackbird. It is chestnut-brown with a white bib on its neck and upper chest; bird-books show a brown belly but this will probably not be seen. The most distinctive feature of the dipper is its continuous bobbing while standing on stones in the river, jerking as if its knees were on the blink. Up and down it goes in short spasmodic moves, in almost constant motion while out of the water, then in a flash it plunges. In Irish it is called 'gabha dubh', the blacksmith — a name derived from this incessant vertical movement perhaps?

Once in the water the dipper walks along the riverbed searching for insects or their larvae. It then emerges, mouth full, to another rock in its territory. The bird normally has a range of about 3,290 feet/1,000 m along a river, within which it stays throughout the year. So once you spot a dipper in an area the chances are that it will be there when you return next time.

The dipper nest is a neat ball of mosses and grass. Crevices in rocks above the water were the sites for the nest in the past. The arrival of humans — and so, bridges — has given these birds a new range of locations. The ledges and crevices of old bridges above mountain streams could be checked for nests if a dipper is seen. As old bridges are replaced with sleek concrete structures these sites may once again vanish.

**Link** Oldbridge, Laragh, Annamoe, Roundwood

The road we are on leads back to the town of Laragh. It winds along the Annamoe river valley, rising high above the valley floor at some points. Extensive areas of mixed deciduous woodland are visible on the eastern sides of the valley. Along the road there are many fine mature trees, possibly the remnants of estate woodlands.

The road from Oldbridge to a coniferous woodland close to Laragh is a section of the Wicklow Way.

On reaching a T-junction with the R755, we take a left and head for Annamoe. We are now on the floor of the valley through which we travelled from Oldbridge. Conifer woodlands predominate on the road as far as Annamoe, where we cross the river and continue north (a left turn). Ballinacorbeg rises steeply above the road, its sides a blaze of yellow when the gorse is in flower. On early autumn mornings this whole valley is a wondrous place. A clear morning sun, frost on the ground and a mist rising gently into the air — after a trip from Dublin it is akin to arriving in a new land.

The road takes us into Roundwood village. To the east and north of the village is the Roundwood or Vartry Reservoir, a supplier of water to the city.

**Link/Diversion**

Just past the village of Roundwood on the road north, there are two choices on the way back to Dublin. A minor road forks left or one may continue north along the R755.

## ROUNDWOOD, DJOUCE WOODS, POWERSCOURT WATERFALL, ENNISKERRY, KNOCKSINK WOODS, THE SCALP AND DUBLIN

**Link** Roundwood to Djouce 5 miles/8 km

Taking the left road brings us along a route that follows the base of White Hill and Djouce Mountain to the left. On the right the land slopes to the east and the Vartry plateau. A number of conifer woodlands line the road; the third and largest is Djouce Woods.

**Stop and walk**

This is a popular place for a walk on Sunday afternoons. There are four car parks to serve the woods, and walks are signposted to the lake within. Below the woods is the valley of the Powerscourt waterfall, though easy access to it is not possible from here. Another walk from Djouce Woods takes one by the southern flank of the forest along the old Deerpark wall of the Powerscourt estate, much of it still intact. To the south of the walk the summit of Djouce itself rises above the surrounding heath. The heather along the walk has been burned on a regular basis over the years to provide fresh growth for sheep, with the result that there is less variety in the upland plants here. The walk brings us to the Dargle River at the point where it is just about to cascade over the Powerscourt waterfall. The valley is Glensoulan ('glen of the stream'), Maulin and Tonduff are to the north and Djouce and War Hill to the south.

The rocks here border on the Wicklow granites. The schists have a swirling pattern as though the constituents were whisked and then frozen. The water of the river has rounded the boulders and rocks along the riverbed and accentuated the schist patterns. The waterfall plunges 400 feet/122 m into the valley below. At one time a glacier poured down over the sides; as it retreated to higher ground, melt-waters along with the rubble and coarse sands were carried into the valley and deposited as a series of fan-like mounds still present today.

The steep cliffs of the Deerpark Valley are home to peregrines, and in spring and all through summer their eerie calls are heard. They dive and swoop high above the valley floor and hunt throughout the region, taking many of the upland birds as prey.

Kilruddery House (*above*) is a fine Victorian mansion near Bray.
Bray itself (*below*) is now in reality the southern-most suburb of Dublin city, but it still retains its popularity as a seaside resort.

In the valleys above Powerscourt waterfall there is evidence of human habitation — not just old huts that may have been used by herders minding cattle or sheep on the high ground in summer, but the scars of cultivation ridges. These ridges or lazy beds were mounds 3 feet/1 m wide and about 18 inches/0.5 m high, on which potatoes were grown. They allowed cultivation of soil that was otherwise too wet or shallow for farming. We can appreciate the pressure that there must have been on the land in the mid-nineteenth century when we see the scars on these slopes, now covered with heather, bracken and grass. We are at an elevation of over 1,000 feet/304 m; winters are cold and harsh. It is small wonder that these areas have long been abandoned by humans and left to the sheep, deer, ravens, kestrels and peregrines.

The walk from the car park to the Dargle and back takes about 2 hours.

**Link** Djouce to Enniskerry and Knocksink Woods 4.5 miles/7 km

The road goes downhill to join the R760. From here into Enniskerry village it twists and winds through mature deciduous woodlands of oak and beech. Lilac and rhododendron as well as holly form a dense undergrowth in places. In the spring and early summer the air is heavy with the smell of wild garlic or ramsons, the flowers standing out star-like and white against the broad dark green leaves.

The village of Enniskerry provides a convenient watering-stop before we continue back to Dublin.

## Stop and walk

Knocksink Woods, on the outskirts of the village on the R117 back to Dublin, is used as a field and study site for the National Conservation Education Centre. Managed by the Office of Public Works, this is a fine example of oak and hazel woodlands. There are also patches of ash, beech and scattered specimens of mature Scots pine. The under storey is mainly hazel and some holly. In damp patches the woodland floor is covered with horse-tail and hart's-tongue fern. The Glencullen River flows through the valley.

Where there have been clearings foxglove appears. A tall plant with pink to purple flowers on a long stem, foxglove is at home on acid soils and shuns areas of a high pH, so its presence tells us that the local soils are acidic by nature. It is a biennial plant. The seed germinates in the first year and leaves are formed. In the second season it produces flowers and seed. This means it must have relatively settled conditions. In forests where clearings take place foxgloves soon become established. The botanical name for the species is *Digitalis purpurea*, purple fingers. In Irish it is 'méaracán dearg', 'red thimble', or 'méirín púca', which may be the 'pooka's little thimble'.

The woods are alive with birdsong in the spring and summer. Tits and tree-creepers are abundant. Flocks of long-tailed tits and coal-tits are seen foraging through the canopy in late summer and early autumn. The bark and stems of the oak and other trees provide plenty of insect food for the birds. The species best adapted to the task of finding it is the tree-creeper, a small brown bird seen on tree-trunks in conifer and broadeaved woodlands; it might even be spotted in parks and gardens around towns and cities.

The tree-creeper locates food by travelling up and down the trunk and probing crevices with its thin curved beak. The motions appear almost mouse-like, an impression reinforced by the bird's brown coloration and small size. One of the toes on each foot points backward, which makes movement a little easier on a steep trunk. The tail is pressed against the tree as the bird feeds, giving further security. Movements are normally in a spiral, with short bursts of activity and then intense probing of cracks in the bark for adult or larval insects.

Nest sites for this bird are usually gaps between the bark and trunk of the tree — not quite holes in the tree, but old trees are generally needed for nesting. Tree-creepers can be encouraged to nest in gardens that they frequent by nailing sections of old bark to trees, which provides an artificial crevice for them.

In the winter months the tree-creeper may join with other small insect-feeders to form flocks of twenty or thirty birds that move as one group through the crowns of conifer and deciduous trees. They seek out larvae and insects that are active in the relative shelter and warmth of cracks in tree-bark. Such flocks are often made up of blue-, coal-, great and long-tailed tits as well as the tree-creeper. Foraging for food in this way allows the birds to find insects more easily. If one bird finds food, the chances are that there will be more available in that spot. The group can cover more ground in a shorter time. During cold spells this is essential as energy reserves are soon consumed while the birds are trying to keep warm and hunt at the same time.

A bird that will be heard rather than seen in summer woods is the chiffchaff. It is a small and inconspicuous bird that is identical to the willow-warbler in appearance. In the hand the expert distinguishes the two species by length of primary wing feathers. In the field the songs of the two are the distinctive features. The chiffchaff has a rather monotonous call while the willow-warbler's song is of a series of descending notes. (Song descriptions in bird-books are at best a frustrating approximation of the real thing. Get a tape to hear the songs if you have not got an informed companion.)

A walk through the woods in the company of a musician can be an enlightening experience. I accompanied one on a trip through these woods a few summers ago. We stopped to listen to one chiffchaff in full song in the heat of the afternoon. The song emerged from a thicket of oak, hazel and ash; of the bird there was no other sign. My companion returned the call as a series of whistles with the same rhythm as that used by the chiffchaff. In an instant the bird stopped singing.

In the mind's eye it was possible to see the little chiffchaff mildly perplexed, head to one side, trying to get a fix on this strange bird. After a few moments the song resumed with a slight variation and continued until once more the strange bird called. Again silence and then a somewhat altered song, this time taking elements of the 'strange bird's' melody.

Among birds, song serves a number of purposes. Many species proclaim territory with song. The male robin carries this to extremes, often singing and holding a territory throughout the year. In towns under streetlights robins may sing through the night, fooled by the lamps into thinking day was upon them and the dawn chorus about to begin. Song prevents direct confrontation among the birds. A vigorous and early singer in the dawn chorus will repel all who dare to move into its territory. Song bonds adult and young. The calls of chicks are already known to the mother bird before they emerge from the egg. Each adult recognises its own young from their call.

But as to what it was the chiffchaff thought it heard that day in the woods we may guess but never know. Perhaps it was just playing with us.

A walk around this wood will take up to 2 hours if you stop to admire the flowers and listen to the birds; alternatively, half an hour can cover a circuit from the car park to the river, across the second set of stepping-stones encountered and back by the first set.

**Link** Knocksink, the Scalp, Dublin 1.5 miles/2.5 km

On the R117 again we enter the Scalp, a long, narrow, steep-sided valley just outside Enniskerry. The valley is one of a number of glacial outwash channels found on the margins of the Wicklow uplands. As ice waters melted in the mountains to the south, massive blocks of ice may have remained intact in the valleys. Water formed immense lakes between the hills and remaining ice. In places it overflowed and gushed out along valleys. The soils on the valley walls were stripped by the passing water and only the huge granite boulders were left.

The vegetation on the slopes is a mix of hazel, oak, ash and sycamore scrub.

The R117 continues north into Dublin city via the suburbs of Sandyford and Dundrum.

## ALTERNATIVE ROUTE

### ROUNDWOOD, SUGAR LOAF, GLEN OF THE DOWNS, BRAY, DUBLIN

**Link** Roundwood to Great Sugar Loaf 6 miles/10 km

Taking the R755 straight on from Roundwood village brings us first down to the Vartry Reservoir and then out onto the level plateau of the Vartry. At the reservoir, whooper swans are occasionally seen but the deep waters are otherwise not suited to waterfowl. On the plateau much of the ground is improved pasture. In places where fields have been neglected, rushes are quick to recolonise.

**Walk** Climb of the Sugar Loaf

The peak of the Great Sugar Loaf is visible for most of the journey. About 5.5 miles/9 km from Roundwood a left turn takes us to the car park, 0.5 miles/1 km down the road, at the foot of the mountain. From here it is a gentle stroll to the summit. Going from an elevation of 688 feet/209 m to 1,648 feet/501 m — or 960 feet/292 m in all — it is one of the handiest mountains to climb in the Dublin area.

The lower slopes are covered in gorse and heathers. In early summer meadow pipit, skylark and wheatear are there in abundance. Once we leave the heather the climb becomes a scramble over the quartzite slopes of the mountain itself. Much of the track to the summit is now in deep gullies. The passage of thousands of people over the years has ground the quartzite to a powder in places. From the summit the view is of Dublin Bay to the north and the coast of Wicklow to the south. On a good day, and with good eyes and maybe a little imagination, it is said that the mountains of Wales are visible due east across the Irish Sea. The most likely summit to be seen is Snowdon, 3,306 feet/1,005m and just behind the isle of Anglesey.

Weathering has slowly broken down the hard quartzite rock to leave the volcano-like peak of the Sugar Loaf. The same hard quartzite rocks form a band that extends to Bray Head and through the Little Sugar Loaf to encompass Dublin Bay on the south. While Bray Head and, on the other side of the bay, Howth Head were overrun by glaciers and their profiles flattened, the Great Sugar Loaf remained above the ice and thus escaped the rub-down Bray and Howth received. Such peaks — called nunataks — may have acted as refuges for hardy plants that could withstand the Arctic conditions. As the climate warmed, these plants, alpines in the main, were able to move downhill, but had to retreat once it got too warm. Today they are found at the summits of a few Irish mountains.

**Link** Great Sugar Loaf, Glen of the Downs 2 miles/3 km

From the car park we head east to the N11, joining it just north of the Glen of the Downs. Turn left if you wish to head for Dublin; otherwise turn right for the Glen.

**Stop and walk**

There is a car park in the Glen and a number of trails laid out through the woods. The woodlands are a fine example of semi-natural oakwoods with an under storey of holly. The valley is, like the Scalp, a glacial overflow channel, the largest of its kind in the country.

**Link** Glen of the Down , Bray 4.5 miles/7 km. Dublin 7.5 miles/12 km

From Glen of the Downs we head north along the N11 to Bray. For those who do not wish to enter Bray, a bypass now brings the motorist on to the Dublin suburb of Loughlinstown. From Loughlinstown Dublin city centre is reached via Stillorgan and Donnybrook.

The Scalp. A V-shaped glacial valley near Enniskerry

# THE BOYNE VALLEY
## INTRODUCTION

The area of the Boyne Valley under consideration here extends from the mouth of the River Boyne at Drogheda to an area upstream at Trim. Only an hour's drive from Dublin, this short section of the valley is steeped in history, folklore and mythology. It was once the centre of power in Ireland, where the High Kings ruled. It is here, too, that the ancient and mysterious burial-grounds of Newgrange, Knowth and Dowth can be found, all of them older than the Pyramids or Stonehenge. But this area, where St Patrick first began his missionary work, was also a great centre for Christianity. Throughout the county, the beautiful ruins of once-great monasteries dot the landscape and many of the finest Celtic crosses in Ireland still stand tall.

Meath, meaning 'the middle kingdom', originally consisted of the present Meath and Westmeath, together with parts of Cavan and Longford. The modern county came into existence in the thirteenth century and its borders were defined in the sixteenth century. As far back as 1172, King Henry II bestowed Meath as an earldom to Hugh de Lacy, who built castles in Trim, Kells and elsewhere. However, English control of the county wavered in succeeding centuries, and only part of Meath remained inside the Pale and under direct control from Dublin. The county's northern boundary was the scene of the Battle of the Boyne in 1690, in which King William III defeated King James II and asserted English Protestant rule over Ireland.

This part of the Boyne Valley is in Meath, 'the Royal County', which lies stretched like some kind of animal hide to the north-west of Dublin. Most of the county consists of rich, rolling farmland, fringed on the south by the Bog of Allen, to the east by a narrow coastal strip and to the north-west by more barren lakeland. The population of the county, now at 95,000, is growing fast as the villages of the southern end

# BOYNE VALLEY

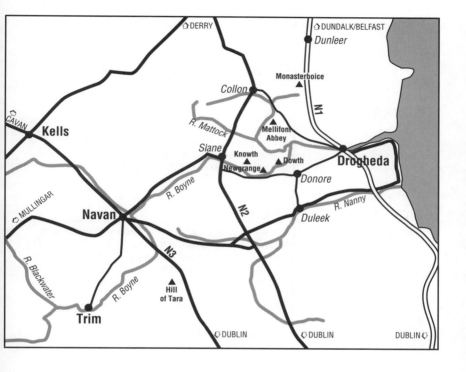

turn into dormitory towns accommodating the irresistible expansion of Dublin.

There is a lot to see here in a concentrated area that can easily be covered by car or even bicycle. Because the region is so close to Dublin, it tends to look to the capital for some services and entertainments, so check the Dublin section if there is no entry below.

# ESSENTIAL INFORMATION

## BANKS

Banks are open Monday–Friday, 10 a.m.–3 p.m. and sometimes longer. The four main banks — Bank of Ireland, Allied Irish Banks, Ulster Bank and National Irish Bank — all have branches in Drogheda, while at least one of them is represented in each of the other towns of the region. Most branches have cash-dispensing machines for after-hours use.

## BICYCLE HIRE AND REPAIR

The rolling hills of County Meath are excellent territory for cyclists who don't mind exerting themselves in return for fine views and quick access to the main heritage sites. Indeed, the bicycle is one of the best means of seeing all the chief attractions in the Boyne Valley, most of which lie within a 25 mile/40 km radius of Drogheda. The Boyne Valley tour covered later in this chapter can easily be undertaken on a bicycle. Bicycles are available for hire from:

Carolan's Garage, 77 Trinity Street, Drogheda, telephone 041–38242. March to September only.

The Quay Cycle Shop, 11 North Quay, Drogheda, telephone 041–34526. All year round.

The following do repairs:

The Quay Cycle Shop

Cycle World, 24 Brews Hill, Navan, telephone 046–22517

Inches Cycles, 2 George's Street, Drogheda, telephone 041–37422

Michael McLoughlin, Bridge Street, Trim, telephone 046–31954

P.D. Cycles, Kenlis Place, Kells, telephone 046–41861

## BUREAUX DE CHANGE

All commercial banks cash traveller's cheques and exchange currency. Traveller's cheques and major credit cards are accepted by most hotels, large shops, travel and transport companies.

## CAR HIRE

Details of all major car hire companies are covered in the Dublin section. One locally based operator is Practical Car and Van Rental at:

Carnacross Motors Ltd, Carnacross, Kells, Co. Meath, telephone 046–45062

Halco (Plant) Ltd, Mell Industrial Estate, Drogheda, telephone 041–36018

Fitzpatricks Garage Ltd, Dublin Road, Kildare, telephone 045–21100.

# CAR REPAIRS

The Automobile Association is at 23 Suffolk Street, Dublin, telephone 01–6779481.
The branch in Dundalk, County Louth, can be contacted at telephone 042–32955.
AA members should make use of the organisation's freefone number, which is
available 24 hours a day.
The following garages offer a 24-hour emergency towing and breakdown service:
Boyne Auto Recovery, Mill Road, Mornington, Drogheda, telephone 041–31966/
088–591812
Nobber Motors, Nobber, telephone 046–52151/046–52170
Post-Haste Breakdown Service, County Meath, telephone 088–591111.

# CHURCHES

Catholic mass times are usually posted outside churches. Drogheda has many
churches of interest, including the churches of St Peter's and St Mary's (both Church of
Ireland) and St Peter's Catholic church, which houses the head of St Oliver Plunkett.

# CRÈCHE AND BABYSITTING SERVICES

Euro-placements, 59 Waterloo Road, Dublin, telephone 01–6603926.

# EMERGENCIES AND MEDICAL MATTERS

In cases of emergency, ring 999 from any telephone, and say which service you
require — fire brigade, police or ambulance. The call is free.
If you are in the Drogheda area, Our Lady of Lourdes Hospital is on call, telephone
041–37601. There is also a hospital in Navan: Our Lady's General, telephone 046–21210.
The main Dublin hospitals are listed in the Dublin section.

# GARDAÍ (POLICE)

If an emergency arises ring 999 and ask for the Gardaí/Police. This call is free.
Otherwise, the area's police stations can be found under 'Garda Síochána' in the local
Golden Pages.
Crime is low in the Meath area, but Gardaí still advise visitors to take care of their
valuables. In particular, they recommend that cars are always locked even when
unattended for only a short period and that all property is removed before one leaves
the vehicle.

# LAUNDERETTES

These are rare outside the Dublin area. Dry-cleaners, however, are more common,
and there is usually at least one in every town.
Eastenders Launderette, 1 Bóthar Brugha, Drogheda, telephone 041–39300
The Laundry Shop, 3 Wellington Quay, Drogheda, telephone 041–38922

# PHARMACIES

Pharmacies generally follow normal shop-opening hours (9 a.m.–5.30 p.m.) though a
few have late-night opening. These include:
John Farrell, Market Street, Trim, telephone 046–36600. Fridays until 7.30 p.m.
Maher's Chemist, 105 West Street, Drogheda, telephone 041–36205. Thursdays and
Fridays until 9 p.m.

The view along the narrow passage leading to the central burial chamber at Newgrange.

## POST OFFICES

Post offices are generally open Monday–Friday 9 a.m.–5.30 p.m. and can be found in most towns and villages. Details of telephone services are in the Dublin section, page 17.

## TAXIS

The quality and availability of taxis varies a lot, with extra charges for baggage and night journeys.
John Bailey, Boyne Hill, Navan, telephone 046–23431
Dial-A-Cab, 4 Church Street, Drogheda, telephone 041–34677
Duke Street Cabs, Orwell House, Duke Street, Drogheda, telephone 041–51839
Frank Dignam, Haggard Street, Trim, telephone 046–31465
Vincent Smyth, Mooretown Cross, Slane, telephone 041–24563

## TOURIST INFORMATION OFFICES

The main tourist office for this region is located at Market Square, Dundalk, in County Louth. It is open Monday–Friday 9.30 a.m.–5.30 p.m. off-season and 9 a.m.–6 p.m. Monday–Saturday during the summer months, telephone 042–35484.
At Newgrange itself, there is an office which operates from April to the end of October, telephone 041–24274. A tourist office is open on Narrow West Street in Drogheda from June to August, telephone 041–37070.
There is also a new tourist office in Mill Street, Trim.

## TOURS

Bus Éireann offers two tours in the Boyne Valley area, which are available from early May to the end of September. Each incorporates visits to the main attractions, including Newgrange, Knowth, Tara, Slane and Monasterboice. Details from Bus Éireann, Dublin, telephone 01–8366111.
The Meath Heritage Centre offers tours around the area, information can be obtained from the centre on telephone 046–36633.
Midlands & East Regional Tourism suggest many tours in their publications, available from any of the tourist offices listed above.

## TRAVEL

Despite its proximity to Dublin, getting about the Boyne Valley can be troublesome if you don't have a car or are not willing to push a bicycle around the hilly terrain.
If you don't take one of the suggested bus tours direct from Dublin (see below), the provincial buses to Drogheda and Slane provide the best starting-points for the area. These leave from Busáras in Dublin, telephone 01–8366111. There are also trains to Drogheda leaving from Connolly Station, telephone 01–8366222. Bicycles are permitted on trains, with rates varying from £4 to £12 return, depending on the number of kilometres travelled.

# FESTIVALS AND SPECIAL EVENTS

## June

Trim Pony Races, featuring the 'International Nun Run', in which horse-riding nuns compete against each other for charity.
The Trim Busking Festival takes place on the bank holiday weekend at the start of the month.
The National Town & Country Fair in Slane Castle is also held in early June.
Laytown Races. An annual horse-racing event held on the strand at Laytown.

## July

Vintage Car Rally, Trim

## August

Moynalty Steam Threshing Festival, which recalls the methods used by farmers for harvesting crops in times past.

# WHERE TO STAY

There follows a list of some of the best hotels, guesthouses and hostels in the Boyne Valley area; information on the many B&Bs can be obtained from Bord Fáilte, or locally. All the accommodation listed below is approved by Bord Fáilte; there are many more unapproved B&Bs, guesthouses and hotels and, although standards vary considerably, some at least offer good value and good quality. They can be found by consulting the telephone directory or by seeking out the premises locally.

Bord Fáilte grades hotels and guesthouses separately depending on facilities. Hotels range from five-star luxury to modest, usually family-run, one-star establishments. Guesthouses are classified separately, from four stars to one star. Country homes and other specialist accommodation are not so graded. As prices vary according to season and inflation, a rough indication is given based on the cost of overnight single accommodation (double accommodation may cost up to 50 per cent less for two people sharing). The categories are as follows:

| | |
|---|---|
| Economy: | £15 to £25 |
| Budget: | £25 to £35 |
| Moderate: | £35 to £45 |
| High: | £45 to £60 |
| Very high: | £60 and more |

When asking the price, check whether a service charge is added.

# HOTELS, GUESTHOUSES AND COUNTRY HOMES

## Bettystown
Neptune Hotel, telephone 041–27243. Grade *. Seaside hotel. Open March to October. Rating: economy to budget.

## Castlebellingham
Bellingham Castle Hotel, County Louth, telephone 042–72176. Grade **. An elegantly refurbished seventeenth-century hotel in beautiful surroundings. Open all year. Rating: budget.

## Dowth
Glebe House, telephone 041–36101. A small country home ideally located for visiting Newgrange, and offering tennis in the grounds, golf, fishing and riding nearby. Rating: economy.

## Drogheda
Boyne Valley Hotel, telephone 041–37737. Grade ***. Family-run country-house hotel in a converted nineteenth-century mansion on 16 acres/6.5 hectares. All rooms *en suite*. Open all year. Rating: budget to moderate.
Rosnaree Park Hotel, Dublin Road, telephone 041–37811/37673. Grade *. Open all year. Rating: budget to moderate.

## Duleek
Annesbrook House, telephone 041–23293. Georgian house 0.5 miles/1 km from the village. Open May–September. Rating: budget.

## Julianstown
Old Mill, telephone 041–29133. Grade *. Situated close to the Boyne Valley, this hotel offers private fishing to residents. Open all year. Rating: economy to budget.

## Kells
Headfort Arms Hotel, telephone 046–40063. Grade **. This homely 18-bedroomed hotel offers TV and showers in all rooms. Open all year. Rating: budget.

## Kilmessan
Station House Hotel, telephone 046–25239. Grade **. Converted from an old railway junction house, this hotel lies in 6 acres/2.5 hectares of gardens and woodland, and is conveniently situated for walks on the nearby Hill of Tara. Rating: budget.

## Navan
Beechmount Hotel, Trim Road, telephone 046–21553. Grade *. Open all year. Rating: budget.
Balreask House, telephone 046–21155. Old-style house on working farm 1 mile/1.5 km from town. Open Easter to October. Rating: economy.

## Slane
Conyngham Arms Hotel, telephone 041–24155. Grade **. This family-run hotel, a fifteen-minute drive from Newgrange, offers good food and friendly service. Open all year. Rating: economy to budget.

## Trim
Wellington Court, telephone 046–31516. Grade **. Open all year. Rating: economy to budget.

# HOSTELS

## Carlingford

Adventure Centre and Holiday Hostel, Tholsell Street, Carlingford, telephone 042–73100. Cheap but basic 11-roomed hostel.

## Drogheda

Harpur House Hostel, William Street, telephone 041–32736. Three bedrooms and two dormitories. Open all year.

## Kells

Kells Hostel, telephone 046–40100. Open all year.

# CAMPING AND CARAVAN SITES

## Bettystown

Bettystown Caravan and Camping Park, telephone 041–28167. 40 caravan pitches and 25 tent pitches. Situated in the heart of the village, two minutes' walk from the beach. Hot showers, children's playground, and nearby local amusements and shops. Open Easter to the end of September.

## Dundalk

Gyles Quay Caravan and Camping Park, telephone 042–76262. Total of 92 pitches, 10 miles/16 km from Dundalk. Pets allowed. Showers, washing and drying facilities, licensed club on site. Open April to September.

## Mosney

Mosney Holiday Centre, Caravan and Camping Park, telephone 041–29200/29000. Turn right 2 miles/3 km off main Dublin–Belfast road after Gormanstown. There's a Mosney in every country — a family-centred beach holiday resort which saw its best days in the 1960s before the boom in popularity of Mediterranean holidays and nowadays looks a bit tatty. Still, this site offers Ireland's largest indoor water playground, a boating lake and amusement park, pet farm, sports facilities, film screenings nightly and baby-sitting services. Open end May to end August.

# SELF-CATERING

## Carlingford

Three-bedroomed townhouse in Carlingford village. Open all year. Further information telephone 042–73116 and 044–48761.
Three-bedroomed cottage overlooking Carlingford Lough, 1 mile/1.5 km from the village. Open all year. Further information telephone 042–21668 and 044–48761.
Traditional old farmhouse, three bedrooms, open fire, beach ten minutes' drive. Open all year. Further information telephone 042–76199.

## Drogheda

Modern self-contained apartment, close to Bettystown. Open all year. Further information telephone 041–38189 and 044–48761.
Three-bedroomed bungalow with patio and garden, good touring base. Further information telephone 044–48761.
Two-bedroomed period house, 5 miles/8 km from Newgrange, adjacent to town centre. Open all year. Further information and booking telephone 041–34045 and 044–48761.

## Laytown

The Cottages, Seabank. Four bungalows and two cottages available, cots and high chairs furnished on request, launderette, tennis court. Open all year. Further information and booking telephone 041–28104 and 044–48761.

# Where to Eat

All restaurants are required by law to display their menu and prices outside the premises. The list below is not in any sense a 'good food' guide, though some indication is usually given as to what can be expected from a restaurant. The ratings used refer to the approximate price of a meal for one person, wine not included. These are as follows:

| | |
|---|---|
| Economy: | under £5 |
| Budget: | under £10 |
| Moderate: | under £15 |
| High: | over £15 |
| Very high: | over £25 |

## Drogheda
Black Bull Inn, Dublin Road, telephone 041–37139. Good pub food. Rating: budget.
Boyne Valley Hotel, telephone 041–37737. Very good à la carte menu. Rating: high.
King's Restaurant, Mell, telephone 041–37144. Open 8.30 a.m.–7.30 p.m. Home cooking and baking, breakfast, lunch specials, teas and snacks. Rating: economy to budget.
Monasterboice Inn, telephone 041–37383. Open for lunch 12.30–3 p.m. and 5.30–10 p.m. à la carte. Famous for fresh scampi, which is served all day. Rating: budget to moderate.
Noble Grape, 3/4 Stockwell Court, Stockwell Street, telephone 041–38333.
Open 6.30–10 p.m. Italian and French cuisine. Rating: moderate to high.
La Pizzeria, 38 Peter Street, telephone 041–34208. Open 6–11 p.m.
Closed Wednesdays. Good pizzas and salads. Rating: budget.

## Kells
Round Tower, Farrell Street, telephone 046–40144. This pub offers a full à la carte menu in the evenings as well as bar snacks. Rating: budget.

## Kilmessan
Station House Hotel and Restaurant, telephone 046–25239. Grade B. Have your aperitifs on the former platform of the train station that closed here in 1952, and dine in the old ticket office. A fish and meat menu featuring local produce. Rating: moderate to high.

## Slane
Bartles Steakhouse, The Square, telephone 041–24664. Open for dinner Tuesday to Sunday and for lunch Wednesday–Sunday. Rating: budget to moderate.
Newgrange Farm and Coffee Shop, telephone 041–24119. Open daily April to October 10 a.m.–5 p.m. Good home-made soups, sandwiches, quiches, etc. Rating: economy.
Slane Castle Restaurant, telephone 041–24207. Open Wednesday–Sunday 12 noon to 10.30 p.m. Nice atmosphere, serves steaks and grills. Rating: moderate to high.

## Termonfeckin
Triple House Restaurant, telephone 041–22616. Open for dinner Tuesday–Sunday, and for lunch on Thursday, Friday and Sunday. Rating: budget to moderate.

## Trim
Bounty, Bridge Street, telephone 046–31640. Reputed to be the oldest pub in Co. Meath, nice place to stop off for a snack, served all day. Rating: economy.

Brogan's, High Street, telephone 046–31237. Food served Monday–Friday 12.30–2 p.m. Set lunch and pub grub. Rating: economy.

Haggard Inn, Haggard Street, telephone 046–31110. Open 12.30–2.30 p.m. and 6–10 p.m. This pub has a reputation for good food. Rating: budget.

# DAYTIME ACTIVITIES AND SPORT

## ANGLING

In the north-eastern part of County Meath there is coarse angling available in Drumconrath. Also game fishing on the River Boyne.

## CINEMA

The Abbey Cinema, Drogheda, telephone 041–30188, has two screens showing popular films. Listings for this and other local entertainments can be obtained in the local newspaper, the *Drogheda Independent*.

## ECOLOGY

Newgrange Farm, Slane, telephone 041–24119. Tours of a living farm for both adults and children. Coffee shop. Open July–August 10 a.m.–5.30 p.m. (weekends 2–5.30 p.m.), May–June 2–5.30 p.m. Sunday only.

Sonarite Ecology Centre, The Ninch, Laytown, telephone 041–27572. A visitor/educational centre which aims to show how man can live in harmony with nature. Open April–October.

## GREYHOUND-RACING

Boyne Valley Greyhound Stadium, Navan, telephone 041–21739. Wednesday and Thursday evenings.

## HORSE-RIDING

Abbeylands Riding School, telephone 041–23641
Briarleas Riding School, telephone 041–29333
Castlehill Equestrian Centre, Julianstown, telephone 041–29430
Pelletstown Riding School, telephone 01–259435

## SQUASH

Star & Crescent Recreation Centre, Fair Green, Drogheda, telephone 041–36148 offers squash, badminton, a games room and a bar. Open 9 a.m.–11 p.m. Monday–Saturday, 6–11 p.m. Sunday.

## SWIMMING

Drogheda, Navan, Trim and Kells all have municipal swimming pools.

There are good sandy beaches at Laytown, Bettystown, Mornington in County Meath, and, further north, at Baltray, Clogherhead and Termonfeckin in County Louth.

# BOYNE VALLEY TOURS

## TOUR 1: DROGHEDA

Drogheda, an industrial town of 25,000 people straddling the border between Counties Louth and Meath, can be chosen as the starting or finishing point of a tour of the Boyne Valley. It is a town with many stories to tell, some of them tragic. The first settlement here on the River Boyne dates back to Celtic times, but the Danish Vikings colonised the site in 911. However, it was under the Normans that Drogheda first gained significance as the strategic northern outpost of the Pale, as the sphere of English influence centred on Dublin was known.

In 1412 the settlements on both sides of the Boyne were united and granted a city charter. By the end of the century, the heavily walled settlement had become one of the four most important towns in Ireland, a fact underlined by the passing in Drogheda in 1494 of the repressive Poynings' Law, which was designed to curb Irish freedoms.

Drogheda was the scene of one of Oliver Cromwell's most infamous Irish massacres in 1649, when the English leader's army laid siege to the town and then extracted a terrible revenge on its defenders by slaughtering 3,000 men, women and children with great brutality. Many more were transported into slavery to the Caribbean.

The savagery continued later in the century when St Oliver Plunkett, who spent much of his time in Drogheda, was arrested in 1681 on trumped-up charges of sedition and then hanged, drawn and quartered. The saint's severed head was brought back to Drogheda from London and is now enshrined in St Peter's Church for public veneration. The door of his prison cell is also in the church.

Many of the medieval buildings remain, giving an agreeable mixture of old and new to this busy town. These include St Laurence's Gate, a thirteenth-century barbican or fortress gate, and one of the few to be seen in Ireland. Originally, there were ten gates in the city walls, but St Laurence's is the only surviving one. The one military action recorded at the gate was in 1641 and probably the principal reason for its survival was that the gate was not on the main route into the town. On the south side of the gate you can still see part of the old town wall.

Standing on West Street, Drogheda's chief thoroughfare, you cannot fail to notice the modern Gothic style of St Peter's Church. This is where the shrine to St Oliver Plunkett — severed head and all — is to be found. The church itself, which was begun in 1881, is unremarkable, so it's fair to deduce that the numerous visitors come primarily to see its macabre contents.

The Tholsel nearby is an eighteenth-century square granite building which used to serve as the town hall.

St Mary's Abbey, reached from Narrow West Street by Old Abbey Lane, is the town's oldest monastic site. A monastery was apparently built here after St Patrick's visit in AD 452. It suffered frequent raids by the Vikings but in 1206 a hospital was established on the site, which was taken over by the Augustinian Crutched Friars. The abbey was surrendered in 1543 by the last prior.

The other side of the river is dominated by the great prehistoric mound of Millmount, topped off by a tower and barracks. These barracks have been transformed into an arts and crafts centre with a town museum that houses a folk kitchen and exhibitions ranging from prehistoric to medieval times and on to the nineteenth century. The emphasis is on the commercial and industrial heritage of the town rather than its troubled history. There is, however, one room entirely devoted to Irish history up to the founding of the State.

These same barracks were stormed by Cromwell's army in 1649, and were used as a prison in 1916. They are well worth a visit. Telephone 041–36097/36391. Open 2–6 p.m. Tuesday–Sunday May–September, 3–6 p.m. on Wednesday/Saturday/Sunday rest of year.

## TOUR 2: NORTH OF DROGHEDA

Before taking the Boyne Valley tour, visitors may wish to make the diversion north of Drogheda, where the coast road via Baltray to the fishing village of Clogherhead is recommended. Look out for views of the Mourne Mountains further north.

From Clogherhead, take the R170 inland to Dunleer, then turn south onto the main Dublin–Belfast road. After 8 miles/13 km, you come to the tiny village of **Monasterboice**, site of the remains of a fifth-century monastic settlement founded by a disciple of St Patrick and one of the finest ecclesiastical locations in Ireland.

The famous ruins here include two churches, a round tower, three high crosses and other remains, but it's the crosses that people really come to see. In the graveyard is the imperfect North Cross, about 16.5 feet/5 m high, displaying a simple crucifixion and a spiral composition. The West Cross is traditionally known as St Bureen's Cross. Over 21.5 feet/6.5 m high, its carvings relate a number of biblical episodes, including David killing the lion, the kiss of Judas, and the baptism of Christ. The South Cross, now commonly known as Muirdeach's Cross, is regarded as one of the finest surviving examples in Ireland. It stands 18 feet/5.5 m high and owes its name to the inscription at the base, which reads: 'A prayer for Muirdeach by whom this cross was made'.

It is incredible to think that these magnificent crosses are over a thousand years old and that they have survived Ireland's weather and troubled history. The Round Tower, 115 feet/35 m high, stands as a reminder of how the monks were constantly under attack and forced to retreat into these towers for protection. The entrance into the tower is a few metres high and could only be reached using a ladder. Monasterboice was finally burned in AD 1097 and abandoned shortly after.

Drive west of Monasterboice to Collon, and then south for 5 miles/8 km until a signpost indicates a right turn down a minor road for **Mellifont Abbey**.

Another ruin, equally rich in atmosphere, Mellifont was the first Cistercian monastery to be founded in Ireland. It dates from 1142 when St Malachy began his reforms to bring the Church in Ireland into line with Rome. His relics are deposited in the Abbey. The ruins, including a large church, a square tower and an octagonal building where the monks used to wash, stand evocatively on the banks of the River Mattock. A map is available giving details of the different structures, such as the baptistry, the chapel and the refectory.

After the closure of the Abbey was ordered in 1539, it was turned into a fortified house by the Moore family and is remembered in Irish history as the place where Hugh O'Neill surrendered to Lord Mountjoy in 1603 after defeat in the Battle of Kinsale two years previously.

Return to Drogheda via Collon and Tullyallen, or begin the Boyne Valley tour below at Slane instead of Drogheda.

## TOUR 3: BOYNE VALLEY

Take the N51 west from Drogheda towards Slane. About 5 miles/8 km along the river, and a little hard to find, is the site of the Battle of the Boyne, fought back in 1690 but celebrated annually with grim fidelity by the Unionists of Northern Ireland ever since.

The Boyne Valley is steeped in history. Oldbridge (*above*) is the site of the Battle of the Boyne, probably the most decisive battle in Irish history. The tumulus at Newgrange (*opposite*) is one of the most spectacular pieces of archaeological restoration in Europe.

The battle, fought on Irish soil but orchestrated by the great European powers, has been thoroughly forgotten everywhere else. However, in Ireland, it is one of the seminal events of our history, and a continuing source of friction and recrimination. While in international terms it was just one more episode in a general political struggle, in Ireland the Battle of the Boyne came down to a bitter fight between Catholics and Protestants which was to determine the course of Irish history for the following three centuries.

Today, these tranquil fields beside the Boyne reveal little of their tremulous past. The tragedy unfolded rapidly after the Catholic James acceded to the English throne in 1685, giving Irish Catholics the hope of retrieving their losses of the previous decades, when their lands and possessions were seized by reforming Protestants. However, King James, who was Scottish, was overthrown in 1688 and fled to France to reorganise his forces. The following year, he landed in Ireland at the head of a French force. The main battle took place on 1 July 1690 (12 July on the modern calendar) on the hilly terrain on each side of the Boyne. The Dutchman William of Orange and his force of 10,000 took up their positions north of the river, from where they crossed the Boyne to engage James's larger but poorly trained and poorly led army. The result was a rout of the Catholic forces, with James the first to flee through Dublin and onto France.

The outcome of this battle was reinforced by further Orange victories in 1691, and for the defeated Irish, the nightmare of the Penal Laws began shortly afterwards. Catholics were stripped of their remaining rights and privileges, and reduced to the status of second-class citizens in their own country. English and Scottish settlers arrived in ever-greater numbers, particularly in the north-east, and the seeds of the current conflict in Northern Ireland were planted.

Continue west for 8 miles/13 km to **Newgrange**, one of the unmissable sights of Ireland and the highlight of this Boyne Valley tour. Newgrange is

a neolithic passage grave, one of the most spectacular in Europe, built around 3200 BC. The site, a huge circular mound of boulders covered with grass, was a select burial-ground probably either for kings or druids. It is believed that at least five people were buried here after being cremated over 5,000 years ago. Just how these primitive people managed to drag 250,000 tons of stones to the site remains a mystery.

Each 21 December, the shortest day of the year, and weather permitting, the rising sun penetrates the chamber through a roof box down the passageway and illuminates the chamber for about twenty minutes. No one really knows why this arrangement is so; most interpretations suggest it was intended as a symbol of rebirth and renewal or a signal of hope at the beginning of the year. At the entrance to the chamber is a large stone carved with spiral and diamond shapes, the meaning of which again defies modern interpretation.

Newgrange has been beautifully restored and the guided tours are most informative. Especially in peak season, it is advisable to get there early in the morning to appreciate the site to the maximum. The adjoining interpretative centre, open during the summer, explains the history of the site. Newgrange itself is open daily from June to September 10 a.m. to 7 p.m. and October to May 10 a.m.–1 p.m. and 2–5 p.m.

Newgrange is just one of the tumuli, or mounds, in the area known as Brugh na Bóinne, which was the burial-ground for Stone Age kings. There are two other principal burial sites, Knowth and Dowth, and numerous smaller remains, some overgrown and others disturbed or plundered.

Knowth is believed to be 500 years older than Newgrange. It contains two burial chambers and is surrounded by seventeen satellite tombs. Currently undergoing excavation and open to the public during summer months only, it is hoped that it will be as impressive as Newgrange. Archaeologists have discovered the remains of two Iron Age men on this site, and 300 of the 600 carved stones in the valley are here at Knowth.

Dowth is about the same size as Newgrange, with two tombs facing westwards. However, the site was badly plundered by souvenir hunters in the nineteenth century and has yet to be excavated properly. It is open only during the summer months. There are some beehive cells which it is believed were added during Christian times.

**Slane**, 3 miles/5 km further east on the N51, is a beautiful little village built around a crossroads with four Georgian houses arranged in a square. Local legend has it that a wealthy merchant built the houses for his four spinster daughters, who hated each other but couldn't bear to be parted. It is a lovely place to stop and browse.

The castle which overlooks the Boyne nearby was built by the Conyngham family and is now home to Lord Henry Mountcharles. Over the last ten years, the grounds of Slane Castle have been used as the venue for rock concerts from the likes of U2, Bob Dylan, Queen, The Rolling Stones and

Bruce Springsteen. The eighteenth-century mansion, which wasn't open to the public, was badly damaged by a fire in November 1991, but concerts continue to be held in the grounds. There was also a restaurant and nightclub housed in the castle and restoration work is being carried out at the moment.

In the distance is the Hill of Slane, where St Patrick lit the first Paschal fire in AD 433 to celebrate Easter. The idea was that it could be seen by the pagan High King, whose royal seat was on the Hill of Tara, a few miles to the south. It must have worked, as St Patrick is said to have converted the pagan King Laoire by using the shamrock to explain the Trinity. Ireland was never to be completely pagan again.

Near Slane village is the Francis Ledwidge Cottage and Museum, dedicated to the farm labourer who wrote poetry but died fighting for the British Army in the First World War at the age of thirty. The cottage is open to the public March–October Monday–Wednesday 10 a.m.–1 p.m. and 2–6 p.m., Saturday 10 a.m.–1 p.m., Sunday 2–6 p.m. More information can be obtained at 041–24285.

With the main attractions of the area seen, the visitor can return on the N2 to Dublin. Alternatively, take the longer way back to the capital via Navan, the Hill of Tara and Trim as detailed below.

## TOUR 4: NAVAN, TARA, TRIM AND KELLS

**Navan**, 6 miles/10 km west of Slane, is the principal town of County Meath, and an important base for mining, manufacturing and commercial activity. However, there's little to detain the outside visitor, so take the main N3 road in the direction of Dublin for 8 miles/13 km until the Hill of Tara is reached.

It was from the ancient Hill of Tara that the High Kings of Ireland ruled the land. The view from the top on a clear day is wonderful. All that remains are grassy mounds and a few markers left by archaeologists to indicate the site of the court.

There were 140 High Kings in all, the most famous of whom was Cormac MacAirt in the third century AD. He was responsible for magnificent feasts held in the banqueting hall, said to hold up to 1,200 people. MacAirt's reign was cut short when he received facial wounds during a battle, as the ancient Brehon Law forbade anyone with physical blemish to rule. His palace is part of the Royal Enclosure, which is the largest site on the hilltop. In the centre of the enclosure is the Lia Fáil (stone of destiny), an old fertility symbol which, legend has it, roared three times when a true High King sat upon it at his inauguration.

The spread of Christianity brought an end to the golden age of Tara. In AD 979 King Malachy defeated the Danes here. Over 800 years later, yet another bloody battle took place on the hill in the 1798 rebellion between an Irish army of insurgents and a British force, which proved victorious.

Centuries after the ancient order, Tara was once again the centre of 'power' when in 1843 Daniel O'Connell chose the site for one of his mass meetings in protest against the Act of Union. It was attended by over a million people. At the beginning of the twentieth century, much damage was done to the site by religious fanatics and amateur archaeologists who believed the biblical Ark of the Covenant might be buried on the hill.

The Hill of Tara, with its fine views westward over the plains of Ireland, is a place for your imagination to wander, as well as being one of the most significant places of historic interest in Ireland.

Return to Navan and take the R161 to Trim. Just off the main road, and overlooking the Boyne, is Bective Abbey, the second Cistercian abbey to be established in Ireland and probably the most beautiful of the ruins to be seen in the area. The ruins of the abbey, which was founded in 1150 by the King of Meath and closed in Henry VIII's reign, date to the fifteenth century, when a smaller abbey was built to replace the earlier Gothic structure.

**Trim**, further west again, is a town dominated by its castle, the largest in the country and one of the best examples of medieval architecture. Hugh de Lacy, Lord of Meath, originally founded the castle in 1172, though the ruins date from fifty years later. In 1649 it fell to Cromwell and from then on was left to decay. At the moment, however, extensive restoration work has begun.

Trim is a pleasant country town with several sites worth visiting. On Loman Street, St Patrick's Cathedral (Church of Ireland) is a remnant of the medieval parish church of Trim. The original church was 149 feet/ 45 m in length but it now measures 87 feet/26 m. Access is by appointment only from the Deanery, St Loman's Street.

The Crutched Friary was built by the Knights of St John of Jerusalem after the Crusades. The knights wore a red cross on their uniforms, hence the name crutched (crossed) friars. It can be found across the river, off the Dublin road.

The 75-foot (23 m) column of the Wellington monument was erected by the people of Meath in 1817 and dominates the southern skyline of the town. The Duke of Wellington, who conquered Napoleon at Waterloo and later became British Prime Minister, was born in 1769 near here, between the family homes in Dublin and Daingean.

Butterstream Gardens feature an old rose garden, a Tuscan temple, a formal pool garden and a white garden. The gardens are open afternoons (except Monday) from May to September and are well worth a visit. Telephone 046–36017.

There is also a heritage centre in the town which assists tourists in tracing their roots. Telephone 046–36633, open Monday–Friday 9 a.m.–5 p.m.

A detour north-west from Navan for 10 miles/16 km leads to **Kells** (or Ceannanus Mór, as it is known in Irish), which of course is most famous

The Hill of Tara, ancient site of the High Kings of Ireland (*top*). Trim Castle, with its outer walls and fortifications in the foreground (*left*)

for the Book of Kells, the best example of early Christian art surviving anywhere in the world. Saint Columba founded a monastery here in the sixth century, but in the ninth century a group of monks sought refuge in Kells after being expelled by the Vikings and it was these monks who undertook the great work that is the Book of Kells, a Latin version of the four Gospels. During the Cromwellian war of the seventeenth century, the book was moved for safe keeping to Trinity College in Dublin, where today it can be viewed in the Long Room. However, there is a fine facsimile on show in St Columba's Protestant church in Kells.

In the main village square stands the stump of a Celtic cross, which in 1798 was used as a gallows. The elaborately carved crosses standing in the graveyard of St Columba's are, in contrast, as unimpaired as they were 1,200 years ago. Also in the graveyard of the church is the 100-foot (30 m) round tower, from where you can see St Columba's house, a small seventh-century two-storey building with a steeply pitched stone roof and a well nearby. It is said that the ancient Irish held the Celtic equivalent of the Olympic Games here in 370.

To return to Dublin from Navan, take the N3 for 30 miles/48 km. The driving time is less than one hour.

## BICYCLE TOUR

The Boyne Valley tour above can be covered easily by bicycle. Cyclists arriving from Dublin are advised to leave the city by Phibsborough and Finglas, taking the (busy and very straight!) Ashbourne road (N2) to get to Newgrange. Alternatively, put your bike on the train and start from Drogheda.

Regardless of which starting point is chosen, the following circuit is suggested: Drogheda — site of the Battle of the Boyne — Newgrange, Knowth and Dowth — Slane — Navan — Hill of Tara (take the N3 towards Dublin; the hill lies on the right) — Trim (via Kilmessan) — Kells (via Athboy) — return to Dublin via Navan, or Drogheda via Slane.

The length of the core Drogheda–Navan–Kells–Drogheda route is about 75 miles/120 km. The terrain along the route consists of rolling countryside, with few difficult climbs.

## ECOTOUR

Meath is noted for its rich soils, which result in an abundance of fine pasture. In the distant past these soils would have supported oakwoods that in turn maintained the soil through a constant supply of leaf litter to the surface. (Leaf litter encourages earthworm activity, which promotes other soil animal activity and the assimilation of organic matter.) The deep soils originated with the passage of glaciers over the local limestone rocks and with material deposited by the River Boyne as it passed through low-lying areas.

The burial chambers at Dowth, Knowth and Newgrange are in all probability there because of the local soils and the River Boyne. The resources required to build the chambers at Newgrange were enormous. Farming must have been extensive at the time in the region. The land along the Boyne is good meadow land that has lately been reclaimed to form rich pastures.

Rather than explore a wide range of habitats within the county, it is better to walk along the river at its heart. In the recent past the Boyne River catchment was subjected to an arterial drainage scheme. These Board of Works schemes have for years been a source of great concern for anglers and environmentalists. During the process, river courses are deepened and often straightened to improve the drainage of surrounding land. The cost of such projects is not just financial: anglers claim that years afterwards these rivers are still not as good to fish as they had been.

Sir William Wilde, in *The Beauties and Antiquities in the Boyne and Blackwater* (1849), commented of Navan in relation to the Rivers Boyne and Blackwater, 'The inhabitants of Navan, like those of most Irish towns through which a river runs, have turned their backs upon the stream, scarcely a glimpse of which can be obtained from its narrow streets.' This reluctance to encroach on the rivers may well have had a touch of practicality to it; the town is situated on a hill above, well away from the dangers of flood waters that, no doubt, rose each winter.

While past inhabitants turned their backs on the river, some did, in time, take note of the potential that lay in the canal network springing up in Ireland through the eighteenth century. Two centuries ago a fundamental change in the character of the river was forged with the building of the canal from Navan to Drogheda. This channel allowed navigation from the coast upriver at all times of the year. Today the canal and river move in tandem at a stately pace from Navan east to Drogheda. The canal, having consumed the energies of hundreds in its creation, is now a faded remnant of past desires for industrial greatness, while the river continues to flow with all its power.

Construction of the Boyne Canal, running parallel to the lower Boyne, began in 1759. The first phase was from Drogheda to Slane and in the following thirty years £75,000 was spent on this section of the project. The line to Navan was completed in 1800. Total cost of the canal was £196,683 or £10,430 per mile. The Boyne Navigation Company ran the canal for many years but was always in competition with the railways. In 1913 the company went into liquidation and sold the canal to John Spicer, who ran it until 1923. Pleasure cruises were one of the money-making ventures attempted on the canal before it fell into disuse.

## Walk

The walk begins in Navan and follows the southern bank of the river, along the towpath between the river and canal. This was, some years ago, under consideration as a long-distance walking route. To date no signs have appeared to guide the walker and at times in the winter, parts of the path are muddy and may be impassable. For the ecotour we will walk about 4 miles/6.5 km along the river to Beauparc. Here we can return to Navan and transport or, more adventurously, continue through Slane and on to Drogheda. The entire route is about 16 miles/25.5 km but, as I warned, not all in good walking condition.

In the early 1980s a linear park was established along part of the Boyne to the east of Navan where the canal enters the town. Unfortunately, being on the town's outskirts, this area is sometimes neglected and an impressive accumulation of cans and plastic bottles may be seen at the beginning of the walk.

To start, we head from the town to the River Boyne along the L21 road; there is a car park just across the bridge and in on the left. Leaving the car park we walk down to the river and the place where the Boyne Canal entered Navan. Our route between majestic river and faded canal is a magical one.

Just yards from the town otters may be seen in the waters of the Boyne. The otter is an elusive animal, though signs of its presence are found throughout Ireland. The signs are spraints, droppings deposited on a prominent rock or mound of soil and grass. Black and mucilaginous with a musky odour when fresh, they contain the scales and bones of fish and the shells of crabs and molluscs when by the sea. The otter is resident along both rivers and the coast, liking clean waters and secluded places. Feeding in the early morning or at dusk, it keeps very much out of the way of human activities. In spite of this reputation for the quiet life there is plenty of evidence of otters living along rivers in towns and cities throughout Ireland.

After many years of keeping an eye out in likely places I had given up on ever seeing one. Then on a March morning, not five minutes' walk from Navan, on the River Boyne I saw three otters in broad daylight.

I first noticed a movement that went against the current along the opposite bank of the river. A rat, I thought but then noted how strong and purposeful the movement seemed. With binoculars I made out three sleek animals swimming against the current. At the time the Boyne was swollen with flood waters. They could have been mink but the wide flat heads and bulk ruled this out. In Irish they are 'cúanna uisce', water hounds; that's exactly what they looked like as they moved with grace and power through the water.

This group of three was in all probability a mother with two young. After mating, the male leaves the female to rear the young in her own territory and does not return. The otters moved upriver and out of sight.

After about ten minutes my attention was caught by a high-pitched whistling which I attributed to a bird in the undergrowth. The sharp whistles grew louder and seemed to be shooting back and forth across the river. Then one of the otters came into view just yards from where I stood. The whistles were calls between the two on the far bank and the one now almost at my feet in the water. Once it caught sight of me it shot across the river with incredible speed. The party then proceeded upriver to Navan.

The walk is an easy one along a very level terrain. The surroundings change gradually from wood-lined stretches to areas of open pastures and back to woodlands.

The kingfisher can be regularly seen on the river. There are few more aptly named creatures: this stocky little bird feeds almost entirely on fish, catching minnows and sticklebacks from a perch above the water. For the fish to be visible the water must be clear and fairly calm, which rules out fast-flowing rivers or areas muddied by pollution. Another problem for this fisher is the winter. Hard frosts can freeze still waters; the kingfisher is locked out of the pantry. In cold spells they may move downriver to the coast, feeding in estuarine marshes where freezing is less likely.

Another reason for the name is perhaps the flashy plumage. No royal robes could match the splendid vibrancy of this bird's rich orange and iridescent blue feathers. In flight the kingfisher moves speedily and in a straight line just above the water. You need a wide river and a good distance of water to catch the display — the Boyne is an excellent site. A blue streak and quickly beating wings is all that will be seen; the orange underbelly is not visible.

The favoured feeding sites are slow-moving rivers. Old canals with plenty of overhanging vegetation and mill races with still water are good locations to check for the presence of a kingfisher. The nest is a burrow dug by the parents in the soil on the riverbank. When in use it soon becomes fairly rancid. Fish-remains and the waste of the young accumulate below the entrance.

It is said of the kingfisher that it is rarely hunted by other birds. The rapid flight and secretive habits may in part account for this fact. Another reason is said to be that the taste of the flesh is unpleasant. The flashy plumage may in that case serve as a warning.

On tall conifers along the river cormorants will be seen standing sentry. Almost motionless they perch atop the trees and seem to be looking to far horizons for some sign or other. They lack the oily preen glands which the mechanisms of evolution bestowed on later bird species and for this reason stand with wings outspread in the sun or wind to dry after fishing.

The river is also a happy hunting ground for swallow and swift. These graceful acrobats of the skies move lightly over the water's surface, rising high into the air when loaded with prey. Old trees along the route of the river will provide nesting sites for these birds in the country. In town they are dependent on gaps and spaces beneath the eaves.

By weirs on the Boyne an occasional solitary heron will be seen. These tall, lean, grey birds with dagger-like yellow beaks and a black crest on the head are unmistakable. They stand alert in the shallow water waiting for the movement of fish or eel. Once prey is within range the heron strikes and swallows it whole. In flight the heron is slow and majestic, the neck is drawn back and the legs extend well beyond the tail. Though a solitary hunter, the heron nests in colonies or heronries in large trees or reed-beds.

For much of the journey the towpath is an elevated walk above the Boyne and the canal. About 1 mile/1.5 km from Navan the River Boyne bows out to the left away from the canal. It is possible to follow the river's banks but you will have to leave it and rejoin the canal after about 0.5 miles/1 km because the way becomes rather wet underfoot.

To be safe stick to the towpath all the way to Beauparc and concentrate on enjoying the peace and tranquillity of the area instead. Retrace your footsteps from the bridge at Beauparc to Navan. The whole walk should take no more than 3 hours at a gentle stroll, allowing time to stand and stare.

# FURTHER READING

Bolger, Dermot: *The Journey Home, The Woman's Daughter* (Penguin). Bleak tales of suffering among Dublin's forgotten underclass.

Brown, Christy: *Down all the Days* (Minerva). Life in working-class Dublin from the viewpoint of the disabled writer on whom the film *My Left Foot* was based.

Craig, Maurice: *Dublin 1660–1880* (Allen Figgis, Dublin). The indispensable guide to Georgian architecture in Dublin.

Cronin, Anthony: *Dead as Doornails*. Memoirs of Dublin in the 1950s and of the troubled lives of contemporary literary giants such as Brendan Behan and Patrick Kavanagh.

Delaney, Frank: *James Joyce's Odyssey – A Guide to the Dublin of 'Ulysses'* (Hodder & Stoughton).

Doyle, Roddy: *The Commitments, The Snapper, The Van, Paddy Clarke Ha Ha Ha* (Minerva/Hodder & Stoughton). The housing estates of working-class Dublin come under the literary microscope for the first time to stunning comic effect.

Durcan, Paul: *Crazy about Women* (National Gallery of Ireland). A collection from one of Ireland's best-known contemporary poets which is based on the paintings in the National Gallery.

Foster, R.F.: *Modern Ireland 1600–1972* (Allen Lane/Penguin Press). A highly respected though contentious reading of modern Irish history.

Gogarty, Oliver St John: *As I was Going Down Sackville Street* (Sphere). Rip-roaring memoirs of the poet, playboy, surgeon and 'friend' of James Joyce.

Joyce, James: *Dubliners, A Portrait of the Artist as a Young Man, Ulysses, Finnegans Wake* (Penguin Books).

Lee, J.J.: *Ireland 1912–1985* (Cambridge University Press). Stirring if polemical account of Ireland's failings in this century.

McDonald, Frank: *The Destruction of Dublin* (Gill & Macmillan). The heart-rending story of how developers destroyed so much of Dublin from the 1960s on, as told by a leading journalist with *The Irish Times*.

MacThomáis, Éamonn: *Me Jewel and Darlin' Dublin* (The O'Brien Press). Affectionate if sentimental memoirs of Dublin from a native son.

Malone, J.B.: *The Complete Wicklow Way* (O'Brien Press). A guide to Ireland's best known walking trail, by the man whose idea it was.

Nicholson, Robert: *The Ulysses Guide — Tours through Joyce's Dublin* (Mandarin Paperbacks, London). An easy-to-use guide with clear maps for the Joyce enthusiast.

O'Connor, Joseph: *Cowboys and Indians* (Flamingo). A tale of Dublin suburban youth, as seen through the eyes of Eddie Virago, one of Grafton Street's original punks.

O'Connor, Ulick: *The Celtic Dawn*. The story, simply told, of the Irish Literary Renaissance at the turn of the century.

Pritchett, V.S.: *Dublin: A Portrait* (The Hogarth Press, London). Dublin in the 1960s, as viewed by an English essayist and writer.

Ryan, John: *Remembering How We Stood* (Gill & Macmillan). More memories of the grim 1950s.

Somerville-Large, Peter: *Dublin* (Hamish Hamilton). A good, all-round history of the city from its earliest beginnings to the 1960s.

Walsh, Brendan: *Irish Cycling Guide* (Gill & Macmillan). Includes a grand tour of Ireland by bicycle, and several day and weekend tours from Dublin.

# Suggestions for Future Editions

While every care has been taken to ensure that the information given is accurate and up to date, changes may have occurred since the authors completed their research. No responsibility is accepted for any such changes, but reports of gaps or inaccuracies are most welcome. Readers who wish to offer comments and suggestions should address them to:

The Authors
Insider's Guide to Dublin, Wicklow and the Boyne Valley
c/o Editorial Department
Gill & Macmillan
Goldenbridge
Inchicore
Dublin 8.

Paul Cullen
Ken Boyle

# INDEX